employi Generation WHY?

understanding, managing, and motivating your new workforce

eric chester

TH BOOKS

www.GenerationWhy.com

Library of Congress Control Number: 2001127124
ISBN 0-9651447-7-1 (cloth)
ISBN 0-9651447-8-X (paper)

Editing: Linda Carlson, Carlson Editing, Erie CO
Design: Bob Schram, Bookends, Boulder CO

PUBLISHED BY TUCKER HOUSE BOOKS
a subsidiary of Chester Performance Systems
1410 Vance St., Suite 201
Lakewood, Colorado 80215
(303) 239-9999
www.generationwhy.com

Dedication

To my awesome wife, Lori, who has shown me true love,

our four Generation Why children who have taught me humility,

and above all, to my Heavenly Father,

from whom all blessings flow.

Contents

PART THREE—CONNECTING POINTS:
HOW TO REMAIN WHY2K COMPLIANT

Acknowledgments

THERE IS NO END to the long list of people who have been the inspiration and driving force behind the book you are holding. First, let me pay homage to my wonderful friends and colleagues, Mark Sanborn, Mark Scharenbroich, Mary LoVerde, and Scott Friedman for their sage wisdom and guidance. Secondly, I am very indebted to my loyal associate and coworker, Sheila Deibler for keeping me on task and for throwing her heart and soul into this project. Lastly, I thank my collaborative Dream Team, Bob Schram, Linda Carlson, Christie Chester, David Avrin, and Dennis Cass, who have done such an incredible job in taking my zany ideas and passionate ramblings and helping me channel them into something I am very proud of.

About the Author

eric chester is the premier expert on Generation Why. In fact, he coined the term. Leading news organizations worldwide (CNN, ABC, MS-NBC, FoxNews, The Denver Post, The San Francisco Examiner, etc.) have come to rely on Eric to provide insight, perspective, and answers into the mind-set of this misunderstood and often-maligned generation.

Eric has spent years in the trenches with the youth of Generations X and Why. He is a former teacher and coach turned motivational speaker and talk show host who has personally worked with more than two million students since the early eighties. Eric's greatest depth of experience with Generation Why comes from living in the trenches with Holli, Travis, Zac, and Whitney in his critical role as father/ stepfather. He is helping to prepare them for the changing world they will help to shape.

As an electrifying keynote speaker and consultant, Eric provides valuable insight and strategies to leading-edge Gen Why employers like Arby's, Legoland, Toys Я Us, and Discover Financial. He presents frequently for the National School Boards Association, the American Society for Training and Development, and the Society for Human Resource Management.

Married and living in Lakewood, Colorado, Eric is the president and founder of Generation Why, Inc.

www.generationwhy.com

WHO ARE THEY?

PART ONE

Why the Label Generation Why?

I 'VE WORKED WITH YOUNG PEOPLE all of my adult life. I was born in 1957, at the tail end of what has since been referred to as the Baby Boom. Like most Boomers, I naturally assumed everyone in America, except for my parents, was pretty much like me. I naively assumed they thought as I thought, believed in the same things I believed in, and felt about most things the way I felt.

My professional career began as a high school teacher and coach, and my naive assumption was quickly laid to rest by the graduating class of 1980. Even though they were only five years younger than me, it seemed like we were light years apart. Born in the early sixties, these students were born after the population boom and had missed out on the prosperity boom and patriotic boom that punctuated my generation. It was a much smaller generation than mine, and one that didn't readily accept the Pollyannaish notion of the virtues of God, Mom, the Chevrolet, and apple pie. And I wasn't the only one who felt that these students were jaded and cynical. The tenured teachers at my school and throughout the country were commenting that *something weird had happened*; that the *new students were a strange breed apart from the norm.* Something had happened alright, but no one could say what or why.

The first moniker given to them, the Baby Busters, signified an end to the U.S. population boom, but it fell short of adequately defining this *strange new breed* that had come into the world. Years later, the graduating class of 1980 (along with the next fifteen that followed) were being referred to as Generation Xers. They were causing a commotion, not only in the classroom as students but also in the workplace as the new labor force.

In time, I found my way with Generation X. I was forced to. I interacted every day with Xers. I started out as a teacher with Xers as my students. Then I entered the business world and managed a workforce composed almost entirely of Xers. Years later I found my calling as a motivational speaker for students, and I'm sure you can guess who I was expected to both captivate and inspire. I grew to love my work with them, and I knew that nothing in my life could ever be more challenging—or more rewarding—than connecting with, and motivating members of Generation X.

Once again, I had made an assumption that was incorrect. Even though I remained a speaker for high school and college students, the Gen Xers grew up and moved on. In their place, they left a whole 'nother breed that, in comparison, makes the Xers look tame.

Indeed, we are experiencing the effects of another significant shift in generations. We are now experiencing the emergence of post-Generation X, and they are far more difficult to reach and even harder to understand than even the Xers were. To distinguish them from their predecessors, they are being referred to with labels like Millennials, Echo Boomers, Generation Next, Boomlets, Generation Y, and the Net Generation. Although convenient and clever, these labels set the parameters of *what* they are but fall short of defining *who* they are.

In our midst there is now an entire generation whose perception of information, reality, authority, respect, privilege, rules, culture, right, and wrong is vastly different than that of those who've gone before them. They simply refuse to do the *what* before they know the *why*. It is as if every child born in America after 1980 has had a microchip surgically implanted in his or her forehead that filters out every command, every request, and every instruction that is not bundled with acceptable rationale. They are a generation that demands to know "why?" Whether you work with them, have tried to get service from them, or live with them, you have undoubtedly been asked questions like these:

Why should I listen to you? Why should I tell the truth, obey the rules, and do as I'm told? Why should I have a dream and set goals? Why should I go to school, study hard, and get a job? Why should I show up for work on time, wear a uniform, and treat the customer like they're special? Why should I work hard and keep my nose to the grindstone for a promise that it might pay off down the line? Why should I believe in you, myself, the government, the future, anything? Why?

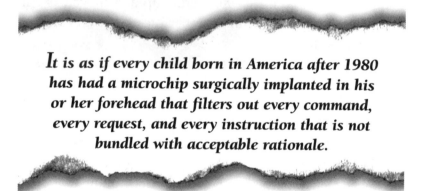

It is as if every child born in America after 1980 has had a microchip surgically implanted in his or her forehead that filters out every command, every request, and every instruction that is not bundled with acceptable rationale.

It is for this reason that I've dubbed the 60+ million Americans born between 1980 and 1994 *Generation Why.* If you work with them, beside them, or even *for* them, you know the name is deadly accurate. They are questioning all the rules, all the time-honored institutions, and all the previously unquestioned questions—and they are doing it loudly!

Let us not forget that although questioning authority has historically been regarded as a lack of respect, it might also be seen as a sign of an investigative mind and individuality. Nancy Reagan ushered in the "Just Say No" campaign. Nike told

Generation X to "Just Do It." The Army tried to get eighteen-year-olds to enlist by prompting them to "Be All That You Can Be!" While these campaigns worked amazingly well with Boomers and Xers, they bombed out with the Whys. Generation Why wants answers, not commands. They demand reasons and rationale, so the traditional "because I said so" isn't going to cut it. This doesn't make them stupid, but rather it proves that they're shockingly bright and discerning. It also makes them extremely difficult to understand and even harder to manage and motivate.

They demand reasons and rationale, so the traditional "because I said so" isn't going to cut it.

Please don't make the mistake of thinking that this book is about teenagers. Rather, think of it as being about an entire generation, most of whom are currently in their teenage years. But the vast majority of the values, attitudes, and beliefs ingrained in them throughout their youth will remain with them throughout their lives, just as most of the values, attitudes, and beliefs you hold to now have their origins in your earlier years.

Mature adults are not warmly receptive to the idea of having to attach rationale to everything they ask their children/students/young employees to do. We think to ourselves, "we did what we were told, and they should, too." When our expectations are not met, we feel angry, confused, and disconnected, and we might even start to blame them for the problems we're having connecting with them. However, instead of fighting them, if we change the way we view them and how we communicate with them, the results are astounding.

Education is rapidly passing this baton to business, and as a result your workforce is being transformed in front of your eyes. Your emerging workforce is causing you to reexamine your hiring practices and revamp your management techniques. This is good—if you're proceeding with insight and a practical plan. However, if you're slow to make changes, or you are making changes without really understanding the root cause—you may be signing up for some serious trouble.

This book will demonstrate that when you and I lay our preconceived notions aside, look for insight, reach out to this generation, and sufficiently address the question "why?" (not necessarily answer it), Generation Why becomes phenomenally attentive, motivated, creative, and empowered. It's then that you'll discover that they can do amazing things for your business.

The Aliens Have Landed

ASPACESHIP HAS LANDED in your company parking lot. The beings coming down the craft's ladder and entering your place of business have assumed human form, but their clothing, their hair, and their skin adornments are obviously not of this world. Communication is a major barrier, as they speak in a language all their own and seem to have difficulty understanding your requests. They claim to have come in peace, but you see signs that they anger quickly, even to the point of aggression.

Your first reaction is to rush to the spaceship and close the door in hopes these aliens will return to their own galaxy, but alas, it's too late and they are too great in number. You have heard tales of these creatures, and you have seen them around your town and your community, but you wonder why they have chosen to invade your domain. Suddenly it dawns on you. They have seen the *Now Hiring* sign in your window; they know you are in desperate need of help, and they have come to apply. Having exhausted all other options, you reluctantly decide to integrate the aliens into your workforce. You hope for the best, even if you have no idea how to bring it about.

Experienced managers thought they had seen it all. Just when they found the answers to working with cranky, apathetic Generation X (now well into their late twenties and thirties), along comes a generation that completely changes their assumptions about how young people come up in the world, and what it takes to connect with them. The managers in my seminars vent their frustrations as if they were in group therapy:

"They don't give a hoot about my customers!"

"If you correct their mistakes, they'll quit on you!"

"I can't get them to show up on time!"

"They picked up the cash register functions in a snap, but when it goes down, they can't count change back from a dollar!"

"You have to watch 'em like a hawk, or they'll steal you blind!"

"She asked for an extended lunch hour to go shopping with a friend, and it was only her third day on the job!"

"He looked okay at the interview, but two days later, he showed up for work with blue spiked hair and a pierced eyebrow!"

"If the pizza joint down the street offers them fifty cents more per hour than I'm paying, they're gone without a word of notice!"

"They assume it's okay to call me by my first name, and they act as if we're buddies. I'm fifty-three, and I'm their boss!"

"When I do something extra for them, they act as if I owed it to them!"

Ready or not, here comes Generation Why. And they're not politely knocking—they're breaking down the door! They are entering the workforce—and society—with a whole new set of attitudes, values, and beliefs.

Gen Why numbers more than 60 million, which is significantly larger than the size of Generation X, and just slightly smaller than the Baby Boom Generation. Here are a few demographic insights:

☞ 1 in 3 is not Caucasian,

☞ 2 in 4 come from a single-parent home,

☞ 4 in 5 have working mothers, and more than 2% have one or both parents incarcerated.

When you take a statistical look at the emerging workforce, the numbers tell the story of a nation in transition.

Ready or not, here comes Generation Why. And they're not politely knocking—they're breaking down the door! They are entering the workforce—and society—with a whole new set of attitudes, values, and beliefs.

☞ There has been an increase of close to 25% in young managers, age twenty to twenty-four.

☞ Jobs in retail are expected to continue to grow 14% in the next six years.

☞ Service jobs are growing at an astronomical 47% rate.

☞ Turnover (employees leaving their jobs at twelve months or less) among young workers is at an all-time high. For twenty- to twenty-four-year-olds, the rate is 54%. Among sixteen- to nineteen-year-olds, the rate is 78%.

Numbers only graph the outline, but when you connect the dots, all of these statistics mean that the new and emerging workforce is presenting a gargantuan challenge and that change will continue as they move up through the organization. Particularly impacted, of course, are the retail and service sectors, but high-tech firms are also struggling to integrate Gen Why into an environment that has already been challenged by prima donna Gen Xers. Gen Why has grown up with a lack of constancy, which means that your current human resource policy of rewards and promotions probably won't cut it—and your current crop of Gen Whys probably won't be around in two to three years, for reasons you have little or no control over. The internal chaos that results from so much turnover has monumental, most often negative, consequences for your long-time employees. This means that you not only have to figure out how to recruit, train, and manage your new employees, you have to re-examine your whole system of managing human and other resources. Business is and will be different, no question about it. The real question is—*what are you going to do differently in your business?*

TAKE ME TO YOUR LEADER!

America's business leaders are baffled. If you've had any experience employing, supervising, or managing young people, you know that referring to your emerging workforce as aliens isn't all that outrageous. After all, they do not see life—much less a job—like you or anyone from a previous generation does. However, because your success hinges on their performance, you cannot afford to ignore them or hope they will grow out of their attitudes and behaviors towards work. Because how can you lead them if you don't understand them?

The best we can do as managers and mentors of Generation Why is to realize how different their coming of age is from the way ours was. The place to start is understanding the kinds of messages they have been receiving that can—and most often do—run counter to the lessons we try to teach them. We can impart our wisdom and our experience, but every day since birth they have been subjected to a radical counter-programming. For Generation Why, this is how the world really works.

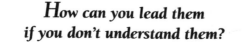

How can you lead them
if you don't understand them?

It is difficult, to say the least, to instill in Generation Why a solid work ethic (patience, determination, integrity, persistence, ingenuity, etc.) when the world around them says that they can get what they want without it. It's no wonder that many Gen Why managers complain that leading them on the job is like trying to push a piece of string across a table. But do not despair! As you will discover in subsequent chapters, the very forces that drive Gen Whys to question the process and to attempt to separate effort from reward can be used to bring out the best in them, creating new and exciting results for your business.

The very forces that drive Gen Whys to question the process and to attempt to separate effort from reward can be used to bring out the best in them.

WORLDS APART

We all occupy the same basic space and have the same basic physiology. So how come they don't seem like they're members of the same species?

They aren't like you, and they never will be. On Maslow's Hierarchy of Needs pyramid, Whys need and want the same things you do (food, shelter, belonging, self-actualization), but they are going to go about acquiring those things in a radically different way. This is where the differences begin.

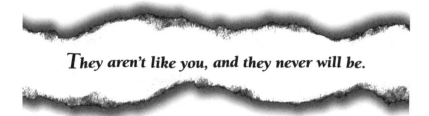

They aren't like you, and they never will be.

Psychologists pretty much agree that our values drive our decisions and that our decisions forge our identities and individuality and shape our lives. They also remind us that our core values are programmed into us during our first fifteen to sixteen years of life, through a combination of five major life-shaping influences: Parents/Family; Schools/Education; Religion/Morality; Friends/Peers; and Media/Culture.

The decisions you make in your professional and personal lives are rooted somewhere in your value system, and that system was predominantly formed before you got your driver's license or went on your first date. Granted, you have matured and changed through the years, but most of your core values (what I'll be referring to from here on out as your value programming or the way you are wired) are probably pretty much still intact.

Do you think today's world and the combination of those five influences that programmed you are the same as they were in the eighties, or in the nineties? Of course not! They're not even close. Odds are, your mother didn't work full time throughout your childhood. You probably never had to worry about a kid pulling a gun on you in school. You went to church or synagogue most weeks. Your friends lived close by, and you spent more time with them in person than you did talking to them on the phone. And you probably recall a time when popular music was more about love than hate and prime time television focused on family relationships instead of sexual ones.

My point is simple. The question here isn't, *"How old are you?"* but rather, *"When were you young?"* Pull off your Traditional/Boomer/Xer glasses and take a look at the world from a different perspective—put on a pair of Gen Why glasses for a few minutes.

Generation Why has no recollection of the Reagan era, and they don't remember the Challenger explosion. They were toddlers during Operation Desert Storm and Black Monday, 1987. They don't remember ET, Mr. T, or McDLTs. They don't remember PacMan, mopeds, or "Who shot J.R.?" They don't remember when every young boy wanted to grow up to be just like O.J., or when being a presidential intern was a respected assignment. Mention *Miracle on Ice* to a Gen Why, and they think you're talking about Tonya Harding. They've never walked across a room to change the stations on a television. They've never used carbon paper. And they've never lost anything in shag carpeting!

On the other hand, Generation Why has never known life without cell phones, pagers, fax machines, and voice mail. Their world has always included minivans, bottled water, cable television, overnight package delivery, and chat rooms. They would have no personal reference for a time before ATMs, VCRs, PCs, CDs, MTV, CNN, SUVs or TCBYs! And sadly enough, Gen Whys have never known a world without AIDS, without crack, or without terrorist attacks. They've never known a world where kids didn't shoot and kill other kids.

Naturally, the long-term effects of these influences can only be predicted at this point in time. However, if you were to take a very broad look at the general influences and resulting attitudes of the last three generations, it might look something like the information in Table 1.

TABLE 1: Generational Comparison Chart

TOPIC	BABY BOOMERS 1946-1964
The Future	*Is ours!*
Television	*Bonanza*
Wealth	*I'll earn it!*
Heroes/Role Models	*Men of Character*
Kids Killing Kids	*Unthinkable*
For Kicks	*Drive-Ins*
Employment for Teens	*Hard to find*
Loyalty to Employer	*I could work my way to the top!*
Parents	*Try to please them.*
Justice	*Always prevails*
School/Training	*Tell me WHAT to do.*
Respecting Elders	*Is automatic*
Credit/Borrowing	*Only if I have to.*
Environment	*Don't litter.*
Government	*Is there dishonesty?*
Communication	*Via parents' phone*
Shock Rock Icons	*Little Richard*
	Elvis Presley
	Alice Cooper
Change	*Dislike*
Streetwise	*Naïve*
Technology	*Ignorant*
Video Game	*Pong*
Pornography	*In Movie Theaters*
Promiscuity leads to	*Mono*

Attitudes and Influences of Adolescence

GENERATION X 1964-1979	GENERATION WHY 1980-1994
Sucks!	Might not happen!
Family Ties	Jerry Springer
I don't care that much about it.	Gimme, or I'll take it!
Men and Women of Character	What's Character?
It's possible	It's everywhere
Drive Thrus	Drive Bys
I'll work if I have to.	Jobs are a dime a dozen!
This could lead to the top!	If I can't take Saturday off, I'll quit!
Try to put up with them.	Aren't around much.
Usually prevails	Can be bought
Show me HOW to do it.	WHY do I need to learn this?
Is polite	Just because they're older? No way!
If I really want something.	How much can I get?
Save the whales.	It's too late now.
There is dishonesty!	Is there honesty?
Via personal phone	Pager/cell phone/E-mail/chat rooms
Boy George	Marilyn Manson
Ozzy Ozborne	Nirvana
Madonna	Eminem
Accept	Demand
Aware	Experienced
Comfortable	Masters
PacMan	Mortal Kombat
In Video Stores	On TV, or a click away online.
Herpes	AIDS

INTERNAL WIRING DIFFERENCES: THE WAY WE THINK

So what mark have these influences left upon your emerging workforce? Perhaps the most profound difference, and the one that is the springboard for most of the other differences we will be discussing in the next chapter, is the way Gen Why thinks and processes information. Where our minds operate more like a VCR, theirs function more like a DVD player. Although they both process complex sights and sounds, one accesses that information in a sequential order, while the other can access and process information sequentially, in reverse, or in random order with no loss of time.

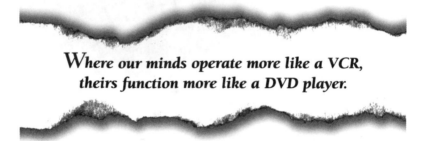

Where our minds operate more like a VCR, theirs function more like a DVD player.

The latest series of interactive video games exemplifies the digital mentality of Generation Why. Players who don't want to go through the effort of actually defeating and mastering the beginning and intermediate levels of these games can simply log on to the Internet and download numerical codes that will give them step-by-step instructions on how to jump ahead to any level. To you and me, that amounts to cheating. To Gen Why, it's just using an external resource to accomplish a goal.

You're probably reading this book much like you do the morning paper—from the front to the back. I bet you eat your salad before your steak, and your steak before dessert. When you took employment with your organization, you expected to begin low and work your way up through the ranks. With any new recreational pursuit, you fully expect to start out as a beginner, pay your dues as an intermediate, and consistently practice hard to move to the next level.

You and I are linear, or analog, thinkers and doers. We move sequentially from left to right, from top to bottom, from front to back. We have been taught to learn, earn, save, then spend. Our parents ingrained into our psyches that we were to work before we could play. You and I believe that there is a natural order to things, and we know that we must adhere to The Law of the Farm: cultivate—plant—fertilize—*then* harvest.

Generation Why doesn't see it that way. For them, life is an all-you-can-eat buffet, offering unlimited choice, few rules, and a pay-as-you-can system. They see absolutely no reason to stick with our analog logic in this digital world. Not when they believe in their ability to leapfrog over the painstaking cultivate/plant/fertilize parts *and go directly to the harvest!*

*F*or them, life is an all-you-can-eat buffet, offering unlimited choice, few rules, and a pay-as-you-can system.

How could any manager expect employees who were value-programmed over the past twenty years to be remotely the same now—or ever? How can we expect them to think sequentially, when they are wired for a pull-down menu of choices and immediate results? And if they're not thinking like us, they're not going to be automatically in sync with our logic, rules, practices, and procedures. Understanding this is the first step towards understanding Generation Why.

WHO MOVED MY CHEETOS?

Some things never change. There are the constants of youth: the rebellion, the self-doubt, and the frustration with the status quo. But every generation has its variables, too. Every generation faces a world that is different from the one their parents and their grandparents inherited. With the dawning of the Information Age, Generation Why has collided with a reality that is radically different than the world of your youth or your parents' youth. The change in their reality is as dramatic as the changes in society and culture that took place when the Industrial Age changed the face of the world about a hundred years ago. The Industrial Age moved people out of rural, agrarian communities and into big cities and industrial centers where the tone and pace of life were radically different from life on the farm.

The change in their reality is as dramatic as the changes in society and culture that took place when the Industrial Age changed the face of the world.

Think about how you struggle as an adult with a dynamic, global marketplace of ideas, where technology, mass media, and the New Economy can change your existence in an afternoon. Think about the pressures of an uncertain workplace, or the speed at which you live your life, always running at full pace just to keep up.

Now imagine if you had never known life any other way. Today the changes brought on by the Information Age affect the mind far more than the body. Whereas older generations have had to learn to cope with the Information Age, Generation Why has grown up with it. For them, all this speed and change and uncertainty are normal. Big city, small city, inner city, small town, uptown, downtown, even in the remotest of areas—parents can run, but a high-tech, media-dominated universe means that they can no longer hide their children from the pervasive and persuasive messages that reverberate through our culture.

These messages may be hard for adults to decipher because our opinions and values are already formed, but step outside the framework of your own life and look at this postmodern world from the viewpoint of Generation Why. You will quickly understand exactly why Gen Why is so different.

Profile: GW—What Can We Really Expect?

WE'VE ALREADY ESTABLISHED that Gen Why is different than any previous generation. We've seen how culture, technology, society, media, and the events of the modern world have powerfully influenced Gen Whys, causing them to approach life—and subsequently the workplace—with a completely different set of attitudes, values, and beliefs. Now it's time to get a better handle on the common characteristics of Generation Why—their specific values, attitudes, and behaviors—so that we can more effectively manage and motivate them in the workplace.

LABELS, TERMS, AND CLASSIFICATIONS

I realize that I'm treading on dangerous ground in this section. I am about to run the risk of stereotyping more than 60 million of our fellow human beings. This is the slippery nature of generational analysis, which tends to paint large groups of people with a broad brush. Making generalizations always raises the question of the exception to the rule, and there are plenty of exceptions—in your workplace, in your neighborhood, even in your own family—to the twelve characteristics we're about to discuss. While many members of Gen Why display several of these traits, not every Gen Why displays all of them, and in each case, it is definitely a matter of degree.

But making observations about the behavior of a generation, even the negative behavior, is a powerful tool for understanding because, make no mistake, Generation Why is different, and the older generations' difficulty in dealing with these differences is already causing friction in the workplace. And that friction shows no sign of stopping.

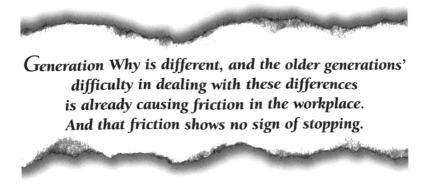

Generation Why is different, and the older generations'
difficulty in dealing with these differences
is already causing friction in the workplace.
And that friction shows no sign of stopping.

THE DOWNSIDE

Six of the twelve following characterizations of Gen Why are
not necessarily flattering terms. They are, however, frank
and honest, and are an essential prerequisite to helping
managers understand their new workforce. These negative
characterizations are not intended to condemn or malign
anyone, much less our nation's youth. There is a lot of hope
and promise in Gen Why, but we also have to confront the
ways in which their attitudes and opinions don't jibe with a
stable and productive workplace. The better that Boomer
and Xer (and even Gen Why!) managers can understand
these differences, the more effective they'll become in dealing with them.

Among the pages that immediately follow, you'll discover
the less desirable traits of Gen Whys. You'll see them
described by such terms as *impatient, desensitized, disengaged,*
skeptical, disrespectful, and *bluntly expressive.* You might be
tempted to say that these are traits of any young American in
the throes of puberty, but the difference is that for Gen Why
these aren't just the results of adolescence. These modes
inform their behavior and their larger attitudes about the
world. Any normal adolescent rebelliousness has been mag-

nified by the cultural influences described in the previous chapter. Gen Whys have been imprinted to be independent, and rather than receiving counter-programming from their parents and from society, their independence and individuality have only been reinforced.

Boomers, and to a growing extent Xers, tend to view Gen Why with dread. Part of it has to do with the natural distrust older generations have for the young—those people who have the audacity to come along, just when adults have everything the way they like it, and upset the apple cart with new fashions, new music, new heroes, new attitudes, and new morals. Part of it has to do with the inherent faults in Gen Why. But this generation, perhaps unlike any before in history, has been demonized.

The same media that has programmed them and undermined their values also constantly portrays them in a negative light. They are taken to task for wallowing in violent music and video games; their tattoos and piercings are sensationalized to the point where they are seen as freaks; and they are shown as disconnected, lazy, even dangerous. Every time the tragedy of violence strikes another school, the papers and news magazines wonder what is wrong with these kids. They have been frequently pictured being led away from a courthouse in an orange prison jumper.

This generation, perhaps unlike any before in history, has been demonized.

While Gen Why's faults might appear easy fodder for casual Boomer conversation, the "whole truth" often goes unspoken. This generation shows an infinite amount more promise and hope than they have been given credit for. Call it a testimony to the indomitable human spirit, or the adaptability of youth, but for all their negative traits, there are counterbalancing attributes that make Gen Why the ultimate paradox.

THE UPSIDE

The good news is that Generation Why is *adaptable, innovative, efficient, resilient, tolerant,* and *committed.* They have the time, the tools, and the talent to create a better world for us. They have more information available to them than any previous generation—and they aren't afraid to use it. They'll research products before they buy them, investigate colleges before they enroll, and do background checks on prospective dates so they won't end up in a dangerous predicament.

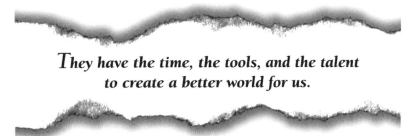

They have the time, the tools, and the talent to create a better world for us.

Studies show they place a much higher emphasis on marriage and family than their parents do and that they will not allow a career to upset a happy home life. I've been told by countless teens that they are not going to make the mistakes their parents did and that their family will always come first. I firmly believe that Gen Whys will be better parents because of what they and their friends have had to endure.

Volunteerism is at an all-time high, thanks to the unprecedented involvement of Generation Why, who are putting their time where their hearts are. It is hard to find an organized student club, sport, or activity where participants aren't involved in some type of community service as a part of their credo. Soccer teams stick around after their games to clean up the park. Student councils visit nursing homes, paint homes for the elderly, and hold canned-food drives. Cheerleaders volunteer to take underprivileged children trick-or-treating. As a part of her graduation requirements, my sixteen-year-old daughter, Whitney, is required to do a minimum of sixteen hours of community service each semester and report her efforts back to her high school counselor.

Both Sides on Your Side

As you read the descriptions that follow, you'll see how they are all interrelated. For example, the fact that Gen Why has been programmed by this ever-changing world to be inherently impatient has led them to be more readily adaptable to change. In other words, for every downside characterization, there is an upside. It is therefore necessary to comprehend the *macro* view of your Whys rather than arriving at a hasty stereotype of their pluses and minuses, relying solely on the sound bite ramblings of the word on the street.

TWELVE COMMON TRAITS AND TENDENCIES OF GENERATION WHY

With that in mind, let's examine the twelve common traits and tendencies that serve as a snapshot profile of Generation Why.

1. **Impatient** Complete these clichés:

Patience is a _____ .

Good things come to those who _____ .

I'll bet if you scored your results on paper, you got 100%. If you scored using your life as the example, the results would not be pretty.

Life in the new millennium is all about speed. We want everything faster today than it was yesterday. Faster commutes. Faster connections. No waiting in service lines. Express delivery. Fast. Quick. Instant everything.

Gen Why has grown up in an instant world, and they don't buy in to the old "patience is a virtue" and "good things come to those who wait" axioms. Many, if not most, people realize that making big changes in your life—buying a house, getting married, starting a new business—takes time, effort, and patience. But Generation Why has not learned those life lessons yet. To them, patience is a sign of being out of step. The patient are glanced over, passed over, and run over. Patience means you might not get what you want. Time has become the ultimate commodity, and success is measured by the speed with which goods and services are acquired.

Part of this has to do with the natural impulsiveness of the young. But where the Great Depression taught a nation of people to make sacrifices and to be patient, the Information Age has taught Generation Why that you never have to wait for anything. First there was FedEx, then E-mail, and then Instant Messaging. The message our Information culture and economy sends Generation Why is that you never have to wait, and if you do find yourself waiting, there's always another company waiting to give you what you want faster, better, and cheaper.

Boomers don't like to wait, and their Gen Why offspring have learned that waiting is bad and that patience is for someone else. We have spawned a generation of Stress

Puppies who are in a perpetual rush to get the goods before time runs out. This is a generation best summed up by the kid that will stand in front of a microwave oven shouting, "Come on, I ain't got all minute!"

We have spawned a generation of Stress Puppies who are in a perpetual rush to get the goods before time runs out.

Gen Whys are perpetual Stimulus Junkies. Where you and I might believe the world is moving too fast, for them it's not moving fast enough. What intrigues us bores them. Their mental diet consists of an endless stream of visual, auditory, and sensory stimulation where everything moves at the speed of light. This presents a huge challenge to managers, teachers, trainers, parents, and anyone else who is trying to get them to focus on that which does not come prepackaged with high-speed graphics and an adrenaline rush.

I use the term *Junkie* because it implies a compelling desire. Generation Why doesn't merely want sensory stimulation—they're addicted to it. When they aren't receiving their minimum requirement for stimulus from a single source or in a given situation, they switch into another mode, foreign to most non-Gen Whys: multitasking. Their brains are programmed to consume information in bulk and process it simultaneously, and they will shut down or go into sleep mode if they experience any degree of sensory deprivation.

Beyond mere stimuli they also crave change. In fact, if change is not a part of their work environment, they will instantly create it. The irony is, Generation Why does not really know what change is. How can they, when they have no real comprehension of what stability is? After all, to truly understand change, you first have to know what constancy is. You'd have to know rules without exceptions, principles without variables, and a world with absolute truths, guarantees, certainties, and constants. Those who were born in the eighties and raised in the nineties have heard about these concepts, but have little or no experience with them.

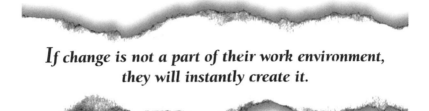

If change is not a part of their work environment, they will instantly create it.

Life for Generation Why is a never-ending sequence of events where nothing stands still. In their world, news that is more than a few minutes old is not considered news, technology becomes obsolete the moment it is introduced, and what was a red-hot trend this morning will be painfully out of style tonight! They have been conditioned to the quick fix and the speedy solution. For them, frustration is what happens when they cannot get an immediate answer or an instantaneous result.

WHYS UP! Don't waste the unique talent your Gen Whys have for multi-tasking and digesting information quickly. Be on the lookout for new trends in training and keep feeding their need to be stimulated by continuing to teach them new skills. Provide them with the freedom to explore new methods for doing repetitive tasks, and they'll show you how to increase productivity and efficiency. Ask them for suggestions to improve processes and shorten learning curves. Let them be involved in the design of new training systems. Keep meetings and internal communication short and to the point and vary the methods for delivering the necessary content. When change happens, let your Gen Whys ride the wave and help you adjust. After all, change doesn't scare them the way it may tend to rock your world. They love change, and they'll help you embrace it and use it to your advantage.

2. Adaptable Gen Whys thirst for change and are programmed to readily accept and adapt to the constantly changing world they are a part of. My dad, a WWII veteran, hates change. He even has trouble understanding why the price of gas constantly fluctuates. He often refers to the good old days when the neighborhood service station (When was the last time you heard that term?) advertised regular gas at 29.9 cents per gallon, and they didn't have one of those big signs with the removable letters. They had the price painted on their exterior wall!

Being born at the tail end of the Baby Boom, I learned to cope with change. I still tend to be mostly conservative in nature, but I know some change can be good. I take change in stride, and I try to make the best of it. My younger sisters, both Xers, actually enjoy change. They tend to be drawn to progressive, forward-thinking ideas and are more open to new ways of doing things than my peers or I seem to be. My children, all Gen Whys, are at the opposite end of the spectrum. They demand change and they will gravitate towards it. They thrive in the type of whirlwind environments that repel my dad, scare me, and shock my sisters.

Even though Gen Why didn't create this sped-up world—they inherited it!—it is encouraging and mind-boggling to realize that instead of complaining or withdrawing, they are making the most of it. The impatience we talked about in the previous section can actually work to their advantage. They know change is coming, and rather than sit back and wait for it to come and then freak out about it, they rush to it. It may seem like they're addicted to change, but often they're just impatient to get through it. And their incredibly adaptive skills let them. A Gen Why is hungry for the latest version of software so they can learn it and put it to use. They aren't so much addicted to change itself as they are especially equipped to process it, and they just don't want to waste any time. They know that life is short and to be enjoyed, and that the people who can adapt quickly can spend less time fretting over what they can't control and more time enjoying life.

The pace of change is not slowing down much, either! Life is only going to get quicker in the years ahead. Business desperately needs to tap into the mind-set of a generation that can think, adapt, and embrace change before it happens. Leading organizations are searching for people who dream in color and are capable of seeing the future before it unfolds. Gen Why brings the ability to instantly react positively to change. Think about the implications of that: faster roll outs, faster training, faster product launches, faster rebounds from a bad year. And they do it happily. That is the power present in Generation Why.

WHYS UP!

Don't shield your Whys from the changes that are taking place in your organization or your industry. Instead, harness their energy. Give them a reference for the way business was conducted yesterday and how it has evolved to its present state. Then share your concerns of how change and technology are impacting your industry and how they will affect your business in the future. Invite them to openly express their ideas and present suggestions for keeping your business in step with—or even a step ahead of—the changes.

3. **Innovative** You cannot keep up anymore by keeping up; you have to think ahead of the competition and invent the rules along the way. In the New Economy, success is the fusion of ideas and technology. The good news is, Gen Why is chock full of revolutionary ideas and has no fear of technology.

Generation Why forgets easily. They don't recall the hard work that it took to build your business from an idea into an enterprise, and they aren't enamored with the people who made the sacrifices to bring it into existence. They only know that it exists today and that it needs to be different tomorrow if it is to continue to exist. Their minds aren't full of thoughts of how it used to be; they're too busy thinking of how great it could be. Sometimes this makes Gen Why seem overly skeptical. They appear to have no respect, or even knowledge, of the past. They seem to exist in a kind of numb state of Now, where their only concern is where the next spike in excitement will come from, and they question everything that gets in the way.

Their minds aren't full of thoughts of how it used to be; they're too busy thinking of how great it could be.

But Gen Why's lack of respect for the old ways is also freeing. They aren't concerned with the past so, unlike a lot of us, they aren't stuck there. Their ability to float freely through the world lets them see things in a fresh way, and because they are always questioning everything, they are naturally innovative. There isn't a day that goes by where I do not find myself in total awe of this generation and the creativity they demonstrate. Because the Gen Whys who make headlines are usually the bad seeds, we often overlook the countless stories of those who are inventing, reinventing, and revolutionizing our world for the better. And while they are frequently referred to as techno-savvy, it is important to note that Gen Whys are often the ones who have created the technology they are savvy with.

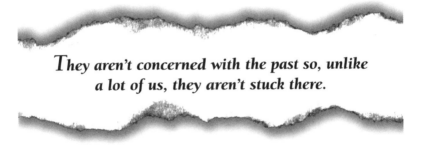

They aren't concerned with the past so, unlike a lot of us, they aren't stuck there.

While many Boomers wish that Gen Whys had more reverence for the history that has given them the prosperity they now enjoy, we should delight in the fact that they are forward thinking and passionate about the future. I am firmly convinced that many of the problems we face as a society today, e.g., AIDS, cancer, terrorism, overpopulation, racism, global warming, and so on, will be solved in the coming years thanks to the innovative nature of our Gen Whys.

WHYS UP! The practices and principles that have been successful for you in the past five years might not necessarily get you to where you want to go in the next five years. The crazy times are not behind us; they are in front of us. Therefore, it will most certainly require fresh, new ideas to remain competitive in the future. The source for many of those ideas is now dressed up and serving as your front line staff. Don't keep them there and discount what they say as inexperienced gibberish. Listen to them. Unleash their weird and wacky way of looking at things and their unconventional approach to solving problems. Remember, they tend to be digital thinkers, not analog, sequential thinkers. In what may initially appear as rubble, you will find a diamond mine of innovation that will keep you in the game for a long time.

Unleash their weird and wacky way of looking at things and their unconventional approach to solving problems.

4. **Efficient** My wife, Lori, an avid cyclist, is quick to remind our children that bicycling is the most efficient transportation known to man. When pedaling a bike, there is virtually no energy wasted, as each stroke produces a result equal to or greater than the energy exerted.

Generation Why will someday be regarded in a similar light. They are simply remarkable at achieving maximum results with minimal effort and minimal resources in minimal time. Whether it is their uncanny ability to multitask or the astounding way they leverage technology to move mountains, Gen Whys have a knack for getting the most out of the least.

Throughout their adolescence, the Whys have been challenged to fit a tremendous amount of activity into a small amount of time. Boomer parents have kept them busy in a myriad of activities, at times racing them from soccer practice to the scout meeting to band rehearsal. Further, they've been assigned to care for the everyday household chores and look after younger siblings while parents are at work. Pressed for higher test scores and faced with stiffer graduation requirements, their teachers have drilled them harder, causing homework loads to increase exponentially from days gone by. Add to this demanding regimen a part-time job, computer time, and a social life, and you can see why Gen Whys have become masters of time management and multitasking.

> **Gen Whys have a knack for getting the most out of the least.**

Gen Why's impatience also contributes to their efficiency. Once they're properly trained, they "have at" their work, because they can't wait to be done. When there is project, task, or assignment that stands between them and free time, they're not going to dillydally; they're going to find a way to get it done. Gen Whys don't get bogged down in the quagmire of details. They simply will not allow heavy workloads and long *To Do* lists to stand in their way. They are not going to sit back and wait for something when they feel they can bring it on through their own efforts. Gen Why is not a bunch of automatons; they have a tool belt full of skills. They assess, analyze, pull the tool, get the job done, and move on.

WHYS UP!

Cater to the task-minded nature of your Gen Whys by looking for ways to involve them in projects with deadlines. If you can break free from using an hourly wage compensation plan, then do so. You'll hit the top of the productivity meter with your Gen Whys when they are trying to reach a goal that is mutually beneficial. If hourly compensation is the only way to go, make sure you reward efficient work with employee incentives. Something like a cash award for completing a task ahead of time or earning a two-hour, paid mini-vacation at the end of the week will really keep your team of Gen Whys motivated.

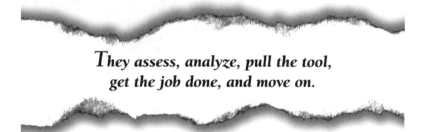

They assess, analyze, pull the tool,
get the job done, and move on.

5. Desensitized Ever wonder why Gen Whys emit the aura of been there/done that? It's because they have. If they haven't been there/done that personally, they've been there/done that virtually, which, in their minds is one and the same.

Generation Whys are the ultimate media-vores. They have grown up with 100+-channel cable TV and the Internet, the combination of which has introduced them to the very best, and the very worst, of everything. They've seen megaton shuttles blast off to outer space and haven't blinked an eye. They've viewed multiple blockbuster movies presented in Dolby surround sound in a single evening while munching on imported ice cream treats. They've been to elaborate theme parks where they've ridden the highest roller coasters and experienced the latest arcade games. The Gulf War was fought in their living room, and they watched images of real war on the same television screen where they had just played a video war game. They've seen students that look just like them savagely die at the hands of heavily armed classmates and endured the horrific visual imagery from every angle in the news coverage. Thanks to the marvel of an information-filled society, Gen Whys have grown up as fast as a radish in a radioactive garden.

What this means to you as an employer is that you cannot break through and stir emotion—positive or negative—with any degree of ease. A rah-rah motivational pep talk at a store meeting is not going to leave your Gen Whys cranked up, ready to bust all sales records. Likewise, you cannot expect them to be deeply saddened and moved to action by a scathing remark, a verbal warning, or a poor evaluation.

Thanks to the marvel of an information-filled society, Gen Whys have grown up as fast as a radish in a radioactive garden.

To make an impact with your Gen Whys, you must first have a connection to their hearts. What's hopeful and perhaps surprising about this generation is that they still have a heart. Just because they're desensitized doesn't mean they are dehumanized. The violence in schools, the drugs and gangs and promiscuity, the rap music, and the outrageous dress can all serve to make Boomers think that Gen Why has had the heart drummed out of them. Not true. In fact, from my experience talking to thousands of Gen Whys across the country, many of them have huge hearts. They only wish they didn't feel the need to defend and shield their hearts so vigilantly. One of the big jobs of managing Gen Why is breaking through these barriers. Once that happens, you'll be pleasantly surprised by what Gen Why has to offer.

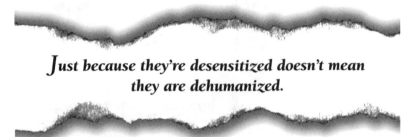

*J**ust because they're desensitized doesn't mean they are dehumanized.***

WHYS UP! The key to understanding Gen Why is that they have grown up in an increasingly impersonal world. Parents phone in to check on their kids instead of being there when they get home from school; teachers spend less and less time with individual students because of overcrowded classrooms; the mass media caters to their every whim, but by nature cannot connect with individuals on a personal level.

Invest time in building rapport. Strive to deepen your relationships with your Gen Whys. Your investment of time will pay huge dividends. Caring is the basis of sensitivity. When Gen Why really believes that you care about them, they will care about you, and even begin to understand why caring is important. When this happens, the hard shell exterior will open up, and you will have a direct link to their hearts and souls. This is where you will have your biggest impact. Instead of been there/done that, you'll develop a teach me/share with me connection. Give Gen Why the personal touch when managing them, and they'll be more than grateful.

When Gen Why really believes that you care about them, they will care about you, and even begin to understand why caring is important.

6. **Disengaged** People who are engaged in something understand the flow of life—everything we do at this moment yields a future result—and they stay engaged out of a desire to effect a result. (Engaged only means actively interested and involved and has no ties to being optimistic, positive, or happy.) Boomers are by nature engaged, having grown up in a time that reinforced the dynamic of choice and consequence. Get a girl pregnant and marry her. Commit a crime and go to jail. Work hard and get ahead. Generation X put a new spin on this principle: make a choice and then deal with it, cope with it, or try to out-maneuver the consequences. For most members of both of these generations, decisions were, and still are, made with the consideration of future implications in mind.

However, to Gen Why, the principle of *choice and conse-quence* has lost its power. They've seen the bad guy get away with it one too many times. Even though they have been cautioned to consider the logical outcome of their actions, they see that there is almost always a way to avoid the con-sequences of their behavior. To further muddy the waters, they are continually bombarded with a dim view of the future. Frequently they hear older people lament about the state of the world. The ambient uttering of their elders that pretty soon no one will be able to afford to own a home, and students won't be able to leave their homes without a bulletproof vest, and the water is no longer safe to drink, etc., etc., etc., ad nauseam, has extracted its toll.

To make matters worse, there is some truth to all this gloom and doom! While the challenges of the world aren't necessarily more severe or more real than in previous generations, we now have 500 channels on television reminding Gen Why, every day, twenty-four hours a day, about all that is going wrong. And given the lack of faith people have in our leaders to solve these problems, it's no wonder that Gen Why has disengaged. They're cynical enough (or smart enough) to see that if a problem can't be solved, then maybe it shouldn't be worried about. Another day means another crisis.

When a manager tells me that their younger workers tend to be disengaged, I rarely argue. But when I ask them what they feel this generation should be engaged about, there is often a long silence. We want our young people to be excited and enthused about tomorrow and to consider tomorrow in what they are doing today. However, the burden is on us to prove to Generation Why that the future is worth the struggle and that they do indeed affect whatever lies before them. We need to show them consequences, both good and bad, and we need to instill in them a sense that life isn't just a series of random events; that despite what we see on television, good is rewarded and evil punished, and that working hard and with purpose does bring rewards.

They're cynical enough (or smart enough) to see that if a problem can't be solved, then maybe it shouldn't be worried about.

WHYS UP! When something good happens in the workplace (a coworker is promoted, a new product is going to be unveiled, the value of your company stock increases, and so on), make sure your Gen Whys hear the good news. Let them know they have contributed to the company's success. If and when opportunities present themselves for advancements, special training programs, or scholarships, make certain your Gen Whys are informed, even if the news doesn't directly impact them. Use bulletin boards, newsletters, company meetings, and personal notes to relate the good stuff, in part just to show that there is good stuff out there. Let your workplace be a place for Gen Whys to come to take shelter from the rain clouds of negative news.

Also, be very aware of issuing empty threats. Attach specific consequences to specific choices and let everyone know the rules of the game. Where there are bad choices, there must also be consequences. Use the news of your company truthfully and honestly to show Gen Why the rewards of good work and the consequences of bad work. Live by a choice/consequence pattern, and you'll engage a generation that has not experienced this phenomenon.

Let your workplace be a place for Gen Whys to come to take shelter from the rain clouds of negative news.

7. Skeptical Despite having lived through many of the same disillusionments as Gen X and Gen Why, Boomers are still relatively gullible. We still believe in the American Dream, that hard work pays off, that a virtuous life is rewarded, and that at the end of the day the bad guy loses and the good guy wins. We grew up in a time when the world around us appeared to be steadily improving and there was an abundance of hope, optimism, and opportunity, and those messages stuck with us. Today, we still believe that most of what we hear and what we read is true. If, on the other hand, we discover that we've been had, we're surprised, shaken, and angry, and we demand an explanation.

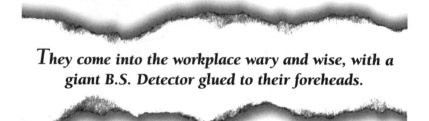

They come into the workplace wary and wise, with a giant B.S. Detector glued to their foreheads.

Xers are far more discriminating. They grew up in the shadow of the sixties mantra "don't trust anyone over thirty" and their adolescence, like that of the Gen Whys, was informed by many of the same falls from grace. The difference is that Gen Why has never known any other kind of world. They have never had an *age of innocence.* They come into the workplace wary and wise, with a giant B.S. Detector glued to their foreheads, and they are capable of sniffing out any crapola that comes within a twelve-foot radius.

Gen Whys are skeptical, and it's no wonder. They've seen their parents downsized and outsourced by the very companies they sacrificed everything to help build. They've been victimized by false advertising claims; they've stood back with shattered spirits as the media disassembled their heroes, and they've heard a president lie to get out of trouble. In short, they've been conned, manipulated, cheated, and exploited. As a result, they do not believe most of what they hear or what they read. If they discover they've been had, they aren't outraged, they just take it as *situation normal.*

So don't be disenchanted with those new hires that don't do everything you tell them to do. Don't be surprised if they don't treat you with fear and reverence, or even respect, as if your commands came directly from On High. And don't be alarmed when your Gen Whys aren't hanging on your every word with a starry-eyed innocence as you parade them around the executive washroom. The *"all this and more can be yours someday if you work hard, fly straight, and stick with the program"* speech won't carry any weight with them. They heard a lifetime of empty promises and overinflated claims before they turned twelve, and they are far too smart for gimmicks and hype now.

WHYS UP! Here's how you can set you and your organization apart from the others, while at the same time creating undying loyalty with your Gen Whys: Tell the truth. Nothing will win their respect and admiration like honesty. Aim for 100% truth, 100% of the time. Because they find it so rarely, truth works like a magnet to attract Gen Whys and helps you to earn their unshakable confidence and trust.

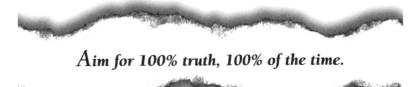

Aim for 100% truth, 100% of the time.

Before you say anything to them, first ask yourself, "Is this true?" Step back and take a look at all of your communication with your Gen Whys. Are promises made that are not well founded? Are any of the standards for satisfactory performance hidden? Are empty threats made as a scare tactic? Are the promises of raises and promotions exaggerated? Are your employees told embellished stories just to get a point across?

If your answer to any of these questions is *yes*, it's time to reevaluate your relationship with your employees. The only person fooled by the games is the manager. Gen Whys get the message loud and clear when they aren't told the truth, and the message they get is not the one we intended to send. They wonder why they should commit their time and energy to any person or organization that has tried to mislead or exploit them, and they won't give the offender a second chance.

8. **Resilient** If there's a downside to innocence, it is that it may lead to a rose-colored view of life, leaving one not really knowing what to do when things go awry. That is not something you need to worry about with your Gen Whys—they know firsthand how to deal with pain and crisis.

Remember when parents had control over what their children were exposed to? Remember when the marvel of childhood innocence lasted into puberty? Ignorance was bliss, indeed!

Today it's the good, the bad, and a lot of the ugly. Thanks largely to the plethora of media and the speed at which information travels, there is very little that Gen Whys haven't already seen or done, either personally or virtually. They gave up believing life was like Sesame Street long ago, and they've since been preparing to take it on, headfirst.

Boomers and Xers grew up believing that the world is supposed to function in a neat and orderly manner. They still have a tendency to panic when things turn chaotic or simply veer off the course of expectation. Gen Whys have no such illusions or grandiose expectations, and they don't shock easily. When the bottom falls out, they don't lie down and call for help. They jump up, knock the dust off, and immediately begin to retool and rebuild.

This resiliency plays well in the workplace. Gen Whys aren't going to get rocked by a bad earnings report or a massive corporate shakeup; they are tougher than that. They believe they can navigate any sea. So while they might quit a job out of pure boredom, seldom will they walk away from one because they find the conditions too challenging.

Gen Whys aren't bandwagon riders, either. Unlike their predecessors, they don't mind making waves. To them, the term *job security* is an oxymoron, so they're not looking to play it safe by diving into office politics and kissing butt just to stay employed. They're the ultimate risk takers, and they possess enough boldness and daring to chart new courses through untested waters. They don't think out of the box—they live there. They feast on change and love it when they are staring down a challenge. If the risk they take doesn't pan out, they're not going to get gun shy. Instead, they'll be in there trying the next time the opportunity comes around.

While they might quit a job out of pure boredom, seldom will they walk away from one because they find the conditions too challenging.

WHYS UP! Resilience is contagious. When the tides turn against you, you'll really appreciate the Gen Whys on your team. Don't assume they are flighty and that you must always paint a rosy picture for them in order to keep them motivated. Instead, let them see what looms on the horizon, good or bad, and rely on their resilience to help you survive the impending storms. Then show your appreciation, and they'll be there through the next storm.

9. **Disrespectful** Respect your elders. How's that for an antiquated expression? Ask anyone thirty or older, and they might roll their eyes and nod along, but they get it. But ask anyone under thirty about respecting their elders, and they'll give you a blank stare. The term *elder* may not even be in their vocabulary!

Boomers and the early Xers were force-fed this phrase and its virtue. Parents, grandparents, and a variety of other authority figures made certain their children—and every child they came in contact with—knew exactly what it meant. As a result, Boomers never questioned this principle; they live by it. Unfortunately, as we matured and had families of our own, we became so preoccupied with work and our own indulgences that when it came to passing down the "respect your elders" maxim to our children, we failed miserably. Proof? When was the last time a kid stood up to give you their seat on the bus, or addressed you as Mr. or Ms. instead of by your first name or, even worse, "Hey you!"

It's not that Gen Why doesn't value respect. On the contrary, they know all too well what respect is, and, more importantly, the power it holds. They live by the creed *"he who has the respect has the power,"* and to them, respect is a prize that must be won. Gen Why craves respect and will go to great lengths to get it, but when it comes to giving respect, they are stingy. They won't automatically respect a person simply because of their age, their position, or their title. They do not want to yield their power or put somebody in a position of control over them. In a strange reversal of the traditional dynamic between youth and age, they believe that they are owed respect automatically but that you have to prove to them that you are worthy of their consideration. In most situations, respect is bartered. "You respect me first," Gen Why seems to be saying, "then maybe I'll respect you!"

They live by the creed "he who has the respect has the power," and to them, respect is a prize that must be won.

Because Gen Why's interests and desires have been catered to by advertisers, media conglomerates, and even parents, they are used to being sought after. Focus groups seek their opinions, marketers listen very, very carefully to what they think is cool and what they think is lame, and parents can spoil them rotten. And because their adulthood is being forced on them at younger and younger ages, in some cases they've needed more power to cope with an increasingly difficult world.

WHYS UP!
Fight the urge to demand their respect. Instead, treat them with the same degree of respect you would have them give you,

and your actions will be mirrored. At the same time, don't let their definition of respect become yours. You are the boss and are in control. They know that, and they'll respect you more for not immediately caving in to their demands. Instead, lead by the example born out of your experiences. As mentioned, they won't automatically respect you because you are older or because you have an important title attached to your name.

You are the boss and are in control. They know that, and they'll respect you more for not immediately caving in to their demands.

Gen Whys respect authenticity, accomplishment, and competence. If you have a strong personality, let it out. Members of Gen Why have strong personalities too, and they are very tolerant of other people's differences. Remember, though, they can spot a phony in a heartbeat. If you are naturally quieter, then *demonstrate* to them that you know what you're doing, and you do what you do, the way you do it, based on experience. When they learn what you did to get you where you are—and they see your hard work and character shine through—you will earn their respect.

10. **Bluntly Expressive** "Children are to be seen and not heard!" "If you can't say something nice, don't say anything at all!"

Remember those little phrases? Gen Whys don't! They've probably never heard them. Instead, they've been taught to speak their minds. They've been told not to keep anything bottled up inside. They've also seen how being overtly verbal— whether or not you have anything valid, interesting, or important to say—has led to fame and fortune for some like Howard Stern as well as countless celebrities of sport, stage, and screen. The new breed of television talk shows has shown them that anyone who might feel slandered, cheated, or disrespected has the right to confront the perpetrator and give them a piece of their mind. Being rude, crude, obnoxious, and insulting in modern day America draws laughter, attention, applause, and sometimes even a fat endorsement contract.

Sadly, the virtues of courtesy, politeness, tact, and diplomacy are on the endangered species list. Gen Whys have their own thoughts, ideas, and opinions—and you are going to hear them, like it or not! They won't stand by passively if they feel they are being disrespected in any way. If a coworker, supervisor, or customer does something to ruffle their feathers, you can bet the conflict is going public. The good news for managers is that they no longer have to wait for an evaluation form to find out how their younger employees are feeling about them or their job. The feedback is immediate. The bad news is that the feedback is often personal and negative and can come out at the worst times and in the worst places.

Being rude, crude, obnoxious, and insulting in modern day America draws laughter, attention, applause, and sometimes even a fat endorsement contract.

WHYS UP! Your Gen Whys want to be heard, so give them a structured forum to do so. Let them know from the outset that you do care about what they think and that you are sensitive to their feelings and opinions. Then inform them that there is a system for airing problems and concerns and that they are welcome, even encouraged, to provide their feedback within the guidelines of the system you have in place.

When a Gen Why does say something inappropriate, try not to take it personally. Again, these are not bad kids. It's just that they have been programmed to let it all hang out and to speak their minds (ironically, oftentimes by their Boomer parents). One thing working to your advantage is the knowledge that for Gen Why, often it's all just talk. Their attitude is often just that: attitude. It's important to figure out what constitutes a real grievance and what is just letting off steam.

Establish firm boundaries for their interaction with your customers and let them know what will and will not be tolerated from them when they're dealing with an irate or insulting customer. Then, sink those fence posts deep. Prepare them for the unpleasant situations they might encounter with your customers and train them how to channel their emotions so that they'll be able to arrive at peaceful and equitable conclusions. Offer recognition and incentives for employees who clearly demonstrate that when it comes to working with others, they can take the heat without getting hot.

11. **Tolerant** Growing up in Wheat Ridge, Colorado (a suburb of Denver), my world was pretty marshmallow. All my friends were carbon copies of me. Their families were like my families, and their houses were like my house. The first black kid I ever had a conversation with was

one I met in college. Throughout my teenage years, I didn't know anyone who had a physical disability, or was Muslim or gay. I didn't know anyone who was extremely rich or extremely poor. My knowledge and opinions of those who were different from me came mostly from my dad, who was raised in the Deep South. I'm not proud to admit it, but it's taken me the better part of the last twenty years to get a true picture of the world and its inhabitants.

There is a refreshing spirit of openness with Generation Why, clearly demonstrated in their willingness to embrace each other regardless of outward differences.

Prejudices divide people, and a divided company will not survive in the new millennium. For decades, business leaders have desperately sought ways to bring people of diverse backgrounds together to create the kind of productivity that is only possible in a united and harmonious workplace. But intolerance is the archenemy of teamwork, and it has hampered the wheels of American progress significantly. Until now.

Perhaps it's a form of positive rebellion, but the majority of Gen Whys have rejected the prejudices handed down to them. They can be rude and disrespectful, but they can also be incredibly understanding of other people's experiences, even if they are radically different from their own. They may be quick to mouth off, but they don't judge others as quickly as it would seem. There is a refreshing spirit of openness with Generation Why, clearly demonstrated in their willingness to embrace each other regardless of outward differences. Credit the civil rights movement or ex-hippie parents, but Generation Why will someday be remembered for erasing hate and being far more tolerant than any previous generation. Race, creed, color, faith, sexual orientation, age, income, status, and the numerous other factors that have often been points of contention for their parents will not stand in the way of progress for Generation Why. In fact, the only thing Gen Whys will not tolerate is intolerance.

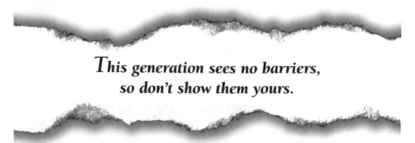

This generation sees no barriers, so don't show them yours.

WHYS UP! Your Gen Whys are the building blocks of a truly effective team. If they are made to feel welcome, they will work with anyone and everyone toward the pursuit of a common goal. Do not segregate them from your established workforce; in fact, integrate them immediately! Give them an opportunity to interact with your most difficult customers and vendors, and you'll be amazed at how quickly they can build rapport and restore torn relationships. Discard your notion of traditional roles for men and women (e.g., the guys carry the boxes and the women brew the morning coffee). This generation sees no barriers, so don't show them yours.

12. Committed Danny is a typical Gen Why who didn't fit in as a mainstream teenager. For years after graduation he bounced around from job to job until Larry, the owner of a small restaurant chain, hired Danny as a cook. Larry took Danny under his wing, befriended him, and went way out of his way to help Danny build a foundation for his life. Larry and this restaurant chain soon became the first real family Danny had ever had. Their relationship has endured many bleak times. To demonstrate his loyalty to his employer, Danny tattooed the company logo on the side of his shaved head and today wears it proudly. When asked how long he thought he might stay with this restaurant, Danny said that he has no plans to leave, ever. Danny truly believes he'll be working with and for Larry for the rest of his life.

Gen Why is fiercely loyal to those institutions they believe in. Get them to buy in to your company's mission, demonstrate that you care about them as individuals, and like Danny, they'll hang in there through thick and thin. Generation Why is searching for a purpose, something to believe in, and someone to believe in them. If they connect with a job that intrigues them and an employer that invites them to be a part of the family, they will be relentless foot soldiers for the team.

The nineties saw the advent of the *free agent* employee, who was always looking for a better deal, and the *fair weather* employee, who deserted the company at the first sign of turbulence. These characteristics are common in Boomers and Xers. Gen Whys are not shaken by chaos nor will they run at the sound of bad news. For managers, this comes as very good news, indeed.

If they connect with a job that intrigues them and an employer that invites them to be a part of the family, they will be relentless foot soldiers for the team.

WHYS UP!

Although it is in their blood to search for the path of least resistance, it is also in Gen Whys' DNA to go down fighting for what they believe in. The trick, of course, is to get them to believe in your organization as they would a friend. Gen Whys need to believe they are wanted, needed, and cared for. When they do, their loyalty shines bright.

FINAL THOUGHT

It's obvious that Generation Why is not going to sit back and watch it all arbitrarily unfold for them. They are looking for opportunities that empower them to use the time, the tools, and their remarkable talents to build a better life. What is not to be missed is the fact that they have an underlying desire to do the right thing, to know the truth of a situation, to have a job that means more than a paycheck, and to live a life that matters.

In the first section, we have laid out a portrait of Generation Why, complete with contradictions and paradoxes. I do believe, however, that the upside clearly outweighs the downside and that we have reason to be optimistic. Surely it's important to recognize Gen Why's negative traits when they pop up in the workplace. A disengaged employee needs to understand they have to give their all in order to succeed, but rather than show managers ways to punish Gen Why, the following chapters will show you how to harness the tremendous talent and energy they bring to your workplace and channel it towards mutually beneficial outcomes. That alien Gen Why you have working for you now might not be meeting your father's expectations, but with your new understanding of them and their world—and the ideas and strategies that follow—you might be able to mold them into your next super employee.

*T*hey have an underlying desire to do the right thing, to know the truth of a situation, to have a job that means more than a paycheck, and to live a life that matters.

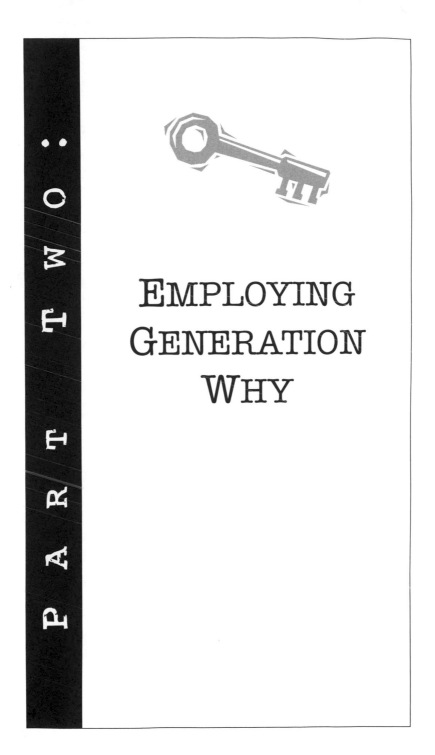

PART TWO

EMPLOYING
GENERATION
WHY

Business strategist Dr. Tony Alessandra reminds us that prescription before diagnosis equals malpractice. In our eagerness to find the remedy to manage and motivate Generation Why, it is imperative that we first have a very clear understanding of exactly what we are up against. We need to know the challenge before us and why it exists before we can ever attempt to find realistic ways to fix what's broken.

In Part One we profiled Generation Why, providing insight and perspective into who they are, how they think, what they value, and why they behave as they do. At this point, you may be saying to yourself: "Okay, so now I understand them better, and I see what I am up against. But what do I do from here?"

The pages that follow are loaded with ideas and action steps that you can take to improve your employment experience with Generation Why. These strategies will help you to realize immediate results as well as long-term performance improvement with your Gen Whys.

Some of these ideas come from personal observation. Others are based in my belief that what has proven successful in teaching, coaching, and motivating Gen Whys through their formal education can be applied with the same successful results in the workplace. Additionally, my clients and friends who, like you, are in the trenches with Gen Why employees every day, have generously shared their ideas and examples. These very wise leaders from diverse industries have discovered a piece to the puzzle and have been gracious enough to share it with the world—even when that world includes their competitors.

You'll also notice how many of these ideas are not exclusive to the chapter they appear in. A good recruiting idea will help you identify your future stars, making it easier to manage them. A well-constructed recognition and reward program will certainly aid in helping you retain the best and the brightest. Simply put, these ideas and concepts are inter-related, but then, so is the nature of motivating and managing employees.

Recruiting

A SK ANY COACH in college or professional sports, and they'll tell you that their ability to win is based primarily on the talent they have on their roster. You can be a whale of a coach and have a tremendous game plan, but if the other team fields better athletes, your chances of winning are remote, at best. The same rule applies in business. If you can't assemble and keep a talented front line staff, your odds of keeping pace with your competitor down the street are slim.

It all begins with recruiting. This is where the rubber meets the road. Ninety-five percent of the personnel problems you face with your employees could be eliminated if you were able to recruit the right people into your company or organization. But with young talent in such short supply, you're competing with businesses of every size and kind and not just with those in your own industry.

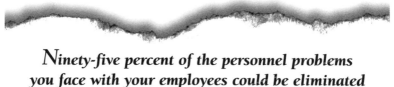

Ninety-five percent of the personnel problems you face with your employees could be eliminated if you were able to recruit the right people into your company or organization.

Think about your expenditure of energy for a moment. If, as a manager, you're spending a disproportionate amount of your time on the hire 'em/fire 'em treadmill, thinking "that's just the way it is with these flaky kids today," you haven't figured out how to attract and hire *good fits* for your business. There are a lot of gems out there to be had. The irony is, they want to work for you as badly as you want them in your employ. Unfortunately, you're misconnecting, and one of you is going to have to seek out the other, or connections will be made elsewhere.

Granted, most Gen Whys aren't coming into your employ thinking *career*—they're thinking *car*. They've got big dreams, and the job you're offering might appear to them to be just a pit stop on the racetrack of their career. This doesn't preclude them from being good bets for long-term employment, it simply means they're not aware—or haven't been convinced—of the long-term possibilities.

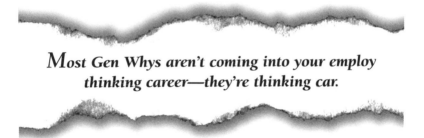

Most Gen Whys aren't coming into your employ thinking career—they're thinking car.

Another challenge of securing good Gen Why help, particularly the part-time, teenage sort, is that they don't value work as much as previous generations did. Part of this has to do with America's record-breaking levels of prosperity. Many members of Gen Why don't have to work at all, or their need to work isn't felt as acutely as it was in previous generations. For Boomers and Xers, work was a way to freedom, but many Gen Why kids already enjoy an unprecedented amount of personal and financial freedom. As for the idea that work builds character, forget about it. How they play is a much better indicator of who they are; where they work is secondary at best. The sports and video games they play, the music they create and listen to, the websites they run—these are more important to them than work. Employers who try to recruit Generation Why with the old attitude that work is good medicine will be met with resistance.

All of this might make Gen Whys look like a bunch of prima donnas playing hard to get, which is partially true. After years of being catered to by the media, many members of Gen Why believe they are superstars. Employers today have to work harder to court them. This is perhaps the greatest challenge managers face, because oftentimes the jobs Gen Why are qualified to fill are entry-level jobs that previous generations were eager take. Gen Why is more picky. They have to be sold not only on the idea of work, but also on why your company is the right company for them.

How can you win at the recruiting game?

There is a line in the action thriller *Face Off,* where John Travolta's character, a cop, implies that *in order to catch the enemy* (the villain played by Nicolas Cage), *he must become the enemy.* To some degree, this philosophy is true for managers looking to recruit Generation Why. Although they are to be viewed as allies and not enemies, to *catch* them you must *become* them—or at least be capable of thinking like they do. The first part of the book is dedicated to that end.

This section contains practical ideas, tools, and processes to bolster your GW recruiting efforts. Incorporating a combination of these suggestions will enable you to put together a strong recruiting plan that appeals to the *good fits* within your Gen Why scope. Of course, to seek out the best, you'll need to weed out the rest, and an effective recruiting plan will essentially widen your funnel, which in turn will increase the flow of applicants into your business. So be prepared. Have a system in place for quickly separating the chaff from the grain, or you're going to trade one problem—

not having enough applicants—for another—training/managing employees that should never have been hired in the first place.

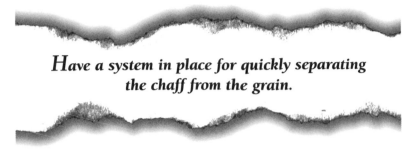

Have a system in place for quickly separating the chaff from the grain.

SELL YOURSELF FIRST

Tom hadn't waited on me for many years. As the senior teller, Tom's job was to supervise the other younger tellers in the bank, but this particular day, the line was long and the bank was short-staffed, so I drew Tom as my teller. "Short-handed today, are you Tom?" I asked.

Appearing stressed and frustrated, he replied, "Eric, we just can't seem to get young people to work here anymore, and I don't understand it, because it's such a great job."

Naturally, I pried a bit deeper. "Tom, what makes it such a great job?"

"Well," he responded, "we offer a competitive salary and a nice benefit program."

I pointed out that so did most of his competitors, and asked, "What makes working at this bank better than working at the one down the street?"

Tom went blank, but his expression spoke volumes. He simply couldn't think of a single reason why his bank—one where he had worked for more than twenty-five years—would be the best choice for potential employees.

Young people in general are very quick to see through

the smoke screens put up by adults. After years of being bombarded with advertising, Generation Why is even savvier at recognizing what is just another marketing gimmick. You cannot move Generation Why into taking an action unless you yourself are absolutely committed. It's like trying to convince someone to go on a lengthy, expensive European vacation when you yourself have never left the country.

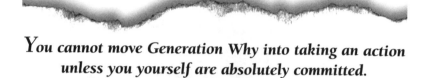

You cannot move Generation Why into taking an action unless you yourself are absolutely committed.

As employers of Generation Why, we need to first convince ourselves of the merits, benefits, and advantages of the jobs we're seeking to fill, and we must know what makes them good jobs. Everyone in our organization who comes in contact with potential job candidates should also be able to do the same. If you're not firmly convinced that you have something really good to offer a potential employee, particularly a Gen Why employee, you need to improve the qualities of the position before trying to find a quality person to fill the opening.

WHYS IDEA Sell yourself first on your company and its opportunities before you post job availabilities. Develop a checklist of specific factors that differentiates working for your business from working for the others your prospective labor pool might also be considering. Then rehearse it and be able to recite it on a moment's notice. Make certain that the members of your entire supervisory staff also know the differentiators and are able to easily repeat them to an interested young job seeker.

To recruit top Gen Why talent, you're going to have to sell them on your company and the advantages of being a part of your team. You must also be familiar with the jobs/opportunities that your competitors are offering so that you can clearly contrast the advantages of choosing *yours* over *theirs* to your GW prospects. Remember: You can't sell something you don't believe in, any easier than you can return from a place you have never been. So convince yourself first!

To recruit top Gen Why talent, you're going to have to sell them on your company and the advantages of being a part of your team.

CAST A WIDE NET

A few years ago I was having lunch with my best friend, who was lamenting to me how difficult it was to find quality women to date. He had been single for about a decade and was looking to meet someone for a long-term relationship and possible marriage. He said he was growing tired of the bar scene and had almost resigned himself to the fact that he would be a bachelor for the rest of his life.

I asked him if it were true that he could potentially meet the woman of his dreams in a bar, and with some hesitation he responded, "Yes, I guess that could be a possibility." I pulled a Sharpie out of my pocket, grabbed a napkin and wrote: *Number 1—Singles Bars.* I asked, "How many other ways are there to potentially meet your future bride?" He said, "Well, I guess I could try more blind dates." I wrote down *Number 2—Blind Dates.* We continued to brainstorm, and when we were done we had a list of fifteen different ways he might be able to meet women. The list included everything from video dating to personal ads to striking up a conversation with a total stranger he found interesting, perhaps in a bank or at a grocery store.

I then spun the napkin around to face my friend. "Any of these methods can be successful in helping you find the woman of your dreams," I said, "but do you know which of these methods will prove successful?" After a long silence (during which he was undoubtedly thinking that if he knew the answer to that question he wouldn't still be single) I answered for him: "Only those that you put effort into."

The same philosophy applies to employers seeking to find the perfect Gen Why employees. If you were to create a list of those strategies and methods you use currently to recruit employees into your place of business, the list might look something like this:

1. Help Wanted/Now Hiring signs
2. Ads in the local paper
3. Post a listing on the Internet

The unfortunate truth is that most of the recruitment tactics we use to attract young workers aren't very creative or effective. If you really want to attract Gen Why, you need to change both the medium and the message. Most of all, commit fully to each effort. Sit down with your key managers and brainstorm about ways you could recruit new Gen

Why employees. When you're finished brainstorming, your list might include twenty to thirty different ways you can recruit employees for your organization. Any of them *can be* successful, but the only ones that *will be* successful are those you put your effort into.

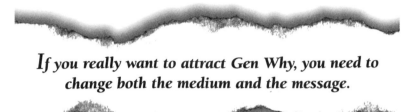

If you really want to attract Gen Why, you need to change both the medium and the message.

WHYS IDEA Cast a wide net. Leave no stone unturned. Use every conceivable method or strategy available to you to increase the number of potential qualified candidates for your business. This will enable you to be much more discriminating when selecting the right employees for your organization.

The balance of this section will present more ideas that will help you widen the net you are currently using. This is just a start. Begin with a list of ideas that have already been successful for you or that you have been considering. When you get to the end of your list, begin brainstorming with your peers and colleagues. Read the best human resource magazines (*Workforce, HR Today,* etc.) to find out what is being done in parallel industries and adapt clever ideas specific to your business. Don't stop there! Ask your current Gen Why employees for their ideas and suggestions.

(P.S. My friend eventually met his bride-to-be on a blind date, proving to me once again that miracles do, in fact, happen.)

CHANGE YOUR GLASSES

The solution to a nagging recruitment dilemma might be closer than you think. By looking at your customer base through a different lens, you might be able to see some potential employee material.

My son Zac and his friends love to hang out at the music store down the street from our house. They have their own band and love to go to this store to try out the new instruments while they fantasize about owning expensive guitars, amps, and drums. Because they are young and aren't going to the store to purchase big-ticket items, the store manager probably sees them as a nuisance, when instead he could view them as a valuable resource.

While flipping through the classifieds of our community paper, I noticed that the music store was advertising an opening for a part-time cashier to work after school and weekends. I stopped in to ask how long they had been looking to fill this spot and was told that they had been running the ad for three weeks and that they'd received a few calls but that no one had come in to apply. "This is strange," I thought to myself. "They're looking outside the store, hoping to lure someone into the store to do something that someone who is already in the store would love to do!" If only the manager were bright enough to make the connection and approach some of the "loiterers," he would expose his cashier in waiting.

WHYS IDEA Open yourself to the possibility that your passionate Generation Why customers might be an exceptional pool from which to draw your employees. Get to know your young customers on a first-name basis. If a Gen Why buys your product, odds are they may want to sell your product. And when they start selling your product, look out! When a member of Gen Why takes an interest in something, they don't just use it, they become experts in it. This is where their media and technological savvy helps them. They can take in and retain enormous amounts of product information. Remember, a Gen Why behind the counter will draw others like him- or herself into your business as both customers and employees.

When a member of Gen Why takes an interest in something, they don't just use it, they become experts in it.

STREAMLINE THE PROCESS

Most of us can remember the days when jobs for teenagers were scarce. I taught high school business classes for six years. In most of these courses, I'd spend three to six weeks on job application and interview skills. My students were more enthusiastic about these units than any other all year, because most had aspirations of getting a job. This job application unit would include tips on where to look for a job, how to dress appropriately, how to ask the manager for an application, what to bring to a job interview, and so on. Then we'd go through the interview process. I'd invite area human resource people and business managers into my class to conduct mock interviews with the students. The underlying message was clear for Generation X—finding a job was a daunting task that took skill, patience, and, above all, perseverance.

Fast forward to the new millennium. Today, the McDonald's in my neighborhood prints a job application on the outside of the bag that hamburgers come in! It is only a six-line application, asking for personal contact information and why you'd want to work for McDonald's. Now, a skeptic might say that with that kind of recruitment policy, anybody could apply for a job, which is true. But that doesn't mean that anybody will get the job. One smart thing McDonald's did was to figure out a step in the application process that wasn't needed. Not surprisingly, other retailers and restaurants have followed suit and eliminated the pomp and circumstance from the application process. McDonald's, a huge consumer of Gen Why labor, has clearly had to modify its recruiting strategies and make it simple for prospects to pursue employment.

McDonald's, a huge consumer of Gen Why labor, has clearly had to modify its recruiting strategies and make it simple for prospects to pursue employment.

WHYS IDEA Tune in to the trends of Generation Why and eliminate all time-consuming, unnecessary, and awkward steps in your recruiting process. Gen Why is not big on jumping through hoops or tearing through red tape. To increase your application flow, decrease the number of obstacles hindering an interested prospect from becoming a new employee.

Test the process by asking a focus group of Gen Why volunteers from a local high school or college to assume the role of job prospects coming into your business. Then ask them to evaluate the processes and how well your staff was trained to help them. Did they make them feel comfortable? Did they offer them an application? Did they take down their name and number for future reference? And so on. This kind of *mystery shopper* tactic can prove extremely revealing!

To increase your application flow, decrease the number of obstacles hindering an interested prospect from becoming a new employee.

SNOOZE AND LOSE

By their nature, Gen Whys are impatient and will typically opt for a mediocre *now* rather than wait for a splendid *later.* Therefore, to remain competitive in the tight labor market, you should look for innovative ways to respond more quickly and you should begin building a relationship with your applicants immediately.

My teenage son set a goal to find a part-time job. He spent a full Saturday and two weekday afternoons traveling through malls and shopping centers filling out job applications and talking to managers from a wide variety of industries. He wasn't trying to find employment for the next forty years, or even the next forty months, he just wanted to find a way to keep gas in his car that was also kind of fun to do and offered a flexible schedule. Later that week the phone started to ring off the hook with calls from the managers of the restaurants, shops, and stores where he'd put in his application. However, these employers were a day late and a dollar short, as the saying goes. Zac had already accepted a job. It wasn't necessarily the best fit for him or even one he really wanted. It was, however, the first one to respond with an interview and a subsequent job offer. At that point Zac felt that changing jobs would be too big of a hassle.

Home Depot Stores are working hard to eliminate the application/recruiting delay by using technology. A prospective job seeker can begin the application and interview process at the local Home Depot by completing a job application and responding to a series of questions at a kiosk inside the store. The application is electronically zipped to the headquarters, where the responses are reviewed and applicants are screened and contacted immediately via phone or E-mail if they are wanted for an additional interview.

Bruce Clifton, HR director for Timberline Lodge in Oregon, claims he has lost far too many solid gold Gen Whys to competing employers who responded faster than he did. He therefore made it his mission to respond to each and every online applicant with a personalized E-mail within two hours of the time the application was submitted. Cutting the response time has greatly helped Home Depot and Timberline Lodge keep worthy applicants from slipping through the cracks.

WHYS IDEA Take steps to decrease the time between application and interview, and between interview and job offer. Don't let any dust collect on an application that comes across your desk. Respond immediately, even if only to say that you received the application and will be in contact shortly. Keep the prospect engaged by sending them an E-mail link to a hidden page on your company website where they can access detailed, insider information about the company. Make certain that you establish immediate contact and maintain active communication from your first contact to the Gen Why's date of hire.

Don't let any dust collect on an application that comes across your desk. Respond immediately, even if only to say that you received the application and will be in contact shortly.

GO WHERE THEY GO

The Swedish furniture maker Ikea is trying a new approach to finding young talented employees: attracting applicants with handwritten ads on the walls of public bathrooms. Spokesman Jimmy Ostholm said that after only four days they had received sixty applications, which was four or five times more than what they would have gotten from a normal newspaper ad. Ostholm added that the unusual campaign was significantly cheaper than a newspaper ad, too.

Ikea has obviously decided to go off the board with its new campaign. However absurd this may seem, the thinking behind it is sound. If you're going to attract a new breed of employee, you have to be willing to go about it using unconventional means and advertising in unconventional locations.

Ask yourself where the best potential recruits for your organization gather and take your campaign to that locale. Consider the visibility of the local skateboard park, public library, or Internet cafe. Form alliances with key people in key locations and work cooperatively to give your message premium exposure. Since you are competing with video games and the Internet for the attention of Gen Why, use both to your advantage. Start a recruitment drive on the web, or take flyers to the local video game store and post them where kids shopping for the latest video game can see them.

Form alliances with key people in key locations and work cooperatively to give your message premium exposure.

WHYS IDEA Clever managers know what is going on in their community, and they take advantage of large crowd gatherings at concerts, games, and rallies with flyers and strategically placed ads. They'll set up booths at festivals and events and distribute flyers at high school, college, and community job fairs. They never miss a chance to be seen, and they consider oddball places to connect that their competitors haven't.

If Gen Why applicants aren't banging your door down seeking opportunity, work on unique ways to seek them out. Consider the skills you want your applicants to have, then seek out both physical and virtual places that hold special appeal to Whys with interests that mirror that skill set. Go where they go.

Consider the skills you want your applicants to have, then seek out both physical and virtual places that hold special appeal to Whys with interests that mirror that skill set.

FORM AN ALLIANCE

Recently I presented for 140 managers of quick-service sandwich restaurants. The meeting planner had taken the preprogram questionnaire and listed as the companies' greatest concern the inability to attract part-time teen labor. I prepared my presentation with this foremost in mind.

Approximately halfway into my presentation, I asked each of the managers to jot the numbers 1, 2, and 3 on a blank sheet of paper. I then asked them to list the three high schools and/or community colleges closest to their restaurant's geographic location. The looks on their collective faces demonstrated that most of the managers had absolutely no idea what schools were in the vicinity of their stores. For those that did know, I continued by asking them to name a contact person, such as a counselor, an administrator, or a teacher, with whom they were on a first-name basis, within each of those three buildings. Once again, I saw looks of utter bewilderment.

To be successful in recruiting Generation Why youth, it is imperative that managers form alliances and/or contacts with those who have an inside track. Managers who are on a first-name basis with key school personnel have a behind-the-lines ally helping them in their recruiting efforts. This also helps the door of opportunity to swing both ways. When the manager needs labor, they can get in touch with the key contacts within that school, to get student referrals, and when the school personnel know of a student who is looking for part-time work, they can contact the manager. Truly a win-win situation.

Managers who are on a first-name basis with key contact school personnel have a behind-the-lines ally helping them in their recruiting efforts.

WHYS IDEA You cannot easily identify the winners from the losers in your potential Gen Why talent pool, so join forces with the people who can. It is worth the investment of time to get on a personal basis with key staff at your local high school or college. Once you know who these key people are, turn them into advocates and allies by keeping in contact with them at least once a month. They want to be a resource for you, because it benefits them as well. Why not take the initiative to invite them to join your team as a talent scout.

BUILD A BRIDGE FOR YOUR FUTURE CEO

Like you, I love hearing a good success story. We've all heard tales of the company CEO who started out as the stockroom clerk. We mustn't lose sight of the fact that our reliance on recruiting good talent is reduced when we can hang on to the good talent we have.

Each year, Hy-Vee, a large supermarket chain in the Midwest, conducts a career day seminar at its headquarters in West Des Moines, Iowa. Hy-Vee invites several hundred of its part-time, college-aged employees to this impressive meeting. The objective of the career day is to entice young college talent to view working at Hy-Vee as a strategic career move rather than as just a job. This gives Hy-Vee an opportunity to showcase its very impressive corporate headquarters to those who might otherwise see only the store they work in and to introduce Gen Whys to the company's high-ranking personnel. The students hear personal success stories from company execs and high-paid store managers, many of whom are not much older than the students themselves. Hy-Vee's CEO, Ron Pearson, who always addresses the Gen Whys, shares how he too began his career with the company as a part-time grocery clerk.

"This program has been remarkably effective," said vice president Rose Kleyweg Mitchell. "It gives those students who are searching for a career path the opportunity to see that their dream job may not be that far removed from their present job."

WHYS IDEA While good managers can entice good people to work for them, great managers have the ability to develop their people into champions. Look past the immature nature of your younger employees and picture how they'll be after a little of your mentoring. Your company's CEO of tomorrow may just be in your stockroom today. Build a bridge for them to get started and keep the path fully illuminated.

*While good managers can entice good people
to work for them, great managers have the ability
to develop their people into champions.*

WORK THE NETWORK

The founding principle for the success of multilevel marketing (MLM) businesses is to involve your friends and family in your distribution network. That is why whenever one of your friends or relatives signs on with an MLM-based company, you are always called and invited to a business opportunity meeting. With Generation Why placing such a high value on social interaction, it doesn't make sense to overlook their social network as a potential pool from which to recruit talent. Companies and organizations that are successful in recruiting this generation have sophisticated employee referral plans in place.

Although Gen Whys won't refer a friend for employment strictly for the money or incentive attached to it, a nice premium always serves to keep their eyes and ears open for future coworkers. This is not something that only large employers can do. I know of a mom-and-pop pizza restaurant that offers its Gen Why employees a pizza party for up to twenty-five of their friends if they refer a job applicant who is subsequently hired and remains with the company for three months. The catch, of course, is that the employee who makes the referral must also still be employed when the ninety-day trial period ends to claim their reward. This is the kind of program that helps to bring more applicants into the workplace while retaining those already there.

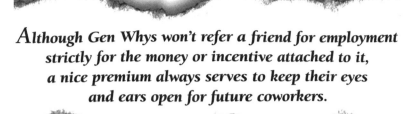

Although Gen Whys won't refer a friend for employment strictly for the money or incentive attached to it, a nice premium always serves to keep their eyes and ears open for future coworkers.

WHYS IDEA

It is not enough to periodically mention that you are looking for good people. Get aggressive and ask your staff to refer specific people for employment. When you call them, use the Gen Why's name and know something about them—it will score many points. Given a choice, Generation Why would prefer to work alongside of their friends. It makes sense to accommodate them by finding unique ways to reward them for referring their friends to your workplace.

STANDING ROOM ONLY

When you call recruits to inform them that you have decided to offer them a position, what is the typical response? If the applicants aren't extremely excited, odds are they don't believe they've accomplished much by getting the job. Further, they may feel that there is nothing special about the job they've been offered and that you would have hired anyone who applied. If this is their first impression and they don't value the job—at least to some degree—they're not going to throw themselves into it.

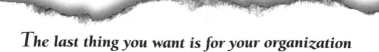

The last thing you want is for your organization to appear desperate for help.

Some people view standing in line as a deterrent to getting involved, but did you know that the appearance of a line can actually help you attract Generation Why workers? Failing to respond promptly to Gen Why applicants is sure death, but the last thing you want is for your organization to appear desperate for help. This is translated in the minds of Gen Why to mean *no one wants to work here.* Instead, project the image that it is not easy to get a job in your organization. (This does not mean you should make the application procedure complicated and thereby create a bottleneck in the process.)

The Marines capitalize on this concept in their campaign: "We're Looking for a Few Good Men." It makes no bones about how difficult it is to get to be a Marine and that only the very best need apply. Instead of scaring off recruits, it creates more of them!

If Gen Why sees your organization as an anyone-can-get-a-job-at-that-place kind of environment, you'll miss out on Marine-caliber talent. Therefore, create an environment where applicants are screened, tested, and rigorously interviewed prior to getting the job, but where the entire process is handled smoothly and efficiently. You'll not only attract a better caliber applicant, you'll discover that the Gen Whys you hire are committed to the job they take.

WHYS IDEA
Make it easy to apply, but not so easy to get hired.

*If the applicants aren't extremely excited,
odds are they don't believe they've accomplished much
by getting the job.*

The First Responder

Gen Whys who apply for employment at Monarch Ski & Snowboard Area in Southwestern Colorado don't get a call from management when they are a prospective hire. The first person they hear from is a peer, and the call comes almost immediately. Monarch has decided that the best people to connect with interested Gen Whys are other Gen Whys who are already committed employees. This immediately puts the applicant at ease. If they have any questions or concerns, the Gen Why staff member can address these issues from the perspective of the applicant, letting them know how the job really works—both the pros and the cons. If the applicant has a question that the employed Gen Why cannot answer, they are referred to management or human resources.

This First Responder program serves Monarch well, while simultaneously aligning it with the specific needs and wants of the Gen Whys. First, it eliminates lengthy delays often experienced when busy managers must try to work in calls to prospective employees. There's literally no time wasted between the time of application and the all-important first contact. Second, it engages the current Gen Why employees, giving them an opportunity to do something they wouldn't normally do during the course of a typical day, satisfying their needs for change and for more advanced responsibilities. Third, it creates an immediate ally for the new applicant, helping them feel as if they already have a friend who works for the company. Oftentimes, the Gen Why employee will serve as a mentor or a trainer for a new employee they helped to recruit.

WHYS IDEA Train your top-producing Gen Whys to be your First Responders to assist you in the initial contact and screening of your Gen Why applicants. Trust them to ask and to answer the type of questions the new job applicants have. Invite your First Responders to sit in on the initial interview. If the applicant is hired, involve your First Responder in the orientation, the training, and the mentoring of the new employee.

A Word to the Wise

Make absolutely certain that your First Responders are solid, committed employees with positive, outgoing personalities. If you have any doubts or reservations about using a Gen Why employee as a First Responder, shadow them on calls until both of you feel comfortable. Make certain to structure a nice incentive-based reward system for First Responders who prove they are capable of helping you reel in good-fit applicants.

CYBER RECRUITING

Your potential Gen Why employees are definitely on the Internet looking for intriguing job possibilities, and you need to have a presence in any medium that commands so much of their time. There are a multitude of recruiting websites that are available to both employers and job seekers—certainly too many to mention and evaluate in this book. My own company recently posted one job opening on

Monster.com, and we received a dozen E-mail solicitations from other Internet recruiting companies by the end of the first day! With so many options available to you, finding the best Internet recruiting sites for your company is something that needs to be done with great care. You need to find those sites that your ideal candidates are using, which in many cases are not necessarily those getting the most hits.

Where you post is certainly a major consideration, but equally important is what you post. Too many companies simply list openings by providing a job title accompanied with associated salary and benefit information, without first trying to form a relationship with the Gen Why job hunter. The best Internet job ads are those that use humor and invoke a thoughtful response as opposed to just a click or two by the cyber surfer. The more targeted you are, the better your chances of finding the right Gen Why for the job.

The best Internet job ads are those that use humor and invoke a thoughtful response as opposed to just a click or two by the cyber surfer.

I mentioned my company as an example, so I'll share what we did to zero in on our exact needs. Our posting gave a three-paragraph description of the administrative assistant position we were looking to fill and also a description of the type of person that would most likely enjoy it (yes, we mentioned enjoyment). We detailed the hours, the environment, and the character traits needed for success, along with the compensation specifics. We then asked each candidate to request an interview by E-mail with the words "Consider Me" in the subject line. This helped us determine who cared enough to read the description and follow the instructions. It also helped us prescreen return E-mails for writing and communication skills.

Even though we were not looking to put a Gen Why through a rigorous and exhausting test, we did want to determine who was capable and interested before taking the next step. Our search, limited to a five-square-mile-radius of our office, netted us sixty candidates within the first week. However, only three applied per our instructions. All three were solid candidates.

Another major consideration in your cyber recruiting campaign is your own company website. Too often I hear Gen Whys complain that when they were looking for a job online, a certain company's website was too slow or too confusing to navigate, so they simply moved on. For the sake of the Whys, it's imperative that your company's website can quickly direct the interested jobseeker to the employment opportunities page and then immediately link them to the job that suits their needs.

Suffice it to say, you must create a strong recruiting presence on the 'Net, if you are targeting the best talent in the Gen Why pool. Of course, all of this might get you a lot of nibbles from Gen Why applicants, but if you want to reel in your catch, a response from your HR/management team (or First Responder) should follow within forty-eight hours or less.

WHYS IDEA
Your Internet application process needs to be simple, painless, somewhat fun and engaging, and user-friendly.

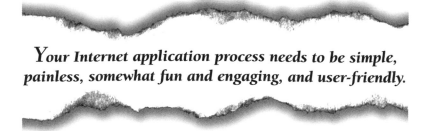

Your Internet application process needs to be simple, painless, somewhat fun and engaging, and user-friendly.

FINAL THOUGHT

When I interviewed with Proctor & Gamble right out of college, they made a proclamation I'll never forget: "Take away all of our buildings, factories, and machinery and leave us only our people, and in ten years or less we'll have it all back—plus some!" P&G certainly had its priorities in order.

Finding the right people to represent your company is a challenging endeavor, especially with the ever-changing labor market. Some of the ideas in this section may seem too wacky for you to consider—and that's okay. But within, or just outside, your comfort zone there is at least one great idea in this chapter that you can build on to help you tap into the talent pool you need. The best advice is to never stop being creative and aggressive in recruiting your new workforce.

Training

I F WHILE RECRUITING GENERATION WHY you felt like you had to work magic, when it comes to training, it can feel like you need a miracle. Rarely will a Gen Why arrive at your workplace armed with the skill set necessary to perform competently in the capacity for which they were hired. While this isn't exactly news to managers employing younger workers, what makes Gen Why different is that they can also lack the fundamental foundation needed to even learn your company's basic skills.

What is incredibly perplexing to managers of Gen Why, especially training managers, is the paradox between Gen Why's lack of basic skills and their incredible technology and business savvy. These aren't kids who set up a lemonade stand for their first business. Many of them trade stock, and they trade it well. Even more have credit cards. While today's new front line employees might not know the basics of supply and demand or even dollars and cents, they have tremendous personal experience with marketing, public relations, new product launches, market research, and advertising. Identifying the skills that need to be trained while making sure there is a firm foundation of understanding for that skill will take all the expertise at your disposal, and then some.

They want to learn, but if the learning process isn't entertaining enough, they check out.

Once the thrill of the application process—the chase, if you will—wears off, your new Gen Why employee is likely to become bored with the day-to-day reality of work, and especially the usually dry training process. Gen Whys will also question you every step of the way: "Why do I need to learn that procedure?" "What is the point of greeting customers at the door?" And on, and on, and on. If they're not doing it verbally, trust me, they're doing it mentally. They want to learn, but if the learning process isn't entertaining enough, they check out. (Of course, the exception to the rule is if a Gen Why really wants to learn a particular skill or if they really need the job, then they will be motivated to learn no matter how bad the training program.) And finally, managers also find odd gaps in Gen Why's knowledge. They can easily learn—and perhaps program—your computerized cash register, but might have trouble counting back change from a dollar if the register doesn't compute it for them.

While today's new front line employees might not know the basics of supply and demand or even dollars and cents, they have tremendous personal experience with marketing, public relations, new product launches, market research, and advertising.

Think back to the twelve common traits and tendencies they bring to the training process, and you can see that you have your work cut out for you. The fact that they are impatient, disrespectful, and skeptical make it all the more challenging for you to instruct new employees in the logistical components of their new job while simultaneously socializing them into the culture of your company. Gen Whys are comfortable around each other, but may have trouble interacting with older coworkers, and even worse, customers who don't immediately treat them as equals.

On the opposite end of the spectrum, when engaged in the training process your Whys will soak up information like sponges, and retain it, too. Because they are very self-conscious about appearing successful and competent, and they'd never want to be embarrassed by not being able to answer a question or solve a problem, they'll very much want to be prepared for any situation they will encounter in the workplace. They are also very future-oriented and are extremely eager to amass the cutting-edge skills that will increase their job-market value. Although they can be the worst learners if they do not see relevance in the subject matter, they are among the best learners when they see personal benefit in the lesson. You'll need to formulate a successful training strategy for your emerging workforce. Here are five basic principles for training Generation Why, followed by examples of how other companies have put them to good use in their own training programs.

Although they can be the worst learners if they do not see relevance in the subject matter, they are among the best learners when they see personal benefit in the lesson.

MAKE IT FUN

Educators are coming to understand more and more how *play* can be used to heighten and enhance learning, and with Gen Why it's more than a theory worth considering—it's a necessity. In their modified version of the Declaration of Independence, it's not the *pursuit* of happiness but happiness itself that is their unalienable right. They are happiest when they are having fun or being entertained.

When that Gen Why trainee walks through your door, he or she has just come from a day that has been sprinkled—or loaded—with fun. Maybe they had some fun at school, as schools are now striving to make learning fun, or at the mall, where they checked out all the latest techno-gizmos, or at a friend's house, where they had the latest and greatest of everything. And you can bet that once their shift is over, they're off to some other activity, or series of activities, in the hunt for more fun and excitement.

It is important to understand that if your training program has a low F.Q. (Fun Quotient) you will not be able to break through their mental barriers and inject your message. Gen Why will simply tune out and shut down. To fight the training blahs, always be searching for new ways to incorporate fun into the training process. Keep in mind that it is important to have trainers that the Gen Why employees enjoy and respect, who can also deliver the content you need to bring in the new workers in a fun and entertaining way.

If your training program has a low F.Q. (Fun Quotient) you will not be able to break through their mental barriers and inject your message.

ENGAGE THEM

Pure and simple, if they're not involved, they're not learning. Although they may pretend to be learning, your Whys won't politely sit back and continue to suck up information from even the most dynamic talking head. They have an innate desire to be actively involved in their own learning, and they're too multi-sensory to absorb much information from lecture-only-based education. For success, every aspect of training must invite them to jump in. If they can't be the pilot, at least let them be the copilot.

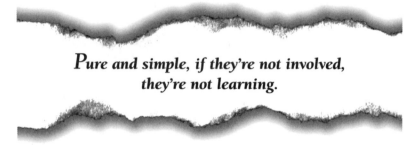

Pure and simple, if they're not involved, they're not learning.

In situations where classroom lecture is truly the best way to deliver the necessary information, Gen Whys should have the freedom to ask questions the second they come to mind instead of holding them to the end of an instructor's monologue. Whys trainers will always look for ways to involve trainees who have experience with a particular subject or skill by allowing them to share their expertise.

MAKE IT FRESH

Even if your company can't afford the latest technology to deliver its training programs, there is absolutely no excuse for being stale. Nothing will turn off a Gen Why quicker than an old joke, a tired cliché—e.g., "think outside the box"—or an example that is painfully out of style or out of touch. They've already heard The Starfish Story, they know that Michael Jordan was cut from his high school basketball team, and they can connect the nine dots with four straight lines. You can't train these new dogs with those old tricks!

Do they need to know every minute detail about your company to be effective at their job? If not, skip what is not important and get to what they really do need to know. But make certain you let them know *why* they need to know. They might have a passing interest in the history of your organization, but they'd rather get the details off the company website than be forced to sit through a lengthy introductory film on their first day in training class.

KEEP UP THE PACE

Courtesy clerks at a nationwide food and drug chain are point-of-contact service providers, whose duties include bagging and carrying out groceries for the customers. Even though this is an entry-level position, new hires range in age from first jobbers to retirees. The Computer Based Training (CBT) module for courtesy clerks is fast-paced and entertaining, and it's effective with Gen Whys and other new hires as well. The training manager commented, "There was one lesson on carryout service that adults tended to like, but courtesy clerks thought was cheesy. But because the lesson was memorable, after it is over they know how to give carryout service and can go out and do it."

Feedback from another lesson in the revised training program pointed out that adults always like the program but teenagers complained that they were being treated like children. This points to something we discussed earlier: treat your Gen Whys like adults and with respect. Check the messages you are sending with your training personnel and training materials to make certain that they do not talk down to or *dis* (disrespect) your Whys.

Be conscious of this generation's propensity for multitasking and allow them the flexibility to progress at a high rate of speed. Whereas going too fast might confuse them, going too slowly will lull them to sleep—and confusion is more easily remedied than boredom. Training materials targeted for an eighth-grade intellect often insult Gen Whys, creating an automatic disconnect. Try to avoid designing your training for the lowest common denominator. Aim to be challenging yet clear, and trust your new hires to let you know where they need more detail. Train a concept and then move to the next. Come back, but only to review or reinforce. Let them apply the new skill they've learned, whether through simulation or in an actual situation, then train another skill. Don't fall into the old school training style of teaching them everything before letting them do anything.

Whereas going too fast might confuse them, going too slowly will lull them to sleep—and confusion is more easily remedied than boredom.

REWARD SKILL DEVELOPMENT

It is very important that your highway of training is paved with frequent pit stops of praise. The most effective training programs build the trainees' confidence and leave them thirsty to learn more. Whys crave recognition, and although they do not want to be patronized, they really like to know when they've mastered a concept or have become competent with a new phase of their job. Each time they acquire a new skill, let them—and everybody nearby—know it. Pause to recognize their demonstrated mastery of each significant skill. When they complete a lengthy program that earns them new responsibilities, or if they gain certification in a specific job skill, make a big deal out of it, perhaps even in front of their friends, coworkers, and family. Recognizing their skill development and training completion ensures that your Gen Whys will be eager to continue learning and growing.

A Word to the Wise

From reading the above, it might sound to you like you're going to have to completely redesign your program from the ground up each and every year to satisfy Gen Why's training needs. It's not that drastic. Gen Why understands that training isn't going to be as exciting as a trip to see MTV's *Total Request Live*. The key is to be smart about what you change. As the stories below show, sometimes it can be something very simple that makes all the difference in the world.

ORIENT BEFORE YOU TRAIN

New employees spend their first day at Influence, LLC, an e-commerce solutions provider, with a smile on their faces. Through a program called Fusion, Influence gives its new hires a taste of the company's progressive working environment by means of a novel, two day orientation program where employees may find themselves in a pasta-cooking contest, socializing with new colleagues, or even hobnobbing with Influence's CEO. The purpose of the Fusion program is to make incoming employees feel as comfortable as possible as quickly as possible and, at the same time, introduce them to the company's mission and values.

The orientation process really begins during the recruitment stage. Companies that are not open about their policies and practices and that do not openly invite discussion about the general nature of their business will battle a high rate of turnover. Companies like Influence that go out of their way to make their Gen Whys feel comfortable from Day One, will find that the investment pays huge dividends down the road.

At this moment, you may have Gen Whys in your workplace who, although they may be very well trained, do not feel like they are part of your team. They have the skills you need and are producing well, but they feel like relative strangers to your organization. It is impossible to get the best they have to offer if they do not feel they are a welcome and necessary part of your family.

Being highly curious and relationship-driven, it is crucial that your Gen Whys meet the staff they will be working with and for in a casual and friendly, nonthreatening environment. It's equally critical for them to learn as much as they can about the nature of your business and how your company makes money prior to being put in the position of contributing to its profitability. To be truly connected to your company, they need to know the history, the rules, the people, the language, and the culture, as well as the performance expectations placed on them. This increases their sense of belonging and their commitment to the job.

An effective orientation program will reduce—if not eliminate—the early job jitters, it will give your new Gen Whys a bird's-eye view of how your company operates and makes a profit; and it will help them establish key relationships with the company's leaders and mentors. Soften the landing into your company, and you'll find that Gen Whys will start their tenure with confidence, a better understanding of their place in the organization and how their work affects the bottom line, and most importantly, with open lines of communication to the people who can help them when challenges arise.

To be truly connected to your company,
they need to know the history, the rules, the people,
the language, and the culture, as well as the
performance expectations placed on them.

WHYS IDEA If you don't already have one, put in place a definable step between the date of hire and the commencement of training. A well-orchestrated orientation program will acclimate your Gen Whys to their new jobs and make them feel connected from the start. If you question whether you need this phase, or if you want to evaluate your existing orientation program, survey your Gen Whys to determine how long it took them to feel comfortable and committed in their existing positions.

EXPLAIN THE WHY

Nowhere is this generation's need to know the *why* before doing the *what* more visible than in the training phase. America's teachers know this truth all too well. Many of them remember sitting in class taking fastidious notes for subjects they did not care about and striving to get good grades for fear of a negative consequence. But now as teachers, they have found that their students don't fear the consequences of poor academic performance nearly to the same degree, and therefore, need a different type of motivation to learn. Successful teachers are those that have mastered the art of attaching the value to a lesson. They teach the *why* so the kid is dying to discover the *what*. Teachers who skip this step and simply teach students in the same traditional way they were taught find themselves in serious trouble.

Trainers who train Gen Why the same traditional way they were trained are discovering that they are also missing the mark. By their very nature, Gen Whys question the validity of each and every step, each process, and each practice they're being asked to remember. They are eager to please, but they want to find the shortcuts and the paths of least resistance, so they will not follow directions just because they have been asked to do so.

Effective trainers attach the *why* to each process. No matter how simple the concept or the instruction, the value always precedes it. For example, the old school of training might go something like this: "At the end of the day, your job is to mop the tiles in front of the cash register. Here's how you should to do it." An effective trainer today would approach the lesson like this: "When our front lobby is spotless, our customers know their food has been prepared in a clean environment and they tell their friends. More business means better wages for our staff. Let me show you our technique for keeping our floors glowing and our wages growing." If this sounds good in theory, but seems like it takes too much time in practice, think how much longer it takes to deal with the turnover associated with improperly trained employees. Managers who only want employees who do what they're told with no questions asked are better off hiring robots than Gen Whys.

They are eager to please, but they want to find the shortcuts and the paths of least resistance, so they will not follow directions just because they have been asked to do so.

WHYS IDEA

Examine your training program from the perspective of a Gen Why, or better yet, have a couple of your existing Gen Whys examine and evaluate your training program. Is there specific rationale behind each action you want them to take? More importantly, are you explaining the reasons behind the important processes? If enough attention is paid to reinforcing the value of each concept, you will be amazed by the manner in which your Gen Whys follow the prescribed procedures. Simply put—explain the *why*, show them how it will benefit them, and they will out-perform your expectations.

LET THEM FIGURE IT OUT

When you enter a Brookstone Store, the first person you encounter is the greeter. The greeter is responsible for both welcoming you and saying good-bye when you leave. They are also responsible for breaking the ice by giving you a quick product demonstration of the item of the week. In many cases, Gen Whys groan when it is their turn to serve as the greeter, because they find the task somewhat boring and gratuitous and definitely not in keeping with their personal image.

Several weeks before Christmas at the Brookstone store in the Flatirons Mall near Boulder, Colorado, greeters were instructed to demonstrate a product called The Chef Fork.

This clever fork has a built-in thermometer, designed to give the user an accurate temperature reading of the food being cooked. "It was like pulling teeth trying to get my young staff to demo The Chef Fork," said Susan Clark, the store manager, who explained that it was because the product was "something that had appeal only to a more mature consumer." Clark explained that one of her young staffers got the idea to let customers test the fork in a cup of hot and a cup of cold water and watch the thermometer reading change. "All customers, young and old, were amused by the demo," said Clark. "And the greeter beamed as though they were performing a magic act in a Las Vegas showroom. This was not my idea; it was all theirs. Therefore, they bought in to it, and soon they were jumping over each other to greet and demo the fork."

Gen Whys are astoundingly creative. They love it when a manager or supervisor acts on one of their ideas. If you present them with a problem and invite them to take a stab at finding the solution, they will both surprise and delight you with their ideas. This can prove to be a terrific way to turn what they may consider an unpleasant task into one they enjoy.

If you present them with a problem and invite them to take a stab at finding the solution, they will both surprise and delight you with their ideas.

WHYS IDEA

What are the Chef Fork possibilities in your workplace? Is there a pressing problem no one in management has been able to figure out? Round up your Gen Whys and turn them loose. Are there certain monotonous or mundane tasks that no one wants to be stuck with? Challenge your Whys to invent new ways for doing repetitive things. Grant them the leeway to make a mistake or two in the process. In the final analysis you will discover a fountain of creative ideas and solutions right in your own backyard.

USE EYE CANDY

Mike David, training director for Mazzio's Corporation, an Oklahoma-based pizza and Italian food restaurant chain, knew that his training materials were not connecting with his Gen Whys, so he decided to revamp them. "We're looking to change from plain black and white to color," he said. "We're moving forward to make everything user-friendly and interactive. Our Gen Why employees are often put off with training materials that aren't fun and engaging."

Leading employers of Gen Whys are in line with David's thoughts. Mazzio's manuals and materials, which used to look like the *Wall Street Journal,* have been modified to look more like the *USA Today*, with bright colors, fun fonts, visual imagery, cartoons, and pullouts. Hypothetical names in the materials that used to reference Bob, Jane, Dick, and Mary are also being modified to reflect names they can more readily identify with, like Jason, Heather, Travis, and Nicole. The stories and scenarios within the text have also changed—once again, to reveal situations representing life in the new millennium.

Forward-thinking training programs blend a variety of instructional methods, and are careful to avoid the overuse of any one technique. The best training programs consist of a full array of instructional methodologies, including, but not limited to, colorful manuals and workbooks, interactive

CD-ROMs, live PowerPoint presentations, classroom lectures, audio cassette programs, web-based training, and professionally produced videos. The idea is to keep the Whys involved by stimulating a variety of their senses.

WHYS IDEA If your training materials are still black and white, by all means, break out the crayons! Examine the names, stories, and examples contained in your training materials to make certain they are up to date. Take advantage of every type of media available to deliver your modules, being careful not to rely too heavily on any one means. Whys are much more inclined to stay focused on the training when they are being entertained and engaged in the process.

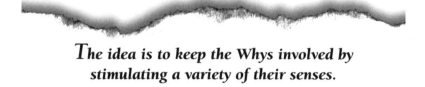

The idea is to keep the Whys involved by stimulating a variety of their senses.

A Word to the Wise

W When training the media-savvy Gen Whys, don't be lulled into thinking your programs must compete with the rapid-fire delivery of television, movies, video games, and sports. Most companies do not have the resources to produce these kinds of materials. Furthermore, the purpose of training is not merely to entertain, but rather to educate, demonstrate, and inform. That does not have to equal boring! Everyone learns more when they are having fun, but entertainment and fun should be incorporated in ways that facilitate learning.

A good rule of thumb is to avoid the grandiose when the simple will suffice. A well-designed job aid—like a colorful instructional poster—informing an employee how to operate a piece of equipment can often be a lot more effective (not to mention much cheaper!) than a sophisticated training module produced to train the same skill. The job aid can also serve to reinforce the skills at the critical point of use where the media-based module is not available. All the advantages of technology and media-based training should be applied if that is the best way to teach or demonstrate the particular job skill, and all of the advantages of more tried-and-true mediums should be used as appropriate, not only for variety, but also for effectiveness.

BRIDGE THE GAP IN SERVICE

As a consumer, you're undoubtedly being affected by America's current customer service gap, what a recent *Business Week* article called the New Consumer Apartheid. Knowing that 20% of their customers account for 80% of their business, or even a more drastic 10:90 ratio, many companies have turned their attention and their resources to providing outstanding service to their top-tier customers while leaving the remaining masses to fend for themselves.

The service the average American consumer took for granted a decade ago has all but evaporated. Now lengthy delays, automated telephone queues, and do-it-yourself service are the order of the day. When you finally get the attention of a customer service professional, they are not the least bit apologetic for their bad service, nor are they concerned when you threaten to take your business elsewhere.

Odds are, you are in the upper 20% with your favorite vendors and service providers and are accustomed to receiving the red carpet treatment from those companies. As the beneficiary of incredible customer service, you know what it looks like and how it feels. Now consider your Gen Why employees in their everyday lives away from your business. Picture them as customers for other businesses in your community and beyond. How are they treated out there? Which side of the equation have they likely been relegated to? Being the newest consumers in the marketplace, Gen Whys stand among the 80% of the buying public who rarely if ever receive good service. However, they do know what it means to wait, to be ignored, to be snubbed, and to be followed by store security officers that think of them as thieves.

As a manager, you treasure every one of your customers and you aren't about to throw 80% of them under the bus. All of your customers want and deserve the best service you can provide, but who is providing that service? Your Gen Whys, that's who. And there is a very real possibility that your Gen Whys do not know what you mean when you urge them to provide good customer service. When it comes to exceptional service, how can your Whys be expected to give it to your customers when they've never seen it, much less received it themselves? How can they give away what they've never had?

Even those Gen Whys who do know what good service is, having experienced it at the side of their parents who have not only expected it but have imperiously demanded it, have only seen it from the consumer side. The notion of serving someone else, in person or on the phone, is a foreign concept to them.

When it comes to exceptional service, how can your Whys be expected to give it to your customers when they've never seen it, much less received it themselves?

WHYS IDEA Before entrusting your customers to a Gen Why trainee, make absolutely certain that your new hire knows what excellent customer service looks like in your business. Have them study the star service provider in your business. Take them on a field trip to a quality restaurant and have them comment on each phase of the service they receive. Suggest they visit a Nordstrom's or similar store to try on some clothes and experience legendary customer service. Show them some of the highly rated customer service training videos that are now available as training aides.

Next, get them involved. Role-play with them the basics of customer service in the various situations and scenarios in which they might find themselves. Let an experienced Gen Why play the role of the worst customer they've ever had and then talk about the various approaches to diffusing the situation. And when they're out in front representing your company to the customers you cherish so dearly, make certain that you reward Gen Whys who provide great service—and do so on the spot! Above all, make certain that you're providing the same degree of service that you expect your Whys to model, because that is what they're most likely to do.

STAY A CHAPTER AHEAD

In my second year of teaching business subjects at Paradise Valley High School in Phoenix, I was given a very difficult assignment. I was asked to teach senior students the Arizona State-required course of economics. Not only had I never taught economics, I had never even taken it as a student. When I alerted the department chairperson of my dilemma, she smiled and said, "Just stay a chapter ahead."

Needless to say, I had to do more than stay a chapter ahead. I recall spending full weekends in the library and creating a lot of note cards to take to class. I simply wouldn't allow myself to be embarrassed by being asked a question that I should have been able to answer, but couldn't. What I discovered in the process was a whole new level of comprehension. Pressured to learn something totally new well enough to teach it to others was all the motivation I needed for mastering some difficult concepts.

Whys don't want to be caught off guard, either. If they know that they are responsible for learning new concepts well enough to teach them to others, that is exactly what they will do. The idea is to share the information power base to facilitate learning. When each member of the training class becomes actively involved in learning and teaching, the retention of the concepts is astounding.

WHYS IDEA
Appeal to your Gen Why's innate desire to be in the limelight and avoid embarrassment by having them serve as the instructors for the material you want them to learn themselves. Give several Gen Whys separate training modules with instructions that they can seek help from you, but that it is their job to master the concepts well enough to train others. This not only keeps them actively involved, but

it also eliminates the tedium associated with traditional training methods. Above that, it will also take you out of the role of being the sole source of information and position you as the learning/training manager responsible for observing the training, filling in the missing pieces, and evaluating the results.

When each member of the training class becomes actively involved in learning and teaching, the retention of the concepts is astounding.

FINAL THOUGHT

In the past, managers and trainers may have envisioned their green recruits as empty neophytes who needed to be filled with vast sums of knowledge before they could be turned loose. Those days are gone. Even if your recruits are green, empty neophytes, they will not sit still and wait for you to cram skills into their heads. Granted, they demand training and they will leave any job where they feel they are not learning critical skills that will help them become more marketable. But if you want them to learn—and not simply to be programmed—then they are going to have to be involved throughout the entire training process. I can't think of a single business that could not benefit from the fresh eyes and ideas that Generation Why trainees bring to the workforce. Being prepared to field those ideas and having a mechanism in place to take advantage of their creativity is something every trainer must be prepared to handle.

Often managers will nervously say to me, "But if I train them really well, they might leave!" To which I reply, "Then you can decide not to train them, and they might stay!" That's when the worried look turns to sheer terror. No matter how you look at it, not training your Whys is tantamount to business suicide.

I can't think of a single business that could not benefit from the fresh eyes and ideas that Generation Why trainees bring to the workforce.

Training Generation Why is about empowering the lowest member on the totem pole, being fun and theatrical, inviting competition among peers to come up with innovative ways to approach work, and letting Gen Why train Gen Why. To remain competitive in today's marketplace, organizations need to become *learning organizations*. While you may have heard the term before, what it means in this context is that whoever has a skill that is helpful to the organization becomes the de facto trainer—no matter what their position or length of time at the organization.

For better or for worse, Gen Whys in record numbers are raising themselves, which makes them much more self-sufficient than we sometimes realize or appreciate. Tap into Gen Why's strengths and insights about how they learn best, learn a few new training tricks and techniques of your own, and your team will be energized and effective.

Managing

I T'S LIKE I HAVE this Ferrari in my driveway and I have no idea how to drive it!" This comment was rendered to me by an exasperated Boomer, during the first twenty minutes of an in-house company management seminar. He continued, "They're much more sophisticated and have a lot more raw talent than I had in my early twenties, but when it comes to getting them to perform like a dependable sedan—much less a Ferrari—I feel like I don't even have a learner's permit!"

Management gurus, marketing whizzes, and dot-com entrepreneurs are fond of talking about how the old rules don't apply. But when it comes to dealing with Generation Why in the workplace it can seem like no rules apply. Some baffled managers are desperately searching for ways to get their Whys to perform at a consistent level. Other managers find getting their front line to comply with even the most basic company procedures a real chore. Dress code violations, lateness and absenteeism, confrontations with customers—the list goes on. The generation raised in chaotic times can create a lot of chaos in the workplace.

It would be a totally different situation if the only problem were an absence of skill. You could more easily manage those possessing the want-to but lacking the how-to. But this isn't the case with the Whys. They have street smarts and book smarts, and they know what they want. What they don't know they can learn quickly—providing they see something in it for themselves. So it's not a talentless crew of morons that you're trying to manage.

What makes yours a daily mountain to climb is that you're leading a new workforce of impatient, individualistic, expressive young people, who have remarkable talent but who are continually questioning authority and structure.

This is not to say that without constant vigilance you will have open rebellion in your employee ranks, but—and this may sound absurd—to get the most out of Gen Why you have to earn their respect. They are not going to promptly take action on your every word, even if you are the one who signs their paychecks. You need to approach managing them with flexibility, creativity, and openness to their attitudes and conventions. Effective managers of Gen Why are willing to deal with them on their terms and to make concessions and exceptions that your boss and your boss's boss would never think to make.

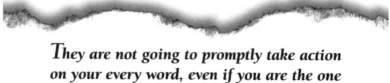

They are not going to promptly take action on your every word, even if you are the one who signs their paychecks.

This doesn't mean you have to sacrifice your authority. In fact, as we will see, Gen Why is quite comfortable with rules and regulations, as long as those rules don't compromise their individuality, their free time, or what they see as their right to have fun. What's hard for a lot of Boomer and Gen X managers is the idea that rules and regulations and company policies are seen by Gen Whys as negotiable. You drive past a reserved spot in the company parking lot and never think of parking your car there. Gen Whys see the same spot and think that it's obviously reserved for them. The rules have to make sense to a Gen Why, or they will blow right by them. Remember, rules before a relationship lead to rebellion!

If it sounds like work is a game to Gen Why, that's because it is. But that doesn't mean they are incapable of working hard or taking pride in a job well done. It just means that they have a low tolerance for rules or management techniques that are arbitrary. And who can blame them? Hasn't everyone at some point or another been suspicious of a boss or manager who told him or her they had to pay their dues before getting more responsibility? While working hard and waiting for the right opportunity is an all-important aspect of the game, Gen Why will smell out a smoke screen or a stall technique in a heart-beat. This will result in a disconnect that will be almost impossible to repair.

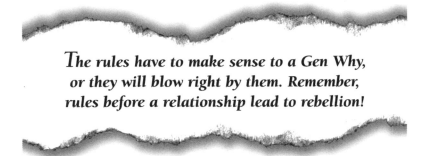

The rules have to make sense to a Gen Why, or they will blow right by them. Remember, rules before a relationship lead to rebellion!

So if you're trying to get the most out of your Whys, be honest and forthcoming, build a relationship with them, and let them see how what you're wanting them to do helps advance both of your concerns. What follows are some specific ways to manage that objective.

LAY OUT THE BIG PICTURE IN SMALL TERMS

Experienced managers tell me that when it comes to working with people, "you may or may not get what you want, or what you deserve, but you will get exactly what you expect." This axiom applies to Generation Why, providing they know what it is you expect. Nothing should be assumed.

You may or may not get what you want, or what you deserve, but you will get exactly what you expect.

During my sixteen-year-old daughter's first week as a hostess at Chili's, the manager gave her a small laminated card that he told her to memorize. The card listed Seven Sizzling Service Standards to give Chili's customers a Sizzling Experience. By memorizing the seven ideals, she would become a true ChiliHead, and he told her that if she could orally recite them back to him by week's end, he'd give her a $20 bill on the spot. The steps were astoundingly simple (e.g., have fun, make eye contact and smile, say "hi" to everyone, etc.), so it took her only few minutes to commit them to memory. Once she did, she clearly knew the big picture of what her job was and what her boss expected from her. My daughter quickly transformed herself into a ChiliHead.

To manage behavior, you first need to clearly articulate expectations. Managers who expect certain behaviors from their GWs but don't clearly spell out those expectations are on their way to a train wreck. Spelling out expectations verbally is less than half as effective as setting them out in writing. Managers who use both written and oral means of sharing big picture expectations are twice as effective.

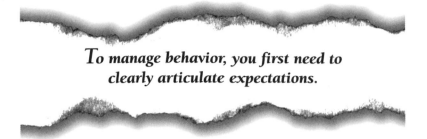

To manage behavior, you first need to clearly articulate expectations.

WHYS IDEA Do your Whys fully comprehend your expectations? (Do you even know what they are?) If not, quantify your list, keeping it simple and easy to memorize and repeat. Make certain all supervisors know the list so that they can both model and enforce those values and behaviors. Reward your GWs for memorizing the list, and quiz them periodically to make certain they retain it. When you see specific examples of the list behaviors being carried out, draw attention and praise to them.

REVISIT YOUR RULES

A medium-size chain of casual restaurants operating in the Midwest called my office recently, seeking a solution to a problem they were experiencing. Their employee dress code permitted khaki shorts, but they were only to be worn between Memorial Day and Labor Day. The restaurant managers were disconcerted because their young Gen Why employees were coming to work wearing khaki shorts in the fall and even in the winter months.

Their question was one of how? How could they get their employees to adhere to their dress code? But before we could address the how, we first needed to address the why. So I merely asked, "Why is that rule on your books?" The first explanation was that the rule had always been there and that it had been enforced for decades. Again, I asked why the rule was there. They again answered with a when, giving me historical perspective on how long their franchise had enforced this particular rule, dating all the way back to this being a rule that had been put in place by their founder.

Realizing that I wasn't getting through to this team of managers, I decided to change my line of questioning. "Does the wearing of shorts have an impact on employee job performance?" I asked them.

"Well, no, not really," was their reply.

"Does the fact that your Gen Whys wear shorts during winter months adversely affect your company sales?" I asked.

Once again the response was, "No, not that we can trace."

I then asked if there was any reason whatsoever why the rule should remain in their employee handbook, and their next response was, "I guess we'd better take another look at this rule!"

Tradition is important in family reunions and passing down recipes. But with Gen Why and the rules in your employee handbook, tradition is suspect. Before trying to get Gen Why to adhere to a rule, a principle, or a practice, first ask yourself if it is necessary or a prerequisite to profit. If the answer is no, don't waste your time on its enforcement. Instead, eliminate the practice and enforce only those rules, principles, and practices that make sense.

Before trying to get Gen Why to adhere to a rule, a principle, or a practice, first ask yourself if it is necessary or a prerequisite to profit.

WHYS IDEA

Know the reason for your rules and be prepared to provide a sound reason for them, even if you're not asked. Gen Why responds to open communication much better than the old "my way or the highway" routine. And if you do decide to throw away or change an old rule that doesn't make sense, celebrate that with your employees. In the story above about the company dress code, the company could have thrown a bon voyage party for the old rule and celebrated the change with employees. A smart leader then takes a moment during the fun to deliver a short serious message about keeping customer service high. Everything's negotiable with Gen Why, and they will appreciate and understand you setting the tone of give-and-take and will respond in kind.

SINK YOUR POSTS DEEP

Football coaches prepare for upcoming games by studying their opponent's tendencies on game films. Knowing how the opposing team will react in any given situation can give one team a decided advantage over its opponent. It serves as the basis for their entire game plan.

As the generation who has grown up learning how to recognize the tendencies of the games that dominate their discretionary time (i.e., video games), Gen Whys are experts in the rapid discovery of patterns. They can quickly spot the give-and-take in the rules set forth by their parents, their teachers, and their managers, and they have no aversion to testing the boundaries. If they discover that their leader is soft on the rules, or has a tendency to look the other way if the process of enforcing a rule is too much of a hassle, they'll waste no time in exploiting that tendency. When looking for ways to go beyond the parameters that have been established for them, if they find there's some give-and-take, they'll immediately embark on a strategy to give less and take more, thereby winning the game.

They can quickly spot the give-and-take in the rules set forth by their parents, their teachers, and their managers, and they have no aversion to testing the boundaries.

My son Zac worked in the sporting goods department of a large retail chain. The store has a very strict policy that calls for the termination of any employee who has two no call/no show absences within the same quarter. Zac is an active student leader who frequently finds himself double-booked for a school-related activity and work. He'd broken the policy at least a half a dozen times over the last few months he worked there. However, because Zac is a good employee and undoubtedly because the store is short on labor, they never once enforced this policy by terminating, much less even reprimanding Zac or any of his like-offending coworkers. When Zac started his employment at the store, he was deathly afraid of violating this policy. Then it became almost an afterthought. Although he wanted to be a good employee with a good attendance record, he no longer feared the repercussions of a no call/no show, and neither did his coworkers. Management has grown soft on the attendance policy, and it has come back to haunt them.

Effective managers keep their rulebook light and tight. They continually edit out unnecessary items, leaving only those policies and procedures for which there is a solid rationale and for which they will grant no leeway. This makes those remaining rules easier to remember, justify, and enforce.

Effective managers keep their rulebook light and tight.

Contrary to widely held thinking, Generation Why does not reject, and will actually embrace, structure. Perhaps it stems from the lack of structure they had growing up in their schools, communities, and families. But when they realize there are consequences for straying outside the boundaries and those consequences will not be negotiated, then their tendency is to adhere to those guidelines and to respect the process.

WHYS IDEA Don't rule out the rules. Instead, identify those rules that are truly important. Then, once you tighten your employee handbook, sink your posts deep. You cannot back down on the important issues to Gen Why, or they will keep taking and taking. As long as you can explain the importance of a rule and as long as that rule isn't arbitrary, Gen Why, even after vocal protest, will ultimately accept reality. Commiserate but don't capitulate.

TUNE IN TO THEIR FREQUENCY

Imagine how difficult it would be to succeed—much less to survive—in a society or a culture where you could not communicate with the natives. There is little doubt you would be ostracized and isolated. Employers feel removed from their Gen Whys due primarily to the ever-widening communication gap. "I just don't understand them, and they have no idea what I'm saying!" is the desperation cry of Boomer and even Xer managers.

Though every American generation has its own version of the spoken word, Generation Why has taken this practice to the extreme. Their use of words, phraseology, gestures, and body language is ever evolving and at a frightening pace. What is considered cool one minute is "so yesterday" the next. As a motivational speaker for thousands of high school assembly programs, I've learned this lesson the hard way. Timely comedy and trendy stories based on pop culture and modern jargon can score a bull's-eye one week, and come across as stale, lame, and totally out of sync the next. Makes for an automatic disconnect and a very long day!

The use of Internet chat rooms and tightly targeted television programs on networks such as MTV have provided an almost instant exchange of the dialogue and fashion. Those who keep up, connect; those who don't, become relics.

Wise managers keep fluent in Gen Why speak. To achieve this result, you need to keep dialed in to the same frequency they are. Permit yourself to stay abreast of current trends, fads, and the pop culture by exposing yourself to their world. Watch what they watch. Tune in to the highly rated teen sitcoms and dramas on the WB and UPN networks, as well as the MTV, VH1, and ESPN 2 cable networks. When you hear of a box office smash that is targeted toward younger viewers, such as the recent movies American Pie 2, Road Trip, Thirteen Ghosts, or Not Another Teen Movie—go see it. Read the books and magazines on their best-seller list. Surf the Internet to find the popular websites the Gen Whys are hitting.

And, yes, even if it is painful, listen to their music. Keeping a "heads up" on the dialogue and the banter and the lyrics of popular rap songs, heavy metal, alternative, ska, hip-hop, and new country will give you that much more of a decided advantage when it comes to connecting and communicating with Gen Why. This is not to say you want to pretend to be one of them—slang can be a dangerous thing in the mouth of an adult—but just the act of trying to understand their culture will put you far ahead of most managers.

WHYS IDEA They know your language, so learn to speak theirs. You'll never really connect with them until you're both on the same frequency. And you don't have to pretend to like their culture, just let them know you're open to it. For Gen Why, pop culture can be almost a religion. You may not share their faith, but respect it and you'll win them over.

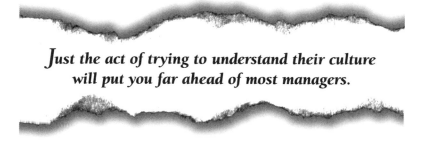

Just the act of trying to understand their culture will put you far ahead of most managers.

GET THEIR HEADS IN YOUR GAME

A friend of mine who manages a Brookstone store inside a newly opened mall told me that involvement was her key strategy for connecting with her Gen Whys. With rare exception, she routes the faxes she receives from headquarters throughout the ranks of her Gen Whys so they can see how the store is doing and whether or not sales are on track.

She makes them aware of the new policies and procedures that are being discussed and considered for implementation. When there is theft due to shoplifting or employee pilferage, she'll have her Gen Whys call the police and file the report. She lets her Gen Whys decide how merchandise should be displayed (within corporate guidelines) and then lets them create the displays. She doesn't play favorites. She involves virtually every Gen Why in almost every aspect of merchandising, marketing, management, sales, store security, and communication—responsibilities that are typically reserved for those in managerial positions.

Her rationale is simple. "My younger employees are extremely curious about why changes are made and why things are done the way they are," she says. "Couple this with the fact that they get bored very easily and that they really feel empowered when their ideas are put in place. Involvement is no longer an option for these Gen Whys—it's a necessity."

If your Gen Whys aren't engaged, they're disengaged. Even if they don't verbalize it, they have a strong need to discover the why behind the what and the how of your operation. To ignore that need is equivalent to pushing their Off buttons.

Involvement is no longer an option for these Gen Whys—it's a necessity.

WHYS IDEA Consider the tasks, duties, and responsibilities of your management position and determine which aspects you're able to share. Take a risk by sharing more information with your Gen

Why employees (all your employees, actually) than you may feel comfortable with. Allow them to interact with your vendors and suppliers and even your colleagues at the home office. Don't just tell them how your business functions; let them experience it first-hand. Satisfy their desire to know the why, and you will have effectively connected on three additional levels: they'll feel important, they'll be stimulated, and they'll be learning and growing.

THE FLEXIBILITY FACTOR: ATTENDANCE AND PUNCTUALITY

Remember back to the twelve common tendencies when we pointed out that Gen Whys are efficient multitaskers, who almost always have two or three activities going on at once? Well, this is where that quality has a tendency to bite.

As you know, this generation isn't known for being punctual. Managers frequently lament that they arrive late and leave early and occasionally don't show up at all. Many companies have enacted strict three strikes and you're out policies only to find they're forced to say good-bye to a lot of good-but-flighty talent.

Current surveys are finding that work schedule flexibility is becoming more important for every class of employee, not just Gen Whys. It may be time to really look at your corporate policies and even your personal work philosophy. Seat time does not equal productive output, especially if your employees are concerned about meeting their personal commitments.

Don't just tell them how your business functions;
let them experience it firsthand.

You need to consider the whole human resource equation, weighing in recruiting and training costs plus staff morale and productivity. Figure out what you really need from your employees and see what kind of flexibility and maneuverability can be inserted into the workplace schedule.

Keep in mind that Gen Why is not easily intimidated with threats and ultimatums for not being on time and/or not showing up. Besides, they know that if they lose this job, there is another one down the street. So instead of (or at least in addition to) punishing the undependable, reward the dependable!

Periodically bring donuts to share with those who show up early for work. Remove everything but the empty box five minutes after the shift officially begins. Arrive a few minutes before closing time with movie tickets for all those still working hard. Single out an employee who routinely demonstrates that they stay within the allotted lunch break time by reimbursing them the cost of their lunch. Structure your compensation program so that at the end of each quarter, employees who've had no schedule violations or infractions will receive an hourly bonus incentive, retroactive to the first date in that quarter. Create a dependability club. Provide special discounts, privileges, and incentives for those who meet the membership requirements.

Instead of punishing the undependable, reward the dependable!

WHYS IDEA

Unless you know something the rest of us don't, you're not going to find a way to completely eliminate the relaxed nature of your Whys and their propensity to push the time-clock envelope. While it is important to have clear standards for attendance and punctuality and to communicate those rules, this process sets up an additional behavioral checkpoint for you to enforce. Furthermore, the stricter you make your consequences, the more arguments you'll encounter from Whys wanting to appeal their sentence. The best thing you can do is to focus your energy on rewarding the Whys who've developed their dependability habit. Create a special status level for employees you can count on and offer recipients special privileges. This will make punctuality and dependability a very desirable goal for your Whys and get the short-staffed monkey off your back.

WAGE A BATTLE AGAINST BOREDOM

Boredom is the archenemy of the more than 60 million, Type A++, Why-Wait, Stimulus-Junkie, Multitasker Gen Whys. If you need to field test this theory, put a Gen Why in a monotonous job with no promise of a change and see how long they remain in your employ. Their need for constant change and continual stimulation is a considerable obstacle for many managers whose front line positions (usually filled by Gen Whys) are laced with mundane, repetitive tasks.

Put a Gen Why in a monotonous job with no promise of a change and see how long they remain in your employ.

Most entry level and/or service-oriented jobs are based on a formula requiring a high degree of sameness in the process. There is no individual creativity or personal artistic expression tolerated when it comes to making a Big Mac. Branding is all about reputation, reputation is based on consistency, and the very nature of consistency requires sameness.

So how do you get Gen Whys to remain engaged in a process that is boring? And how can you shift gears to go from boring to fun without damaging the brand? Here are three variation techniques that can help you accomplish this mission:

1. Vary the task. Don't stick 'em behind the grill all day no matter how much they may say they like it. Rotate them frequently between tasks (e.g., cashier, shake machine, front lobby maintenance, stockroom, etc.). The Gen Why is thinking, "It's fun to do something different!"

2. Vary the procedure. Give your Gen Why the expected outcome of the task (e.g., a delighted customer, a spotless floor, an orderly stockroom, etc.); explain the why; and invite them to create, alter, or improve the existing process. They may choose to follow your method, or they may find a better one. If they can't find a better way, they'll buy into the existing procedure, and they won't try to skip corners. The Gen Why is thinking, "It's fun to target success and figure out how to get there on my own!"

3. Vary the environment. Go ahead; rearrange the furniture. Change the radio station. Alter the schedule. Relax the dress code. From subtle to radical, there are a number of ways clever managers can throw a change into the physical working environment to create variation. While these changes might rock the world of your older workers, they'll be viewed as stimulating or amusing changes by your emerging employees. The Gen Why is thinking, "This is a fun place to work!"

WHYS IDEA

Boredom is the ultimate party crasher. Fun happens at the intersection of Variation and Surprise. Make a checklist of the series of tasks that make up the various individual jobs of your Gen Whys. The shorter the list, the greater the element of boredom. Try weaving new tasks into each job. Experiment with new methods for achieving the desired results of each task, or at least open yourself to letting your Gen Whys do the experimenting. If you feel that these efforts are unnecessary and a waste of your time, the time you save might well be spent recruiting and training new employees who'll need to be hired to replace those you've lost due to boredom.

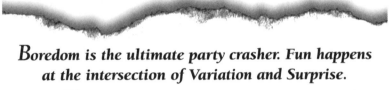

Boredom is the ultimate party crasher. Fun happens at the intersection of Variation and Surprise.

FINAL THOUGHT

To be a truly effective manager of Gen Why employees, you must be part coach, part parent, part mentor, part coworker, part friend, part teacher, part boss—and you must use each of those parts in varying degrees, depending on the specific Gen Why employee you are working with and the specific work position they are in. As individuals, they have fewer, but more unique, tools in the toolbox they bring to the workplace. They may be able to fix the nagging computer server problem you've been having in less than an hour, but they may lose their temper with a nagging customer in a matter of seconds. They may be used to breaking the rules because no one has ever taken them aside and shown them the advantages of occasionally playing by the rules.

If putting all those parts together in the right combination at the right time seems like a sure recipe for disaster—think again! The people skills that helped you get where you are now will surely be your bridge to success with Gen Why—with a few simple modifications and updates. You will need all of your people skills, plus some new ones, as we turn our attention to their on-the-job appearance.

The people skills that helped you get where you are now will surely be your bridge to success with Gen Why— with a few simple modifications and updates.

Appearance

U NLESS YOU WERE a completely abnormal teenager, your parents hated the way you dressed; they were embarrassed by the way you wore your hair; and they didn't think much of the music you listened to either. It doesn't matter what generation you are from, your fashion sense was questioned and disparaged by your elders. But for you, your personal style was your membership card to your generation.

Hair, clothing, and music—think of any recent decade, and you can conjure up a sense of who these youth were, based on these three criteria. From Buddy Holly to Elvis, from the Beatles to KISS, from Michael Jackson to Marilyn Manson and Eminem, pop music stars set the dress code standards for each new generation. Skin tight pants, duck-tail hair, tie-dyed shirts, bell bottoms, afros, poodle skirts, mood rings, saddle shoes, leather jackets, hot pants, under-wear as street wear—the list of outrageous fashion could go on and on (but we're all better off forgetting some things!).

Like all generations before them, Whys also use hair, clothing, and music as identity markers. However, it should come as no surprise that their expression of those factors is radically different than yours. If popular styles are somewhat disconcerting to you, relax. You're just having the same reaction your parents, teachers, and managers had with your generation. The difference between your youth culture and Gen Why's is very apparent on the surface, but what's much more subtle is what is underneath. Back in the fifties, sixties, and even seventies, youth culture belonged to young people. Today, youth culture is a multi-billion-dollar industry.

The difference between your youth culture and Gen Why's is very apparent on the surface, but what's much more subtle is what is underneath.

Self-expression has been marketed to Gen Why since they were in diapers; it is not something they discovered or even truly defined for themselves. This is the MTV generation, after all—a group of kids who have been taught to be outrageous, spirited, and rebellious. For many members of Gen Why, personal style isn't just a part of their identity—it is their identity. It is so ingrained in them that any discussion of it has to be dealt with more sensitively than you might expect.

Coming back to the surface differences, Gen Why has taken personal expression far beyond their counterparts of previous generations. When Boomers and Xers entered the workforce, managers could demand a change—a more conservative haircut, shined shoes, more modest clothing, and so on—and it was easy for the employee to adapt. If it were just for the multicolored gelled hair, saggy pants, or difficult-to-listen-to music, we could simply shrug our shoulders at Gen Why and chalk it up to the temporary insanity that accompanies youthful rebellion. But the generation markers of the Whys go far beyond temporary forms of expression to permanent, physical assertions like tattoos and piercings.

While it may be hard for your customers to accept the reality that their waiter is wearing pants that are three sizes too large, they can usually keep in mind that what truly matters is the service they receive. But when the server has a bullet in his ear or a tattoo running down her neck, some customers may have a difficult time focusing on the service!

Although these trends have roots dating back centuries ago and have even made periodic appearances in American pop culture over the past sixty years, they are back with a vengeance and are drawing gasps of horror from Boomers. In the eighties and early nineties, Xers who engaged in these dramatic forms of self-expression were considered edgy or "club kids." Today, the youth who proudly boast tattoos and metal facial ornamentation include jocks, preppies, 4.0s— even the nerds. To a Gen Why, being pierced or tattooed is not a sign of rebellion—it is merely a sign of the times.

Many companies now feel as though they are between a rock and a hard place. On one hand, employers need to be sensitive to their customers. At the same time, in a competitive economy, especially in the service sectors where payroll is the biggest and most adjustable expense, the cheaper workers tend to be unskilled and/or young—that is, Gen Why. Employers need fresh, young talent and realize that if they rule out applicants based on appearance, the choice set gets incredibly small indeed. Employers are also confronted with the willfulness of Gen Why, who are used to being catered to, to getting their own way, and to being the ones served, not the ones doing the serving. Managers raising the issue of dress or personal appearance in the wrong way and at the wrong time risk dealing with even higher turnover.

To a Gen Why, being pierced or tattooed is not a sign of rebellion—it is merely a sign of the times.

It would be impossible to bring both sides together under a bilateral treaty of agreement, but perhaps we can find a way to call a truce. And while the differences between the generations, when it comes to agreeing on acceptable appearance, will certainly transcend the shelf life of this book, what follows are three tools for working more comfortably and cooperatively with this particular generation when it comes to this sensitive area.

INSIDE OUT

If you went to an investment-banking firm and your broker was wearing a clown suit, you'd have a hard time talking about mutual funds. Without a doubt, dress codes serve a useful purpose. They help customers quickly identify who is working at the store. Dress codes also help set the tone, be it playful or professional, which is an important part of creating a good customer experience. And finally, dress codes help keep customers and workers focused on the task at hand. Even if you have a dress code that seems to be working for you, it may be time to revisit your dress code from the inside out.

Many older managers feel resentful about having to relax the company dress codes to accommodate the young workforce. They instantly put themselves on the defensive, wondering how they are going to get Gen Whys to conform. Even thinking about the problem can seem galling in a time when companies are finding that they already have to bend over backward to recruit, train, and retain Gen Why. After a while, managers start to wonder how much more they're going to have to give to make this sometimes-difficult generation happy.

If this rings a bell with you, let me suggest a paradigm shift. Analyze your dress code to determine the rationale behind your policies. Try thinking about the issue as a Gen Why would, looking at it with extreme skepticism. Question each item of the code to determine its validity. Think back to what we've said about being truthful with Gen Why. Is the dress code in place for the customer's comfort—say, for instance, at a restaurant, or for management's comfort—say in a call center? If there is no face time between your employees and customers, you might want to consider loosening your requirements.

Analyze your dress code to determine the rationale behind your policies. Try thinking about the issue as a Gen Why would.

Pay special attention to any rule that has been in place five years or longer. Just remember that there was a point when long hair for men was completely unacceptable. Today we don't bat an eye at a man with long hair, and employers don't automatically rule out such a person as a deviant, as they might have in the sixties. Think about your Gen Whys in the same way. Just because they have tattoos doesn't mean they aren't bright, honest, resourceful, hardworking kids.

When face time with customers is involved, it can be hard for managers to look past the fashion and hairstyles, because they are afraid of what customers will think. It's a valid concern. But rather than judging for yourself what is acceptable, try the following method for putting prospective employees in the context of what is actually going on in society. Grab a few popular mainstream magazines (People,

Time, Cosmopolitan, etc.) and your employee handbook. Turn the handbook to the section that addresses your current dress code. As you read the rules governing the appearance of your employees, turn to an advertisement in the magazine for a Gen Why product, like Calvin Klein, Nike, Swatch, Levi Strauss, Nokia, and so on. According to your rules, how many dress code infractions do you see among the models? You'll need a calculator to keep count!

Think it's just the particular magazine you're looking at? Try the same experiment with a Business Week, Forbes, Fortune, or better yet, your own industry trade publication. You'll probably detect numerous discrepancies between what the world is telling your Gen Whys to look like and what your handbook is saying. You cannot change the message the world is sending; you can, however, change your employee handbook.

You'll probably detect numerous discrepancies between what the world is telling your Gen Whys to look like and what your handbook is saying.

WHYS IDEA
Consider modifying the dress code you're asking your Gen Why employees to follow to one that is, at least to some degree, reflective of the styles that are fashionable and widely accepted by society. However, do not feel that you must compromise your corporate image to cater to their every whim. There is common ground and it's easier to reach than you think. Target Stores still require employees to wear

red tops and khaki bottoms, but they've shifted from uniforms to uniformity. They now allow for a certain flexibility within the red top/khaki bottom parameters so that workers are distinguishable from customers, but are able to maintain individuality.

If you're willing to periodically revisit your dress code and make alterations (pardon the pun) that keep in step with generally accepted fashion trends, you'll have an easier time keeping your Gen Whys in step with your code.

COMMUNICATE THE CODE

Young men who enlist in the Army expect to have their heads completely shaved. Applicants at Chuck E. Cheese's Pizza Restaurants are told during the interview that they are not permitted to have visible tattoos or facial piercings when they are at work. Those who want to work in the retail fabric industry for Jo-Ann Stores, Inc., know that they are to wear khaki slacks, shorts, or skirts and a white, collared shirt. Gen Whys don't like surprises, especially when it means altering their image. You'll find them much more agreeable to your dress code when they know the rules ahead of time.

During a seminar for the assistant managers of a conservative retail chain in the Midwest, one of the participants expressed his extreme frustration at getting his Gen Whys to adhere to the strict dress code. I asked if they were aware of how they were expected to look on the job before they were offered the job. The manager told me they never mentioned it in the interview process and they assumed the new employee would pick up on what they're supposed to wear by seeing what everyone else is wearing. "The only thing you can assume about your Gen Whys is that they are going to try to push the boundaries," I said, and suggested that the company have a strategy in place before making a job offer.

Through brainstorming we decided that what the company needed to do was to create a series of professionally photographed life-sized posters of employees wearing their uniforms in an acceptable way—clean, pressed, shirttails tucked in, and so on. Gen Why models, who were actual company employees, were chosen for their complete compliance with respect to jewelry, tattoos, hair, and hygiene. Now, during a hiring interview, managers show applicants the posters and point out the dos and don'ts of the dress code. They ask each applicant if they are willing to sign a form indicating a willingness to abide by that specific set of standards, which leaves no guesswork or creative interpretations of the policy. Gen Whys are also told the consequences for breaking the code, which range from a verbal warning for first-time violators to dismissal for third-time offenders.

To ensure compliance, these posters are placed next to a full-length mirror in the employee check-in area. This empowers employees to police themselves first, long before management has to get involved. Now the countless minor violations never have to be dealt with at all, because the employees take care of it themselves. And when there is a problem, store managers can take decisive action by simply escorting the offender back to the break room to perform a quick comparison of their appearance with that of the examples in the posters.

WHYS IDEA Clearly define your appearance standards to your Gen Whys. Eliminate all guessing games and personal interpretations of your dress code by showing them photographed images of what is acceptable. If there are any questions, this is where they can be addressed. Have them sign a very simple form indicating their willingness to abide by the code.

When you spot a dress code infraction, have a system in place to deal with it. Make certain that you alert a dress code violator in private so as not to embarrass them. Ask them to compare what they are wearing to a photo or poster of what is acceptable and point out the differences. Have a system in place to deal with repeat offenders and be certain to enforce any of the consequences you established ahead of time.

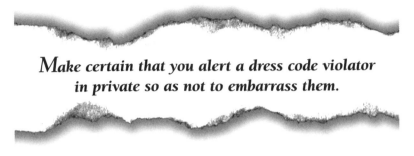

Make certain that you alert a dress code violator in private so as not to embarrass them.

DEBUTING A NEW CODE

ADS, a large call center in the Midwest, decided to update its conservative dress code to make its working environment more comfortable and appealing to Gen Why. Upper management came to an agreement on what they felt was a fair code that gave some strict parameters, but that also left room for creative expression. The vast majority of their associates were already Gen Whys, and they hoped their new, relaxed appearance code would help attract new talent while also serving to retain their current employees.

ADS management then designed and launched a campaign to promote the new code to their associates. They used a variety of interoffice communications to alert the staff to the modifications and to the date the changes would officially go into effect. This hype gave the new dress code policy the look and feel of a significant event for all employees.

On the date the new dress code took effect, management put on a fashion show. The associates entered the workplace to the eighties song "You've Got the Look." The commons area was decorated to resemble a fashion show setup, complete with a runway and chairs. Throughout the day, associates gathered around the runway to see their peers strut down the ramp, while the HR manager assumed the role of The Dress Code Queen to judge whether or not the employee was in compliance. The Dress Code Queen had the authority to throw dress code offenders into a paper streamer Fashion Jail with a mere wave of her Fashion Wand. She tossed a shoeless Gen Why in the brig for twenty minutes, while a girl wearing a halter-top was jailed until she agreed to put on a shirt. A guy who had his boxers peeking over the top of his beltline was also given the maximum twenty-minute penalty, while his coworkers looked on and howled with laughter.

As you might imagine, the fashion show concept met the Whys' need for participation, recognition, visual stimulation, and, most of all, fun. It hammered home the new dress code without making it feel like homework. Best of all, ADS found it much easier to enforce the dress code because the Gen Whys didn't resent the new code from the start, as they surely would have had they just been handed a new employee handbook with a list of do's and don'ts.

Don't lead your Whys to the idea that having a dress code is a bad thing. Let them know how it plays a part in your company image—and how that image serves them!

WHYS IDEA

Don't lead your Whys to the idea that having a dress code is a bad thing. Let them know how it plays a part in your company image—and how that image serves them! Have fun with any changes or alterations you make to your new code, and by all means, get them involved in the roll-out of anything new. Think of a creative way to get them to buy in to your company policies, and always allow some margin for personal expression.

FINAL THOUGHT

Your corporate image is important to you, and your Gen Why's images are important to them. Common ground can be found! Image can become something that unifies rather than divides your workforce. It may mean widening the boundaries to allow for individual difference within a very specific framework. It may mean making your long-term employees slightly uncomfortable as you apparently cater to this new generation. It will probably help to hold each appearance code rule up to this standard: Does this rule have a clearly demonstrable, positive impact on the bottom line? If it does, keep it on the books. If it doesn't, celebrate its demise.

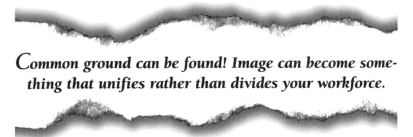

Common ground can be found! Image can become something that unifies rather than divides your workforce.

Fun

VIRTUALLY EVERY PIECE OF RESEARCH about Generation Why highlights the extreme importance they place on having fun. What may be surprising is the extreme importance Generation Why places on having fun while on the job. Perhaps this need is the result of feeling deprived of the carefree childhood fun and innocent games that other generations enjoyed. Many experts think that a society filled with recreational drugs, casual sex, and violence in the media has forced Generation Why to grow up and get serious too fast. On the other hand, maybe their heartfelt need for fun is born out of a spoiled-rotten childhood filled with video games, VCRs, computers, junk food, and loving but permissive parents who cater to their desire for immediate gratification. Generation Why doesn't just love fun; they're addicted to it.

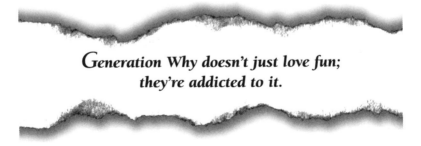

Generation Why doesn't just love fun; they're addicted to it.

Regardless of the reason, there is absolutely no doubt that Gen Why has no interest in a working environment that is not heavy on fun. This is in startling contrast to Baby Boomers, who generally believe that work is a sacrifice you make in order to enjoy your life away from work. Boomers are willing to work long hours, to struggle to succeed, and to take pride in the status of difficult, involving, and high-paying jobs. Generation X, on the other hand, is less likely to run the rat race. They are more interested in finding work that is meaningful, even if it doesn't necessarily pay very well. Managers of all kinds of businesses have noted how difficult it can be to manage Xers because they seem reluctant to work hard at unfulfilling jobs.

At first blush, in this respect, Generation Why workers can seem like Xers, but their seeming reluctance to work hard comes from a different place. Although Gen Why wants to feel that they are making a difference, they aren't necessarily on a quest for meaning in their work. Nor are they primarily interested in riding a rocket to the top. Think back to previous chapters and the stories about the companies that encouraged Gen Why employees to recruit their friends and to dress to their own tastes. This is important because Gen Why thinks about work as an experience. For them, work is no different from going to school or a friend's house or even an amusement park. Even though it's work, they still expect to be able to socialize, to dress the way they want to, and above all, to have fun.

For them, work is no different from going to school or a friend's house or even an amusement park.

Effective managers search for innovative ways to incorporate fun into their workplace, realizing that this serves them well on several fronts. With rare exception, most of today's entry-level positions and part-time jobs claim to offer candidates a fun working environment. Those businesses that can cut through the hype and support their claim of fun are finding it much easier to recruit and to retain top-notch Gen Whys. They also discover the benefits of a fun environment. Fun is the antidote to stress, anxiety, and boredom. Workers who are having fun are also more productive, their morale is higher, and they are less likely to complain about wages, benefits and time off.

Granted, it's easier to incorporate fun into a job at a roller rink or video game arcade than it is into jobs involving maintenance or assembly line work or food preparation. However, it's not so much what a Gen Why is doing, but how they are approaching their job that is important. And as we'll see, fun can come in many forms, and they don't have to be disruptive, decrease productivity, or hamper discipline. In many cases, a fun atmosphere is all it takes to make a Gen Why feel at home, which is why it's important that managers embrace this concept wholeheartedly. If creating a fun and playful work environment is something management is only paying lip service to, then Gen Why employees will leave in droves (and worse, they will tell their friends). But try these simple-to-incorporate techniques, and you will increase the "Fun Quotient" in your working environment and earn the loyalty of Generation Why.

Workers who are having fun are also more productive, their morale is higher, and they are less likely to complain about wages, benefits and time off.

MAKE FUN THROUGH COMPETITION

If your quiet evening at home is interrupted by an annoying solicitation phone call, and the young voice on the other end is trying to convince you to subscribe to your local newspaper, there might be a free throw riding on it. That call could very well originate from the office suite located directly below mine, where a boiler room telemarketing operation employs fifty or so disenfranchised Gen Whys. Take one look at them out on break in the parking lot, and you'd enthusiastically endorse my use of the term disenfranchised. Cutting-edge individuality is the message of their mullets (a type of hairstyle that's "business in the front and party in the back") and their clothes (mostly black), but hopelessness is the message in their eyes. These are obviously hard kids employed in a hard job. Just think of the way you or people you know treat telemarketers who irritate them. Then imagine an eight-hour shift of that kind of constant rejection. Then imagine what it would be like to be a young outsider dealing with all those hang-ups and worse.

But day in and day out I see the same "phonies" in the lot, which tells me that the turnover rate is low. I also hear a continuous stream of cheers and laughter coming through the heating vents, which tells me that there is more than work (at least as I know it) taking place. All this made me wonder what it was about this job that attracted these malcontents and kept them so amused. I decided to go on a high-level, undercover, recognizance mission.

The telemarketing business, a Colorado mom-and-pop operation, has the only vending machines in the building, giving me a legitimate reason to stop by. On my first visit, I noticed a Nerf basketball game set up at one end of the telephone bullpen. On a chalkboard next to the hoop, there was a message that read: "Four sales = Two shots. One basket = $10." Moments later, I heard a voice from a corner of the room cry out, "Got it!" A young, heavily pierced, Hispanic woman ran to the shift supervisor excitedly saying she had just completed her fourth sale of the day. The manager then pulled out a cheerleader-type megaphone and shared the news with the other workers, who applauded and then turned their chairs to watch the action. As she approached the free throw line—a piece of masking tape on the carpet— her coworkers started cheering. She missed her first shot, drawing an "Awwww" from her peers, but before her next attempt they started chanting, "Jo-dy, Jo-dy, Jo-dy." When she made her second shot, the entire room erupted into spontaneous celebration. The supervisor immediately opened his billfold, took out a crisp $10 bill and presented it to Jody as if she'd just won the lottery. At the rousing cheers of the other Gen Whys, she threw up her arms in victory, took a bow, and literally ran back to her cubicle to begin her quest for a repeat performance. I noticed the ripple effect throughout the room as the other phonies began to work even harder toward earning their opportunity to compete.

"Amazing!" I thought. "This place recruits retailing's rejects and gives them the opportunity to be world beaters! They are in a less-than-desirable job, and they are having the time of their life!" What really impressed me was that the company was doing it without quotas and threats, the usual methods of telemarketing firms. Instead of posting goals like a death sentence on the break room wall, the managers had made it fun. The time lost out of the employees' shift was negligible, and better yet, the employees were motivated by one of their peers instead of by management, which is something else that appeals particularly to Gen Why.

A few days later, I returned for another soda and more reconnoitering and found that the managers were tuned in to another important need of Gen Why: variety. This time, the Nerf hoop was down and in its place was a pin-the-tail-on-the-donkey game and a blindfold. The chalkboard read "Three sales = One attempt. Pin the tail for two movie passes." You should have seen the way the Whys were going for it!

WHYS IDEA

Appeal to the game-playing nature of Gen Why. They absolutely love to compete, especially when the winner is recognized and rewarded. If a rejection-based job like telemarketing can take on a game show flavor and simultaneously increase productivity and profits, imagine the possibilities in your business. If you're at a loss for competition ideas, ask your Gen Whys about games they like to play—they'll have plenty of ideas.

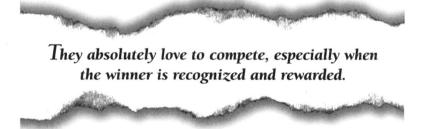

They absolutely love to compete, especially when the winner is recognized and rewarded.

A Word to the Wise

Be leery of contests where employees continually compete against each other for a single prize. Instead, get them to support each other by pitting them against a very achievable goal where everyone can eventually do the victory dance.

MAKE FUN THROUGH PARTICIPATION

The following is not a restaurant review, although it may read like one. As of this writing, I have never worked for the company profiled here, but I have become an avid fan of their concept and approach to Generation Why. For her twentieth birthday celebration, my daughter Holli got to choose the restaurant where her mother and I would take her to celebrate. Without hesitation, she asked to be taken to Joe's Crab Shack. I had never eaten there and didn't understand why Holli was so sure about her choice, but twenty minutes into our dining experience, I not only shared Holli's enthusiasm for Joe's, I also knew the reason why that restaurant boasts the lowest employee turnover of any national chain.

Most major restaurant chains encourage their employees to make birthday celebrations (and the like) special to their guests. I've sat through my share of family occasions at chain restaurants where the staff was about as enthusiastic about performing their scripted celebration cake/song routine as they were about getting a parking ticket. When there's no room for personal creativity or expression, the employee participation wanes and actually works against the desired outcome. But Joe's Crab Shack turns these celebrations into truly unforgettable experiences for its guests.

When there's no room for personal creativity or expression, the employee participation wanes and actually works against the desired outcome.

We notified our server that we had come to celebrate our daughter's twentieth birthday. He got a gleam in his eye and said, "I'll be right back." Moments later the entire restaurant was transformed into a live theater, and we were center stage. Country Western music filled the place, as the mirrored disco ball above our table started spinning wildly. Then eleven Generation Why employees, each attired in crazy cowboy garb, emerged from the kitchen. Singing, hooting, and hollering, they circled our table and then pulled Holli out of her seat. They tossed a giant foam rubber cowboy hat on her head and made her climb aboard a broomstick pony. The DJ alerted the crowd that it was "Holli's Twentieth Roundup" and that "she was gonna rope her a young buck!" At the far end of the restaurant, they introduced another diner, a boy named Kyle. The DJ said Kyle was turning nine today and that "he'd better learn to run from girls while he was still young!" The place went bonkers as Holli began to chase young Kyle around the restaurant while twirling her rope and riding her stick pony. The eleven employees followed behind. The diners were laughing and clapping so hard, the roof nearly came off the place!

I sat there thinking that the routine was so well done that they must do it a hundred times a night, and that they use the same bit whenever somebody comes in for a birthday. But that evening we watched as four other birthdays, two anniversaries, and even a first-day-on-the-job were celebrated, and the celebration was completely different each time. The servers were not the only ones in the show, either. The hosts, cooks, bus help, dishwashers, and even the managers got into the act. The staff appeared to be having as much fun as—if not more than—the diners as they got totally wrapped up in the various characters and roles they assumed. But they didn't neglect their duties. The food was hot and delicious, the service was fast and friendly, and the bathrooms were spotless.

Joe's Crab Shack has little trouble recruiting, retaining, or managing its Gen Why employees. It has found the secret: don't let the action stop, and keep employees actively participating. Joe's appeals to Gen Why's innate desire to be in the spotlight and uses it as a differentiation point.

***Don't let the action stop,
and keep employees actively participating.***

When Generation Why is participating, they're engaged. When they're not, they're disengaged. It's that simple. Companies that learn how to appeal to their innate desire to express themselves through creative participation in the process—regardless of what the process is designed to yield—find that they can capture the soul and release the imagination of a very inventive resource.

WHYS IDEA

Make room in your operation for your Generation Why employees to unleash their creative potential through participation in what makes your company unique. If you're not a restaurant, don't automatically dismiss the principle in place! Gen Why wants the opportunity to show off their talents, skills, and ideas to an audience—even if the audience is just a small team of their coworkers. Find a way to point a spotlight in their direction, and you'll get a command performance. They'll have fun, and you'll get them at their very best!

*Find a way to point a spotlight in their direction,
and you'll get a command performance.*

A Word to the Wise

Use the energy and creativity of your Gen Whys to relight (or ignite for the first time!) the enthusiasm of your more senior employees, whether they're Gen Xers or Boomers. Try not to focus on the rank, title, or seniority of your staff, but rather on what will make your workplace more fun, and ultimately, more productive.

MAKE FUN THROUGH INTERACTION

Kick the can, hide-and-seek, touch football, run-sheep-run—growing up in the suburbs, our block was a hotbed of inventive fun for kids. But for the past fifteen years, suburban neighborhoods have been much quieter. The reason? Gen Whys have been raised on a steady diet of action figures, movie rentals, Nintendo, and computer games. Today's quiet neighborhood streets are a reminder of the impact mass media has had on children everywhere.

The things that you don't get in your childhood can become a driving force behind how you live your adult life. Today's twenty-something members of Gen Why are starting to demand social interaction. This makes sense. You could take away every Nintendo and VCR and satellite dish from every Gen Why's house and they would still get plenty of screen time at school and on the job. Gen Why is the first generation to enter the fully computerized workplace, and everyone, regardless of his or her generation, knows how isolating an eight-hour day in front of a computer monitor can be. As a result, Generation Why is trying to compensate by seeking jobs where they can work alongside their friends and where social interaction isn't penalized. When surveyed, most Whys admit they'd accept less money and work longer hours if they could just work with their friends.

This is almost impossible to comprehend in the success-at-any-cost mind-set of their Boomer managers who would transfer to Antarctica if the money were right. And for older managers, the idea of socializing on the job seems like a recipe for low productivity, mistakes, and poor customer service. It's not unusual for a Boomer manager to react by saying, "No way will I stand back and see my production/service/sales, and so on go down the tubes because I let my staff socialize while they're on the clock!" But remember, we're talking about multitasking Gen Whys. Unlike some other employees who have only two gears—talk and work—Gen Whys can handle the dual action and will literally shift into overdrive when their friends are on the same team. Of course, you need to have clearly stated guidelines defining acceptable coworker socialization while on the job, but if those posts are sunk deep, Gen Whys will adhere to your boundaries at the risk of being separated from their friends.

When surveyed, most Whys admit they'd accept less money and work longer hours if they could just work alongside their friends.

Hy-Vee Supermarkets have facilitated employee social interaction this way: Employee break rooms in its stores are being converted to a rec.-room-like setting. Rather than an industrial look that screams, "Get outta here and get back to work!" its break rooms encourage social interaction, with an environment that includes carpeting and comfortable furniture, cable television, a computer kiosk with Internet access, kitchenettes with refrigerators, microwaves, and more. The walls are lined with pictures of the young staff and descriptions of their schools, families, and hobbies. This is a sure-fire conversation starter, enabling coworkers to rapidly meet and find common ground.

WHYS IDEA
Take the pressure off of your having to be the guru of workplace fun. Instead of being the ringmaster, empower your young employees to create their own fun by simply providing an atmosphere conducive to social interaction. Redesign and redecorate the break room to be more club-like. Lower the walls of the cubicles. Structure an intranet E-mail system that enables employees to stay connected. Plan frequent off-hour (and even on-the-clock) social events, where they can mix, mingle, kibitz, and just hang out. In other words, get out of their way and let them enjoy the social aspect of work.

Instead of being the ringmaster, empower your young employees to create their own fun by simply providing an atmosphere conducive to social interaction.

A Word to the Wise

W Look at your work environment, especially areas where your employees take their breaks and lunches, with new eyes when you go in tomorrow. How does it look and feel to you? Is it cluttered, junky, worn-out? Or is it a place that's clean, comfortable, and relaxing? A new coat of paint, a couple of comfortable chairs, and a boom box may be all that is needed to upgrade a dingy break room into a great place to reenergize your Whys. But whatever it takes, creating a pleasing break area should not be considered an avoidable cost; it should be thought of as a necessary investment.

FINAL THOUGHT

As a manager of Generation Why, especially the younger members, it's hard not to feel like a parent. You don't want to be perceived as a softie, because you're afraid you'll be taken advantage of. The idea of introducing fun into the workplace may seem like a sign of weakness, but if a sense of fun is balanced out with clear rules of conduct and well-outlined responsibilities, it will actually become a source of strength. The confident manager allows fun and creativity but also makes it clear that there is work to be done.

The telemarketing firm I used as an example builds fun so seamlessly into their business plan that employees might not even notice the incentive plan. In the case of Joe's Crab Shack, employees get to cut loose during the special evening celebrations, but to have time to play, they also know that the service, food prep, and cleanup have to be top-notch. Hy-Vee managers know they can get more out of their employees during work because the managers give more by providing better, friendlier break rooms. These examples just serve as the springboard for what you can do with your particular company. Jump on in!

Recognition and Rewards

PERHAPS YOU'RE FAMILIAR WITH the tale of the fisherman who was out one day by himself in his boat. After several hours alone, he heard a rap on the side of his boat. He glanced over his shoulder and noticed a snake glaring up at him with a frog inside its mouth. Feeling compassion for the soon-to-be-eaten frog, the fisherman quickly grabbed the snake and set the frog free. The frog was obviously elated, but the snake was distressed because it had just lost its noontime meal. Feeling guilty, the fisherman reached into his picnic basket, pulled out part of his sandwich, and fed it to the snake. Now the frog was happy, the snake was happy, and the fisherman was happy. Pretty soon the fisherman heard another knock on his boat. When he turned around he saw the same snake, only this time it had two frogs in its mouth!

As a manager, you certainly have systems in place to deal with employees who demonstrate negative behavior or unacceptable conduct in the workplace, but even more important is how you recognize good behavior. You know just what to do if an employee shows up late for work, does not arrive properly attired, or is caught stealing from the cash register. You have a system in place when you see one of your employees do a job unsatisfactorily or lash out rudely at one of your customers. But what system do you have in place to recognize and reward outstanding performance? The story of the fisherman, the snake and the frog would have a completely different ending if the fisherman had saved the frog and given the snake a smack and told him to go away. Unfortunately, correcting bad behavior can take up the lion's share of a manager's time, but when it comes to Gen Why, it's vital to reward the good, lest they swim away.

Baby Boomers, by their very nature, find that hard work is a reward in and of itself. They need only know that they are meeting expectations and are being fairly compensated to maintain a consistent level of productivity. Gen Whys are on the opposite end of that spectrum, crying out for management to praise them when they meet expectations and to tip them when they exceed normal performance levels. They are drawn to environments that offer frequent recognition and are repelled from those that don't.

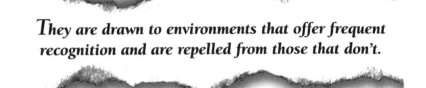

They are drawn to environments that offer frequent recognition and are repelled from those that don't.

In a way, Gen Why is wired to need a lot of praise. After years of being in the marketing spotlight, it's a shock for them to enter the workplace where they are treated like just another drone. It would be easy to criticize them for their selfishness, but who can blame them? When you're the star of the show, when multinational companies have been telling you your whole life that your opinions and ideas and tastes are the most important thing in the world, you're bound to have skewed expectations of the world. This doesn't mean that managers have to kowtow to every Gen Why whim, but it does mean that the emerging workforce requires different handling than previous waves of workers.

The good news is that Gen Why responds with gratitude. A well-recognized Gen Why employee is more loyal, more creative, and harder working than what many managers are used to. And the rewards don't have to be extravagant or expensive. But stroke them the right way, and you will go a long way toward creating a valued employee.

Correcting bad behavior can take up the lion's share of a manager's time, but when it comes to Gen Why, it's vital to reward the good, lest they swim away.

THE FOUR PS OF WISE RECOGNITION AND REWARDS

There are obviously numerous ways to give an employee a pat on the back. However, whatever system you use for recognizing and rewarding the positive performance of your Gen Whys, these four criteria can ensure your Why2K Compliance.

Personal

Regardless of the type of recognition and reward given, the perceived value escalates when it is individualized for the employee. Although this takes more time and consideration for a manager, the resulting benefits certainly justify the extra thought and energy. Yes, this does mean that you've got to know your Gen Whys on a different level. You need to know what they like to do in their personal time away from work. This information enables you to reward an employee in a way that demonstrates that you went out of your way to honor them.

A department manager at a Wal-Mart wanted to give a special reward to a young associate who loved horses. She gave her Gen Why associate the gift of a picture frame for a photograph of her horse—and the frame was engraved with the horse's name! That $30 expenditure registered with the young employee far more than the equal or even double amount of cash would have. When it comes to giving a reward, with Gen Why the thought really does count!

Proportionate

Overzealous managers who are quick to heap praise and incentives on Gen Whys for minor things find it hard to continue to show proportionate enthusiasm for bigger accomplishments. Any recognition or reward should always match the level of performance being recognized. By giving too much of a reward for a small accomplishment, you could paint yourself into a corner when it comes to rewarding more significant achievements. On the opposite end of the scale, giving too little might serve to deflate a Gen Why's enthusiasm and start them thinking about other employment possibilities. Therefore, it is imperative to pre-plan your recognition and reward program to make certain that you have various levels of incentives to reward specific levels of achievement.

By giving too much of a reward for a small accomplishment, you could paint yourself into a corner when it comes to rewarding more significant achievements.

Punctual

Gen Whys live in the moment. Rewarding them with a dollar today is far more effective than giving them two dollars tomorrow. Consequently, wise managers are prepared and keep incentives and rewards on hand. Managers who are ill equipped to reward on the spot find the effectiveness of their incentives drops off dramatically. Given a choice, Generation Why will opt for the delivery of something real today as opposed to the promise of something even better down the road.

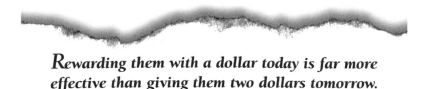

Rewarding them with a dollar today is far more effective than giving them two dollars tomorrow.

Public

The value of the reward you present will multiply exponentially if it is given to a Gen Why in the presence of their peers. They want to know they are doing well, and they want their friends and coworkers to know as well. When a situation prohibits the praising or rewarding of a Gen Why in public, consider sharing the news on the company website or message board, or posting a congratulatory announcement in a highly visible place.

While dining at Ed Debevak's (a fifties-style diner) in Phoenix, I commented to the manager that my server had been exceptionally fun, kind, and friendly. The manager immediately jumped up on a chair in the middle of the restaurant, blew into a noisemaker, shared the story with the rest of the diners, and then called for a round of applause and three cheers for the server—and then a cheer for the entire wait staff.

Let's take a look at some specific recognition and reward programs and ideas. The following require little or no money, just a lot of thought and a touch of creativity. In some ways, it all comes down to educating yourself about Gen Why's attitudes and tastes. You don't have to become an expert, but a little research into what they like will go a long way. Also remember that your recognition and reward system should capture behavior that plays by the rules, that is achievable and self-directed, and that stretches them to high performance.

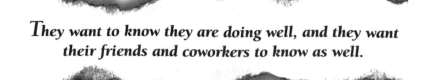

They want to know they are doing well, and they want their friends and coworkers to know as well.

THE MAGIC OF SENDING A LETTER HOME

Dear Mr. and Ms. Franklin:

As you are aware, your son Joel has worked for Alcott's Fine Foods since March. During these six months we have been extraordinarily pleased with his performance.

Joel has an outstanding attendance record with us and has only been late to work on one occasion. He has never missed a day, and in those rare cases when he needs to work out a scheduling conflict, he does so well in advance. Joel brings a positive and enthusiastic attitude to our store and always demonstrates an eagerness to learn something new. When training new employees, the management team at Alcott's frequently uses Joel Franklin as an example of what we'd like to see in all of our new employees.

On behalf of Alcott's Fine Foods, we want to commend you for raising such an outstanding young man. We sincerely hope that Joel feels as strongly about his association with Alcott's as we do about him, and we also hope that he'll consider the career opportunities our company offers in his long-range plans.

Please ask for me next time you are in our store; I would be honored to meet you.

Sincerely,
ARNOLD PECHEK
General Manager,
Alcott's Fine Foods, Store #340

It is hard to imagine the depth of the impact that a simple, sincere letter of praise will reach. Though it only took a few minutes to write, it may someday be read by Joel's great grandkids. It costs only a few cents to create and to send, but it is priceless in its ability to build confidence, reinforce positive performance, and strengthen a long-term relationship. It may even change a part-time mentality into a career mind-set.

If you have any doubts as to its effectiveness, ask yourself this. How would you feel if you received this kind of letter from your son or daughter's employer? How would you feel if your boss sent a letter of this nature to your parents—even now, at this stage in your life?

So would your Gen Whys.

A Word to the Wise

Some of the greatest recognition and reward strategies are those that cost the least. In your desire to build a strong R/R program, don't overlook the simple things. In fact, start with the simple things and build your program around them. Personal letters are also an ingenious way to specify what kind of behavior you want reinforced. If punctuality is an overall problem, single out the Gen Whys who are always on time for personal praise and you'll find that the word spreads fast. Sending these kinds of messages home via E-mail is easier, cheaper, and faster; however, when compared with the tangibility of a signed letter on company letterhead, an E-mail doesn't carry nearly the same weight.

THREE FREEBIES THAT STRIKE GOLD

Name Identity

Gen Whys may not remember Cheers, the smash hit television sitcom of the eighties, but they certainly get revved up when everybody knows their name. It is critical that you know your Gen Why's name, and how to spell it and pronounce it correctly. Ask them how they want to be addressed—Gen Whys are big on nicknames—and refer to them in that manner. Although this sounds basic, many Boomers use the military approach of expressing authority by calling Whys by their last name. This is an immediate disconnect.

Home Depot uses name recognition to inspire excellence by posting signs in the aisles proclaiming, "This Aisle Maintained by Trevor Johnson." This is a unique and memorable form of creatively using your Whys' names in the workplace. If Toby is always punctual, tell the others you want them to arrive at the meeting on "Toby Time." If Jenna is exceptionally good at dealing with angry customers, title a section of your training manual or program "The Jenna Method of Defusing an Unhappy Customer."

About Face

If a picture is worth a thousand words, then getting your mug noticed all over town has got to be worth a library! Rock Bottom Brewery, a popular chain of brewpubs, recently used a large city bus in Denver to display the faces of several Gen Why employees. The fifty-foot-long bus was completely covered, windows and all, with an attractive mural, depicting a dozen smiling staffers with a caption that read "Come have fun with us at Rock Bottom!" This not only served to increase customer and job applicant flow, it also rewarded those Gen Whys who had been with the restaurant the longest. The campaign gave Rock Bottom employees the kind of face recognition typically only given to local news anchors and celebrities.

Wal-Mart, AT&T, and Ford are among a growing list of companies that use actual employees in their ads. United Airlines uses actual flight attendants in its preflight safety videos. Giving your exceptional Gen Whys the chance to appear in one of your print or broadcast ads, or even in your annual catalog or seasonal mailing, is a sensational way to reward them, as it plays into their desire to be in the spotlight.

Giving your exceptional Gen Whys the chance to appear in one of your print or broadcast ads, or even in your annual catalog or seasonal mailing, is a sensational way to reward them, as it plays into their desire to be in the spotlight.

Golden Rule

A great way to honor a high achieving Gen Why employee is to do for them what they do for you, and then some. You might say, "You've been doing such a great job the past few days, Sarah, that I am going to round up the carts in the parking lot. You take an extra twenty-minute break and kick back."

If you really want to reward Gen Why and build your relationship in the process, do something for them that is outside the boundaries of the workplace. "You've really made this place shine, Todd, so toss me your keys and let me shine your ride up for you!" To further the impact, perform the task while the honoree and his/her coworkers look on.

If you really want to reward Gen Why and build your relationship in the process, do something for them that is outside the boundaries of the workplace.

WHYS IDEA

Gen Whys are not bashful by nature. Nothing makes them happier than getting name and face recognition. Let your Gen Whys earn a place in your company's history by having their name associated with doing something outstanding. Take photos of your high-achieving Whys, write stories about what they did that was great, and post them in high-traffic areas. Create an Employee Wall of Fame and give your Whys an induction ceremony for doing continued outstanding work. Seek promotional opportunities where you can use the names and faces of your best Gen Why staffers. Capitalize on the Golden Rule by seeking innovative ways to Do Unto Them. You'll discover that these kinds of quick, simple, and inexpensive ways to recognize and reward your Gen Whys are among your most effective.

THE PRIZE PATROL

Alliance Data Systems employs thousands of Gen Whys in its central call center in Kansas City. Prepared to reward exceptional performance, the management team maintains an award basket loaded with premiums. The basket contains an array of goodies that a committee of Gen Whys has helped to select, including decorated candles, picture frames, lotions, books, daily calendars, long-distance calling cards, fast-food gift certificates, and movie passes. When it's time to celebrate the good work of a GW, here's how they achieve maximum impact:

The Prize Patrol (composed of other Whys) arrives at the honored associate's desk, carrying a giant helium Thank You balloon, and affixes it to their desk so that it is visible from all the other cubicles. An announcement is then made over the PA system alerting all coworkers of the star's special accomplishments. After the applause fades, the honoree is invited to select a prize from the basket.

Even though the incentive is not costly, the celebration is not soon forgotten. In the process, excellence is acknowledged and peers are reminded that excellence pays dividends.

WHYS IDEA

Instead of selecting incentives for your Gen Whys, give them a menu of options and let them decide. Solicit the opinions of your Whys as to what needs to be in your basket, or better yet, give them a budget and let them do the shopping for you. Who knows better than they do what will make them smile? When the time is right for a reward, splash the event with fun. With a little enthusiasm, you can turn receiving a reward into a reward in itself. This process can come in handy on a rainy day to help you divert attention away from a stressful situation and onto a ceremony honoring outstanding performance. Make a big deal out of the occasion with simple and inexpensive touches like balloons, kazoos, streamers, and so on. Encourage your other Gen Why employees to create a quick song or a skit to use as a standard award presentation, and then teach every-one on your staff the lyrics and actions. When you honor an employee in this manner, make certain you take pictures and/or videos and send them home with the honoree.

With a little enthusiasm, you can turn receiving a reward into a reward in itself. This process can come in handy on a rainy day to help you divert attention away from a stressful situation and onto a ceremony honoring outstanding performance.

CASH IS KING

In my youth, I rarely got money in my birthday cards. Of course, life was simpler for adults back then, and they took the time to find out what a kid might like and they'd try to get it for him. Naturally, there were not as many toys and gifts on the market, so shopping was easy, and most kids were happy to get anything that came in a wrapped box.

Gen Whys, on the other hand, have grown up with busier parents and relatives who often don't have time to sift through the countless aisles of the toy superstore and get the exact match on the kid's wish list. Oftentimes, the birthday child is given a pile of envelopes in lieu of presents, and they've come to love the paper inside.

In today's world of unlimited choice, it's difficult to know just what size, type, color, and model of gift to bestow on a deserving Why. That's why paper gifts (money, vouch-ers, certificates) make such good sense! Gift certificates are great rewards for Gen Whys, but their favorite certificates are green, have pictures of dead presidents, and are redeemable anywhere.

If you want to balance your recognition and rewards with some cash incentives, make sure you have fun with it. Johnny Carrino's Italian Restaurants are pros at this. Its managers love to give cash incentives to employees, and they've created some fun and unique internal promotions to do just that, through a game called Smokin' Marbles. Each store in the chain is sent a bag of marbles and a color key from headquarters. Deserving employees get to reach into the bag and pull out a marble. The color of the marble equates to a specific cash award for that period. Cash awards generally range from $5 to $50.

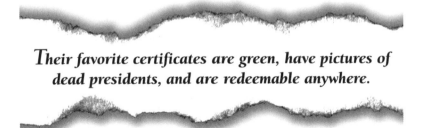

Their favorite certificates are green, have pictures of dead presidents, and are redeemable anywhere.

Carrino's also likes to use cash as a retention incentive. Its Loyalty Lottery promotion is held at each store twice each year. Each employee who has worked for the company since the prior drawing gets to put their name on a ticket and enter it in the next drawing. One name is selected, and that lucky employee receives a $600 cash award.

WHYS IDEA

Although it is not a good idea to use cash as your only incentive, it is a good idea to include it in your mix of rewards. Cash awards are most effective when they are the green stuff—not checks. Gen Whys love it when you "show them the money!" However, don't just walk up to a Why and hand them a twenty-dollar bill. Add some excitement by enclosing it in a card, paper-clipping it to their time card with a note, or making a game out of it, as mentioned in the examples above.

KEEP TRACK OF THE EXCELLENCE

Frequent shopper programs have become a sensational way to maintain customer loyalty for restaurants, supermarkets, coffee shops, and the like. The idea is to have a customer keep track of his purchases by accumulating punches on a small card, and to present the customer with a premium or a freebie when their card has accumulated a designated number of punches.

The punch card concept can be adapted and modified to reward your regularly achieving Gen Whys. Simply give each staff member a punch card and tell them that each time you or your management team sees them going above and beyond the call of duty, you will punch their card. A completed card (six to ten punches) will get them a free meal, a paid day off, a choice of something in your prize basket, and so on.

Fun technicians (general staff members) at Paramount Carowinds Amusement Park are given a STAR Card when they are seen doing something that really personifies the company values. The cards are designed like a mini report card, so that the supervisor can check the box next to the company value that the Gen Why employee was caught exemplifying. The STAR Cards can be exchanged for merchandise within the park.

Chuck E. Cheese's employees earn pull-tab cards similar to lottery scratch-offs for exceptional sales, attendance, uniform compliance, cost controls, and so on. Each card has a random point value that is revealed when the associate pulls the tab. The recipients accumulate points and then trade them in for prizes like gift certificates, small electronics, and paid time off. The more elaborate the prize, the higher the number of pull-tab points needed. This kind of recognition and reward program incorporates fun and competition, while doubling as an excellent retention tool.

Pizza Hut Restaurants in Pennsylvania have instituted the CHAMPS program to emphasize and reinforce company values of Cleanliness, Hospitality, Accuracy, Maintenance, Product Quality, and Service. Managers present team members with a CHAMPS card whenever they see them do something special that reinforces one of the CHAMPS values. Customers also get involved in the promotion as they share feedback about employee performance on Guest Response Cards highlighting the six values.

Each restaurant has a large board in the employee area where both Guest Response Cards and those given by management can be seen side by side. Team members can clearly see how their individual performance impacts customer satisfaction. By region, individual restaurants are evaluated and ranked, and those getting the highest CHAMPS scores are awarded cash prizes for employees to share. This enhances teamwork and camaraderie among employees as they support each other in a joint mission to achieve CHAMPionship goals.

A Word to the Wise

 Although these scorecard programs are an excellent way to keep employees achieving on a consistent basis, it is important to clearly spell out the rules of the program in advance to avoid any confusion. If one manager is quick to give acknowledgment and another is more discriminating, the program can backfire and your Gen Whys may cry, "Foul!" Match the amount of effort required to earn a premium with the value of the premium given. For example, don't make someone redesign the store layout just to get a free video rental coupon; and don't give a Ferrari to a Gen Why who shows up for work on time five days in a row. Also, be certain that you maintain a tight control over the punching or marking device so that unearned punches don't mysteriously show up on an employee's card.

Match the amount of effort required to earn a premium with the value of the premium given.

FINAL THOUGHT

The behavior that is recognized and rewarded is always the behavior that is repeated. While it may be clear to you what the performance standards are and what behaviors are acceptable in the workplace, it is not as obvious to your Gen Whys. Take some time during training and on the job to explain why one particular performance is not adequate, but another behavior is. Once Gen Why knows what the standards are, they are more than able to figure out how to achieve them. A carefully developed recognition and reward plan will cost you relatively little, while reaping you huge rewards in employee satisfaction, performance, and retention. And don't be surprised if you get more in return than you gave!

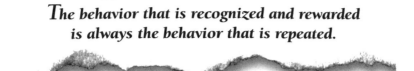

*The behavior that is recognized and rewarded
is always the behavior that is repeated.*

Retention

NOW THAT YOU'VE LASSOED some great young talent and you've trained and managed them into good and valued employees, your job has just begun. Because right when you feel as though you've squeezed a diamond out of a lump of coal, your superstar Gen Why hire comes into your office to tell you they're quitting to work in their brother's lawn service, or worse yet, for your competitor down the street. It's nothing personal, nothing you've done, they just got a better offer, more money, better benefits, a better location, a chance to work with their best friend. It could be anything. And the worst part is that you're going to have to start all over again, and you didn't even know anything was wrong in the first place.

In a market where employee loyalty is fast becoming an oxymoron, smart managers know they have to work harder than ever to keep their talented but fickle young workforce from walking out the door. A client of mine says that Gen Whys exist in the workforce in a stealthy but perpetual job-seeking mode. They are always actively seeking a better deal somewhere else, without showing a single sign that they're discontented where they are now.

They are always actively seeking a better deal somewhere else, without showing a single sign that they're discontented where they are now.

If you want to be hard on young people, you could say they have no sense of loyalty, but let's take a look at the world around them. Big name athletes hold out in the preseason so they can renegotiate their contracts, and team owners are just as fast to trade a player. Many of Gen Why's parents, in an effort to better their careers, job hop all over the place, while many corporations, with all the downsizing and mergers and acquisitions, are quick to reassign or lay people off. Talk to Gen Why, and you'll find that they can in fact be intensely loyal to their friends and families. It's the rest of the world that they are wary about, and perhaps with good reason. Their loyalty must be won, and winning that loyalty starts with the recruitment process.

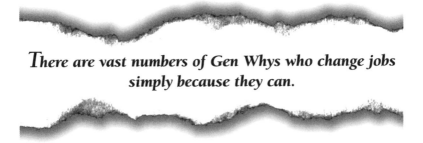

There are vast numbers of Gen Whys who change jobs simply because they can.

In his first year out of high school, my son Travis had ten W-2s to report to the IRS, representing the ten very different jobs he had worked that year alone! Like Travis, there are vast numbers of Gen Whys who change jobs simply because they can. Think about the messages they've received while growing up in a technology-based culture, where CEOs and politicians and even educators talk about how change is good. Some Gen Whys are going to leave because they want a change, and if you can't provide enough change internally, they'll find it elsewhere.

Gen Whys are also much less likely to believe in employee loyalty. They don't get as emotionally involved with work as Boomers and Xers do, so for them leaving a job, or getting one for that matter, doesn't seem like a big deal. Gen Whys don't see leaving a job suddenly as a bad thing, but as a natural one. They often don't see the consequences of abrupt departures. Gen Why has also been taught—or has learned the hard way—that mobility is a good thing. Staying in one place for too long feels to Gen Why like staying somewhere forever. No one, regardless of his or her generation, wants to feel trapped.

Gen Whys don't see leaving a job suddenly as a bad thing, but a natural one. They often don't see the consequences of abrupt departures.

Despite these obstacles, you can hang on to your solid gold Gen Why employees. In fact, when managed effectively, they will be the most loyal workers you have on your payroll! But only if employee retention becomes an area of continual strategic focus, and not just a statistic you glance at on a report. Smart Gen Why managers give employee retention the same amount of energy they give customer service. In fact, in a way, that's what retention is all about—treating your employees like you would treat your best customers. And believe me, without an active retention strategy in place, your Gen Why employees will slip out the bathroom window during break time! Here are some ways to stop them from leaving before they even think about it:

FILL THE RUTS

Many Gen Whys start grazing other opportunities because they find themselves in a rut. It doesn't matter if their particular rut took only weeks to form; to their way of thinking, a rut is a rut, and any way out is a good way out. To defeat this thinking before it turns into a turnover problem, you must be open to some unconventional tactics. The upside is that breaking ruts can be as fun for you as it is for your Gen Whys.

Naturally, you have to recognize the trouble spots as quickly as they develop and keep alert to the stagnant patterns and behaviors that your Gen Why employees exhibit. If there are typical times and/or events that seem to trigger undesirable attitudes and behaviors, then a rut-busting opportunity is within your grasp.

A midsize accounting firm that has begun recruiting Gen Why talent combats a heavy case of the ruts during tax season (January 1 through April 15). Rather than lose its key young people to the monotony and stress associated with this chaotic time as it has in years past, it now designates every Wednesday as Cinema Day. The firm closes its office at 2 p.m. sharp, and the entire staff carpools to the neighborhood movieplex. Once there, they see a movie together on the firm's dime.

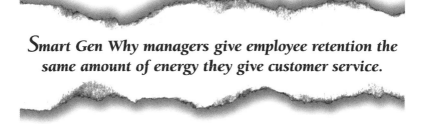

Smart Gen Why managers give employee retention the same amount of energy they give customer service.

The specific movie has been predetermined by a movie trivia game they played during the prior week, pitting the men against the women; the winning gender gets to pick the movie the entire group sees. To begin the Thursday morning company meeting, several staff members' names are randomly drawn from a hat, and they are then called upon to give an ad-lib movie review. This process provides an opportunity for all staff to get involved, play a game, interact socially, strengthen the team, and bust a rut each week.

WHYS IDEA

Ruts left untended become trenches, from which your best Gen Whys will most certainly escape. When they are detected in the early stages and dealt with accordingly, ruts are easily filled. Close your doors for business on a Thursday morning and challenge your staff to a game of Twister or Trivial Pursuit. Preside over the weekly company meeting in a gorilla costume and offer complimentary bananas for the entire day.

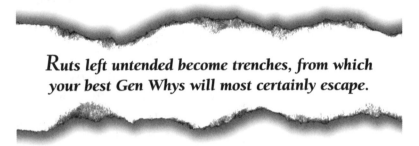

Ruts left untended become trenches, from which your best Gen Whys will most certainly escape.

Where and when is your company most susceptible to developing ruts, and what is your plan for filling them in? Ask your Gen Whys, or better yet, chart negative behaviors and employee complaints to see when stress or boredom is the most common. Then set your course to bust it up by filling in the ruts.

THE MAGIC OF THE SLOW REVEAL

One of my best childhood friends is Jewish, and at the end of the holiday season we would always compare our respective piles of gifts. Even though I often made out a little better than he did, I was forever envious of the way he got his gifts. I opened all my Christmas presents within the span of one hour or less. He got one Hanukkah gift a day for eight days. My holiday was over in a matter of minutes; his lasted for more than a week.

In an attempt to lure, entice, and/or motivate Gen Why employees, some managers are quick to reveal all of the company perks and benefits. While it is undoubtedly important to lure Gen Why employees with clear reasons why they should want to work for your company, giving away too much information actually works against you in the long run.

I work out at a 50,000-square-foot health club facility that offers every kind and brand name of fitness equipment available today. What amazes me, however, is that this club keeps its members and membership active without the use of long-term contracts. I'm convinced that one of the secrets of its success is how it introduces new equipment. Whenever it upgrades, it never puts the entire line of machines out at once. Instead, members will periodically notice a brand-new piece of equipment sporting a big red ribbon. A week or so later, another new piece appears, also adorned by a ribbon. This process continues over several weeks, until a full line of ten to twelve brand-new machines span the workout floor.

While it is undoubtedly important to lure Gen Why employees with clear reasons why they should want to work for your company, giving away too much information actually works against you in the long run.

Throughout that three-month process, the members' morale escalates and the subsequent referral business goes through the roof. I highly doubt they'd experience the same level of continued enthusiasm and extended success if the club management elected to put out all ten to twelve new pieces of equipment at one time. The way the management draws out the new-machine introduction process keeps people coming into the gym more frequently to keep up with the latest piece of equipment, trying out new exercises, and talking to their friends about all the great improvements the club is "continually" making.

Smart managers never show all their cards at once. Perks and benefits, spread out over time, keep Gen Why employees producing at a higher level because they're always looking forward to the future. Along these lines, it's also important to change your smaller benefits and perks frequently, so that new hires learn from your other employees that they never know what goodness to expect or when to expect it.

Smart managers never show all their cards at once. Perks and benefits, spread out over time keep Gen Why employees producing at a higher level because they're always looking forward to the future.

A Word to the Wise

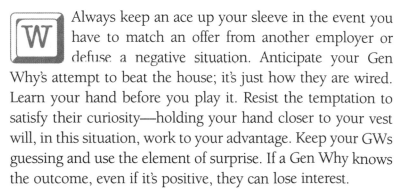

Always keep an ace up your sleeve in the event you have to match an offer from another employer or defuse a negative situation. Anticipate your Gen Why's attempt to beat the house; it's just how they are wired. Learn your hand before you play it. Resist the temptation to satisfy their curiosity—holding your hand closer to your vest will, in this situation, work to your advantage. Keep your GWs guessing and use the element of surprise. If a Gen Why knows the outcome, even if it's positive, they can lose interest.

READ THEIR MINDS

What if you could read the minds of your Gen Whys? Then you'd really know what they thought about their jobs and about you. You'd know if they were seeking other offers or growing bored with their responsibilities or work environment. You'd know what they thought of you as a manager and if you were connecting with them. You'd be able to resolve small issues before they became big ones. Well, there is a way to get all the inside information about your Gen Whys you need to make informed managerial decisions! You don't have to be a mind reader, eavesdropper, or a spy, and you don't even have to be a good guesser. All you need to do is ask them.

Whys are chomping at the bit to tell you what they think and how they feel. If you ask them, they won't hold back and they won't sugarcoat the truth. They are blunt, expressive, and remarkably honest. Effective managers use this generational characteristic to their advantage by encouraging feedback.

Whys are chomping at the bit to tell you what they think and how they feel. If you ask them, they won't hold back and they won't sugarcoat the truth.

Tokyo Joe's restaurants in Colorado thrive on staffing edgy Gen Why kids that other chains turn away solely based on appearance. These quick-serve Japanese restaurants have a remarkably low turnover, in part because their employees feel loyalty to the company that gave them a chance. But they go a step beyond that. Once very few months, the owner, Larry Leith, surveys his entire GW staff to find out what they like and dislike about their jobs. He encourages them to be open and speak frankly about all aspects of their employment and their supervisors. He says his management teams try hard to learn the individual leanings of each employee, and they indeed make a lot of organizational and operational changes based on that feedback.

The easiest way to get them to open up is to open your door. When your staff feels confident they can communicate with you and that what they say will not come back to haunt them, they'll begin to speak freely. You need to establish a practice and reputation of keeping confidences and acting on information in a way that is not punitive to the source or their teammates. Gen Why places a very high value on truth, trust, and authenticity. Once they know they can trust you, they'll feel free to tell you their concerns and issues directly.

One technique to consider is dual-purpose performance reviews. Just as you request feedback from your customers to find out what they like and dislike about your business, products, and services, survey your Gen Why employees to find out what they're thinking. Ask where they see themselves with your company in three months, six months, a year down the road, and so on. Ask what new skills they are eager to learn. Ask when they expect to be promoted. Their answers and responses will enlighten and empower you.

Gen Why places a very high value on truth, trust, and authenticity. Once they know they can trust you, they'll feel free to tell you their concerns and issues directly.

WHYS IDEA Create a new employee response system. Frequently survey your Gen Whys and discover what they really think. Don't be lulled into thinking you're adequately staffed simply because you have a sufficient number of bodies today. If you don't also have the same number of hearts and minds, your staff could leave any day. Find out what they're thinking.

KEEP TABS ON YOUR COMPETITORS—AND ALWAYS OFFER MORE!

The greatest robbers of your business aren't after your merchandise or your money, they're after a far more valuable resource—your trained GW staff. I talk to a lot of frustrated managers who are grasping for a quick fix to their turnover woes. "Your young employees may be leaving your company," I say, "but they're not retiring, are they?" I then ask managers if they know where their employees are going, and more importantly why. Part of the secret of keeping Gen Why employees is in determining what Gen Why defines as *more,* figuring out what *more* others are offering, and finding new ways to trump that *more.*

The concept of *more* often worries Boomers and Xers because they think that means they have to spend more. But more isn't necessarily about money. It may be in the form of more flexibility, or more opportunity for advancement. When more does mean money, it doesn't always mean a higher salary. It might translate to ongoing training and career development programs, 401(k) or other pension plans. More might also be access to technology like cell phones, laptop computers, and other technology. Sometimes, as we'll see below, more can mean bonuses and perks.

Part of the secret of keeping Gen Why employees is in determining what Gen Why defines as more, figuring out what more others are offering, and finding new ways to trump that more.

Savvy managers of Generation Why never stop asking questions, especially when a Gen Why terminates. They want to know what they're up against, so when they lose a valued employee, they find out where that employee is going and why. If they recognize a pattern (i.e., numerous Gen Whys quitting to go to work for the ABC Company), they find out exactly what it is that ABC Company is doing to lure the Gen Whys away.

When you know the reason behind the turnover, you can go to work on securing your employment base by sweetening your offer to meet or beat the wages, perks, benefits, conditions, and so on that your competitors are offering. If you can't meet or beat the wages, you can work to offer more in different ways that are just as attractive. When you feel like you're offering more, make certain your Whys are aware of it. Just as you promote your products and services to your customers, you should also promote the advantages of the jobs you offer to your existing employees.

WHYS IDEA

When it comes to your workforce, do you know what your competitors are offering? Your Gen Why employees do. You undoubtedly keep tabs on your direct competitors in the marketplace, but you also need to keep tabs on your competitors in the employment marketplace. A few hours of investigative research can yield amazing information that can help you create a defensive strategy to help you fortify your business against employee robbery.

EXPAND THE CIRCLE OF BENEFITS

One of the fastest growing supermarket chains in America, Hy-Vee, offers its employees a generous discount on merchandise and services. This isn't unusual in retail, but what sets Hy-Vee apart is that it offers the same discounts on merchandise and services to an employee's family. Imagine your kid, a Hy-Vee employee, coming to you, the parent, and telling you they want to quit their job. If you enjoy your discount privileges at Hy-Vee, you're more likely to encourage your Gen Why to remain employed there. By bringing parents into the loop, employers have an ally in the war against turnover. Gen Whys find it harder to be selfish about their jobs, thinking instead in terms of how their jobs impact not only themselves but also their parents. It might not prove to be the sole determinant when your Gen Why employee gets itchy feet, but expanding the circle of benefits to include their parents could very well work in your favor.

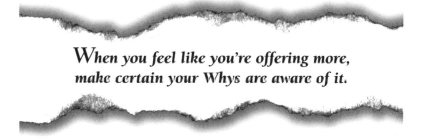

When you feel like you're offering more, make certain your Whys are aware of it.

This is nothing revolutionary, actually. For years, most of the major airlines have extended flight benefits to an employee's parents, spouse, and children. As a frequent flyer, I know that airline employees—especially those in direct contact with angry passengers—might not be doing what they are doing if not for the fear of disappointing their loved ones with the loss of travel benefits. Extending employee benefits to friends and family members is a powerful tool for both recruiting and retaining good help.

WHYS IDEA Rather than looking for ways to expand the list of benefits, look to expand the number of people who benefit from your current list of employee perks and benefits. Creative managers can even find a way for a Gen Why's friends to benefit from a discount on certain days. Don't limit these to the boring list of items like insurance coverage. Instead, offer employees' families significant discounts on merchandise and services, use of your club privileges and amenities, and invitations to special events and celebrations. The savings you'll enjoy from reducing employee turnover will offset any additional costs you incur for extending benefits to family and friends.

Extending employee benefits to friends and family members is a powerful tool for both recruiting and retaining good help.

ROTATE TO MOTIVATE

On most Mondays, I meet a friend for lunch at a nearby Country Buffet. As you might imagine, this self-serve, sit-down buffet restaurant is heavily staffed with Gen Whys as cashiers, bus help, cooks, and food runners. I often see Fred, the manager, walking through the dining room greeting guests and putting out fires. One day, I saw an elderly customer drop his tray and spill his food on the way to his table. Several young employees rushed out to do the cleanup, but Fred, a fiftyish Boomer, smiled and thanked them but took the mop and vacuum and said, "Hey guys, I'll get this one."

"But it's my job to clean up," said one of the teen employees. "No, it's the job of everyone who works here to make certain this place is sparkling clean," replied Fred. "We all need to chip in where we can to achieve that goal." And then he said words that worked like magic on his Gen Why employees: "I'll get this one, you get the next one."

It was a simple gesture, but it spoke volumes about how Fred handles his Gen Why employees. Think about the dirty jobs in your business. Every operation has them, and the old managerial school of thought is to let the low person on the totem pole handle those jobs. But as we've already stated, boredom is the ultimate de-motivator with Generation Why. And though it is no secret that they will tire easily of monotonous tasks, they will tire even more quickly of monotonous, dirty tasks. Smart managers don't delegate the dirty jobs from the bottom of the totem pole up, but instead sprinkle them throughout the organizational chart to make certain everyone supports these assignments. Then nobody gets stuck doing the "same old, same old" all the time.

Rotation also tends to make the new Gen Why employee feel less like a buck private recruit and more like an equal member of a valued team. They like to know that they are not being singled out and dumped on simply because of their youth and inexperience. They'll pledge allegiance to any environment where the dirty work—as well as the cake jobs—are circulated through the ranks.

Gen Why will tune out if they feel they are being disrespected or their personal image is being tarnished. They won't object to doing dirty work as long as they feel that it is not being thrust upon them in the spirit of disrespect or punishment, but rather as something that is shared and it just happens to be their turn in the rotation.

They'll pledge allegiance to any environment where the dirty work—as well as the cake jobs— are circulated through the ranks.

A Word to the Wise

 Roll up your shirtsleeves and take out the trash. Show your Gen Whys that dirty work is beneath no one and that you won't ask them to do anything you aren't willing to do.

CHRISTMAS IN JULY

The bad news is your Gen Whys expect a company Christmas party in December. The worse news is that it's probably not incentive enough to keep them employed through a hectic season. Most companies plan an elaborate employee celebration once or twice a year. Smart companies sprinkle their calendars with frequent celebrations, realizing that their Gen Whys are socially oriented and are more likely to remain in an environment that provides for frequent social interaction. Businesses and organizations that are proactive in their planning of extracurricular activities and social functions for their employees find that they create a community of loyal workers who will think twice prior to accepting employment with a company or firm that does not offer the same environment—even if they pay a higher wage. If your business cannot offer a Joe's Crab Shack atmosphere of fun (refer to the chapter on Fun), it probably can schedule frequent activities outside the boundaries of work. Softball teams, bowling leagues, picnics, river rafting, and holiday parties are just a few of the functions and events that leading Gen Why employers sprinkle throughout the calendar year.

Businesses and organizations that are proactive in their planning of extracurricular activities and social functions for their employees find that they create a community of loyal workers who will think twice prior to accepting employment with a company or firm that does not offer the same environment—even if they pay a higher wage.

WHYS IDEA Keep your Gen Whys on the payroll by having them look forward to a social event in the not-too-distant future. There's nothing they see as uniquely special about having a company Christmas party or Fourth of July picnic; in fact, they expect that. But there's nothing like a bowling night in celebration of National Potato Day or a Remember Elvis's Birthday Bash to keep a Gen Why amused and engaged in their job.

Remember how they like to be in the epicenter. Get as many Gen Whys as possible involved in the planning of these events. If you're stuck for an idea, they've got ten to share with you. Just don't wait for the end of the year to celebrate, and by all means, never let your company's social calendar appear blank or empty.

There's nothing like a bowling night in celebration of National Potato Day or a Remember Elvis's Birthday Bash to keep a Gen Why amused and engaged in their job.

FINAL THOUGHT

You may be thinking that these ideas are going to cost you a lot of money or that they are frivolous expenses. But with today's revolving-door job mentality, employers are realizing more than ever before that keeping that great Gen Why employee you worked so hard to recruit is significantly cheaper than hiring and training a replacement. And it's not just the hard costs that we need to look at, but also things like project delays, reduced morale, the costs for temporary help, filling the open position with the wrong person—the list goes on.

Gen Whys can do amazing things for your business and will be remarkably loyal to you if they are engaged in the right manner. But you cannot afford to take your eye off the ball. You need to know what your competitors are doing and what your Whys are thinking, so talk to them—or more importantly—provide them an avenue to talk to you. Find out what they consider to be more, and see if it makes sense to help them get whatever it is.

Gen Whys can do amazing things for your business and will be remarkably loyal to you if they are engaged in the right manner.

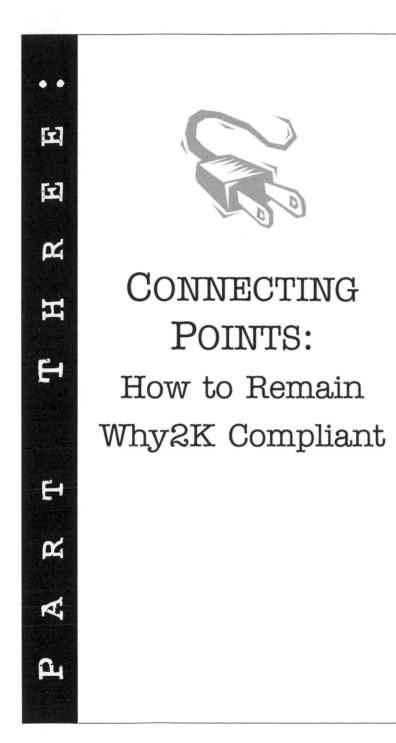

PART THREE

CONNECTING POINTS:
How to Remain Why2K Compliant

"Catch me a fish, I eat for a day. Teach me to fish, I eat for a lifetime."

The science of attracting the very best Gen Whys to your team and getting the most from them once they are there can be summed up in one word: connection. Simply put, if you aren't connecting with your Gen Whys, they literally become obstacles that stand between you and your success. Connect with them, and they become catalysts for helping your business reach beyond its goals. This is an either-or proposition without any middle ground.

Part Two of this book is filled with specific ideas and tools for connecting with Gen Why and for strengthening those connections. These examples are often intertwined, meaning that a properly applied Gen Why training concept will also double as a good tool for managing them. Spiking the Fun Quotient in your workplace will certainly help you to recruit and retain Gen Whys, and so on. However, if your goal is to develop a long-term strategy that will serve to keep you connected with Generation Why over the uncertain future, it is imperative that you look beyond these specific ideas and tools and firmly learn the principles that support them. Below are attitudes and behaviors that will help you connect with Generation Why, followed by sure ways to disconnect. Although they are effective management philosophies for dealing with employees from any age or walk of life, they are essential for successful employment interaction with Gen Whys.

Eight Surefire Ways to Connect

1. **Keep Positive Today and Be Optimistic about Tomorrow** Gen Whys have heard the Chicken Little "Sky Is Falling" routine since they were infants. They know things are not the way they once were, and that life in the fifties, sixties, and seventies was simpler, safer, and happier. But that doesn't give them much comfort now. They want to know the future is bright (even if the future means fifteen minutes from now), and they are drawn to optimistic people.

When I interview Gen Whys and ask them why they like or dislike their boss, the first thing they say is, "He/she is so negative/positive that it makes it unbearable/awesome to be here." Obviously, they're looking for a beacon of light to illuminate the darkness that accompanies the six o'clock news.

Leadership is a trickledown concept. At the risk of sounding too simplistic, certain fundamental attitudes need to reside in you before you can expect them to reside in your employees. At the root of meeting all the challenges you encounter, you must truly believe in yourself, your company, and the opportunities that each new day brings. Remind yourself (and let it be seen on your face!) that today is a gift and tomorrow is going to be even better, and you'll have a profound and long-lasting impact with your Whys.

At the root of meeting all the challenges you encounter, you must truly believe in yourself, your company, and the opportunities that each new day brings.

2. **Know the Why/Show the Why** Your Gen Why employees are inherently inquisitive, questioning the logic and reasoning behind almost everything. Even though they don't always ask why, they're always wondering why and they appreciate a leader who will explain the why. This is exponentially more effective when the why is tied to a direct benefit for them.

Even though they don't always ask why, they're always wondering why and they appreciate a leader who will explain the why.

This does not mean that they need everything spelled out for them. Those who patronize them create distance from them. But it is a good practice to invite their questions and to respond to their curiosity. Know the rationale behind what you ask them to do, and when appropriate, share it with them. However, if you are unsure of something they ask you, don't fabricate an answer. Simply tell them you don't know and that you'll work with them to find the answer. Which leads to the next point...

3. **Tell the Truth** In your effort to lure them, break through to them, or hang on to them, whatever you do—don't deceive them! To connect with Gen Why you must be totally straightforward and honest. From the moment you meet, instill in them the confidence that, in what can be a deceptive world, they can always count on you to deliver the truth. Although they might appear hesitant to swallow everything you say at first, they will grow to trust you over time.

Do not confuse their desire to know the why and their right to know the truth with an obligation to tell them everything. They are not entitled to know every aspect about you or your business or every reason behind your requests, but that which you do tell them must be true. They are resilient and can handle bad news. They will not, however, trust, respect, or confide in anyone who has manipulated the truth, even if only a wee bit.

From the moment you meet, instill in them the confidence that, in what can be a deceptive world, they can always count on you to deliver the truth.

4. **Get to Know Them** Harvey Mackay, the author of *Swim with the Sharks without Being Eaten Alive*, built a successful business empire on the simple principle of getting to know the people you do business with, inside out. His innovative approach to developing relationships with others revolves around the Mackay 66 strategy, which encourages his salespeople to learn sixty-six things about their prospects and clients. These sixty-six items are personal things (e.g., favorite movie, alma mater, names of children, etc.) that require his people to take an active interest in their prospects. MacKay discovered that when his salesforce spent time getting to know and care about their prospects as people, they always found common ground and forged lasting friendships, which led to increased business.

How much do you know about your Gen Whys away from work? They'd love to tell you about themselves, if you care enough to ask. Don't assume that you understand them or that you are communicating on the same wavelength if you haven't made a sincere effort to reach out to their world. Just as MacKay's sales staff discovered, when you do your homework and really get to know your people, you'll discover a whole new level of mutual admiration, respect, and—most of all—connection.

*D*on't assume that you understand them or that you are communicating on the same wavelength if you haven't made a sincere effort to reach out to their world.

5. **Look for Rewarding Opportunities** Organizations and companies that equip their managers with unique and spontaneous ways to reward positive employee performance are the same companies and organizations that will survive the next twenty years. Those that expect high achievement as a standard feature and that only focus attention when employee performance dips are—well, let's just say I wouldn't advise holding their stock.

Although the phrase *Catch 'Em Doing Something Right* is not new, it has never been more appropriate than it is today. Gen Whys demand immediate positive feedback for positive performance, and if the feedback includes a perk or a benefit, then it's all the more effective. Managers who are as prepared to reward the good as they are to pounce on the bad feel less like a prison warden and more like a game show host. Profits and productivity increase in direct proportion to morale. Morale increases when praise is abundant.

6. **Zag** Zig. Zig. Zig. We get caught up in procedures. Procedures become our systems. Systems become routine. There is a sense of safety and security in a routine. So we have the inclination to continue to Zig. Zig. Zig.

Along comes a generation that hates the predictability of the Zig. In fact, they thrive on the Zag. For Whys, variety is not the spice of life; it's the main course! To discourage their need to Zag from routine is to extinguish their flame of creativity, and a reduction in productivity is certain to follow.

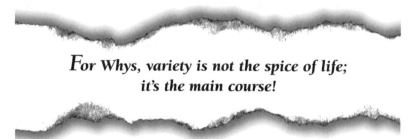

For Whys, variety is not the spice of life; it's the main course!

Can business survive without standards and routines? Of course not. In those situations where adhering to a structured routine is required, explain to your Whys the rationale of the procedure and continue to Zig. But in those routines that have become routines simply out of comfort and security, be open to the Zag! Your GWs could prove that the Zag is a better way.

Keep bobbing and weaving. Never be too predictable. When Gen Whys get to the point where they are fully trained and have nothing new to learn and nothing much changes from day to day, they are going to check out. They might remain on your payroll, but their minds will not be focused on your business. If they get to the point where they are finishing your sentences for you, it's time to Zag.

7. **Make Them a Star** It's been said that Generation Why values self-expression over self-control. Like no generation before, they crave the spotlight; so cast it in their direction. Give your Gen Whys a chance to shine. Give them an orientation video or CD Rom before they start to eliminate the awkwardness of the first day on the job. On their first day, welcome them with their already prepared nametag, locker, workstation, and personalized manual. Then introduce them to their coworkers by sharing why you hired them, "Meet Jason. We're very lucky to have him. He's an honor student and varsity soccer player at McKinley High School, so he's a smart team player!" or "This is Melanie. She's fresh out of MSU with a degree in computer graphics. Melanie is going to help us punch up our E-commerce sales by keeping our website one step ahead of our competitors."

Generation Why values self-expression over self-control. Like no generation before, they crave the spotlight; so cast it in their direction.

When your Gen Why employee masters a skill or does something well, find a way to let others know about it. Better yet, let them present at a company meeting and train others on the skill they've mastered. Praise them in public and never miss a chance to brag on them in front of your superiors. Actively seek out opportunities to put their photo on your Wall of Fame, and post their name on your marquee. Don't just tell them how much you value their efforts; tell the world!

8. **Be the Example** Treat your Gen Whys the way you want them to treat you, each other, and your customers. Take an occasional turn doing the grunt work. Be punctual, polite, and appreciative. Smile every chance you get. Speak well of your supervisors and sing your company's praises. The greatest way to get model employees working for you is to model great employee behavior.

Generation Why doesn't follow advice; they follow example. The days of the do-as-I-say-not-as-I-do leader are over. A parent of a Gen Why cannot have a radar detector on their dashboard and expect that their child will obey the law. Likewise, you can't come to the workplace burnt out and expect them to be fired up about their job. As the old adage goes, what you're doing speaks so loudly that they can't hear what you're saying!

A parent of a Gen Why cannot have a radar detector on their dashboard and expect that their child will obey the law. Likewise, you can't come to the workplace burnt out and expect them to be fired up about their job.

In this chapter we focused on eight connection principles—attitudes and behaviors that will serve as conduits for a limitless number of ways you can get connected and stay connected with your Gen Whys. But just as there are certain connection principles, there are also definite dividers that need to be avoided at all costs. In the next chapter, we'll discuss seven automatic disconnect buttons—the attitudes and behaviors that will create immediate distance between you and your Gen Whys.

Seven Surefire Ways to Disconnect

1. **Be Inflexible** The success of your organization hinges on being properly staffed, and you rely on your Whys as your front line. But when business is booming, everyone has got to be willing to work longer hours than scheduled, right? After all, you always appreciated the chance to work more to make more money. Shouldn't they?

This is a prime example of a disconnect between generations: the assumption that their thinking is in line with yours and that they would make the same money-for-time choices you made at their age. It doesn't play out that way.

Don't automatically assume Gen Whys want to work overtime for a bigger check. Granted, they want the freedom to choose and most will opt for the rewards of overtime over playtime. But if you require overtime hours from them on a consistent basis, you're appealing to your values, not theirs. Force them consistently to choose work over their friends and other activities, and you're bound to lose them.

They've seen what workaholism has done to their folks, and they're not signing up for that program. If they don't have a voice in their scheduling, you're going to experience problems. They've already figured out that they can enjoy time without money, but they cannot enjoy money without time.

They've already figured out that they can enjoy time without money, but they cannot enjoy money without time.

2. **Be Rigid** Want to make your dealings with Gen Why pure hell? Simply insist that it's "my way or the highway!" and that when you say "Jump!" they need to promptly respond "how high?" That management style went the way of the CB radio.

Gen Whys have no shortage of ideas, and they are firmly convinced that there is always going to be another upgrade or a new-and-improved version. They know that there is a better way to do almost everything, and they enter a new job licking their chops for an opportunity to show you. Appear overly rigid and you'll put an "Out of Order" sign on their drive to improve and succeed. Whys resist environments where people are stuck in repetitive patterns and are closed to new ideas and methodologies.

If you are in love with your present systems and are not willing to examine new ways to doing things, don't hire Gen Whys. They are completely turned off by rigid environments and stiff managers who will never give an inch.

3. **Prejudge Them** "Urbanite teens who blare rap music from their low-rider car stereos are homey gang-bangers." "4.0 nerds are video game techno geeks." "Young women with tight pants and bleached hair are promiscuous." These are just a few of the things that you might hear when listening to adults talk about today's youth. The fact that generalizations such as these are ridiculous does not stop them from being bantered about in many circles. Gen Whys loathe stereotypes. They appear destined to prove once and for all that when it comes to their generation, it is impossible to judge the book by its cover.

If you're looking to create distance between yourself and your young workers, let them hear you belittle their music, fashion, media heroes, or culture. Stereotype them or their peers and you've got a fight on your hands, for sure. Those that don't rise up and challenge you on the spot aren't agreeing with your assertions; they're simply voting you off their island without your knowledge.

Gen Whys loathe stereotypes. They appear destined to prove once and for all that when it comes to their generation, it is impossible to judge the book by its cover.

4. **Strip Their Identity** Whys accept the fact that they need to assume a visible role in your company and that they need to put on your team's uniform: just don't ask them to completely remove theirs. They'll see it as a sellout. They won't resist representing your company image, as long as they're not required to put their own image on the line in the process. They're not stupid and they know that they cannot dress for work as they would for a night out with friends. Gen Whys will respect your image standards, provided they know the rules up front and know that everyone else in your employ is also complying with the same standards.

If you depend on Gen Why as your labor source, you're going to have to allow them some leeway to express themselves as individuals. They are nobody's clones, no matter what the salary. Strip them of their identity, and you'll spend a lot of time interviewing new applicants.

Gen Whys will respect your image standards, provided they know the rules up front and know that everyone else in your employ is also complying with the same standards.

5. **Put Profits First** A large department store chain was experiencing dangerously high turnover with its Gen Whys in one of its stores. The reason for this high turnover becomes obvious when you observe a typical Saturday morning sales meeting. The forty-five-year-old general manager elected to begin the meetings by playing the seventies disco hit "Money, Money, Money…" over the store's PA system. Then, after a Knute Rockne-like pump-up talk, he'd dismiss the meeting with a motivational challenge: "Okay team, let's leave 'em broke in the aisles!"

The problem here is that this manager's agenda didn't match that of his Gen Whys. Even though they were commissioned on their sales, his young associates were left to feel that their purpose was all about profits and that the store's gain was the customer's loss. Besides the fact that Gen Why is sensitive to the plight of the needy, they want to know that they are making a positive difference, not taking part in a scam to take advantage of others.

Your Whys do like material things. But if they see that you care more about the dollar than you do the people you do business with, you'll not only erode your customer base, you'll alienate your most important ally.

If they see that you care more about the dollar than you do the people you do business with, you'll not only erode your customer base, you'll alienate your most important ally.

6. **Pigeonhole Them.** Virtually every study that has been done on what Whys are looking for in a job, stresses the importance they place on training. To them, every job is a transition to the next step, and they want the assurance that they are learning something that will prepare them for a future opportunity. Managers who operate under the if-I-train-them-they'll-outgrow-this-job-and-leave assumption are stuck in the Dark Ages. If they're not learning, they're yearning.

Whys will not accept being pigeonholed into a mundane, monotonous, dead-end job. That doesn't necessarily mean they'll quit their job; but it does mean they'll stop caring about their job. And while retaining good GW employees presents a challenge, reviving those who have grown stale in their job is nearly impossible. Train your Whys or they'll go where they can get training.

Whys will not accept being pigeonholed into a mundane, monotonous, dead-end job. That doesn't necessarily mean they'll quit their job; but it does mean they'll stop caring about their job.

7. Put Them on Hold Although they have grand expectations and plans for what lies ahead, Gen Whys are not future focused. They are wired for the here and now. They want instant feedback for their performance, immediate compensation for their efforts, and rapid results on promises made to them. Organizations who play wait-and-see or tell them to "keep up the good work and good things are bound to happen" are likely to alienate this digital breed.

You're certain to disconnect with Gen Whys if you: have a long and tedious job application process; offer performance reviews only every ninety days; make them jump through hoops to get their paychecks; or make a promise that you cannot deliver on quickly. A generation that sees time as its primary commodity will not respect anyone or anything that infringes upon it.

Organizations who play wait-and-see or tell them to "keep up the good work and good things are bound to happen" are likely to alienate this digital breed.

ONE LAST FINAL THOUGHT

Changing your managerial techniques and employment practices to cater to the whims of Gen Why can, on the surface, make you feel like you are caving in to the enemy (spoiled brats, some might say). However, all of the dos and don'ts in this chapter are about connecting with a constituent group, one that is going to become even more important to you in the next five years than it is today. It's not really caving in at all, but rather retooling for the next step—and that's just good business. You need the energy and talent of the emerging workforce and therefore must create an environment where they will thrive and help you grow your business. Connecting with them is the only way to achieve that result.

It is my hope that this book has challenged your managerial philosophies and prompted a change in your methodologies. Every good book I have ever read has done this for me. I have been bold and assertive in my comments and opinions here, I hope to your immediate and ultimate benefit. After spending most of my professional life in the trenches with Gen Whys, I'd be foolish not to encourage you to make bold and assertive changes, too.

Undoubtedly, you've agreed with some of the material and ideas presented in this book and questioned some of it as well. Perhaps at some point you found yourself wondering about the author and where my loyalties lie. It appears that I am maligning Gen Why one moment and defending them the next. Rest assured, I believe in Generation Why and all they can and will become. I have to. I am the father of two and the stepfather of two.

Globally, one of every four hearts beating today beats inside the body of a Gen Why. Although as employees they can cause us distress, we must always remember that this is not a throw-away generation. They are the ones who will care for us in our older age. They are voting in our elections, sharing our highways, and tightening the bolts on the airplanes we fly in. And guess who makes up the front line of the war we are now fighting against terrorism? That's right. Generation Why.

You need the energy and talent of the emerging workforce and therefore must create an environment where they will thrive and help you grow your business.

I wrote a poem about Generation Why that I recite to conclude my live presentations. Because it speaks my heart—and the truth—I'll also conclude this book with it.

Generation Why©

An Original Poem by Eric Chester

Our kids are so different from the ones our folks raised.

They don't obey without reason; they're not easily fazed.

Their test scores have fallen, about school they don't care.

They're street smart, brand conscious, and socially aware!

They don't leap to their feet to show elders respect,

    after all, there's that image they've got to protect.

They often make headlines, and the news is not good—

Yes, Generation Why is surely misunderstood.

The Boomers cry out *"Teens don't know their place—*

    when you try to correct them, they're right in your face!

They're lacking in patience; they are easily bored.

They don't put forth the effort, yet they demand the reward!

We've given and given and what's so unnerving . . .

    they keep asking for more—as if they're deserving!

They don't understand me—so who is to blame?

'Cause I'm doing what I've always done, but the results ain't the same!"

But let us be cautious, nonjudgmental, and wise

    and draw on compassion to see the world through their eyes . . .

The airwaves are jammed with sex, violence, and rage.
It's brought to extinction The Innocent Age.
Real heroes among us, but who gets applause?
Celebrity icons with character flaws.
You can break all the rules, and if you get caught
    a "not guilty" verdict is easily bought.
The music is bleak and the lyrics keep humming—
"Just live for today, 'cause tomorrow's not coming!"

Though often maligned—what reports fail to mention
    (about these sixty million youth craving love and attention)
    is the talent they possess and the drive to make better
    the world where we live and our time here together.
What they need are role models who'll turn on the light
    —and show by example what is morally right—
    who know they seek answers and will attend to that need.
You and I are those people, and it's our time to lead.

There's promise, I tell you, just look in their eyes. . .
You'll see hope for the future in our Generation Whys!

TABLE 2: Ready Reference Summary

PART ONE:
Who Are They?

Chapter 1: Why the Label Generation Why? This segment of our population will not follow advice or respond to authority without first knowing why and what is in it for them.

Chapter 2: The Aliens Have Landed Generation Why can often seem like an entirely different species! Here are insightful facts and statistics to provide a framework of understanding.

    ➤ TAKE ME TO YOUR LEADER! Gen Why's drive to question any process and to separate effort from reward calls for supernatural understanding from their leaders and managers.

    ➤ WORLDS APART Value programming is shaped by the world we grow up in, and Gen Why's world has been radically different than ours!

    ➤ GENERATIONAL COMPARISON CHART Compare and contrast the attitudes and the influences of Generation Why with Generation X and the Baby Boomers.

    ➤ INTERNAL WIRING DIFFERENCES: THE WAY WE THINK We think in a sequential, chronological fashion. Gen Why thinks and processes information in an unstructured, non-sequential pattern. We think analog, like a VCR, whereas they think digital, much like a DVD.

    ➤ WHO MOVED MY CHEETOS? Generation Why not only accepts change, they thrive on change.

Chapter 3: Profile GW—What Can We Really Expect? You can expect to have your work cut out for you with this generation. There is an upside, and also a downside, to working with them.

☞ IMPATIENT They equate waiting with losing. Having grown up in a fast-moving world, they demand instant results.

☞ ADAPTABLE Unlike mature generations who resist change, Gen Why moves in sync with change and is not rocked by the unstable events of the New Economy.

☞ INNOVATIVE Gen Why sees the world from a fresh perspective and is always looking for a better way to get things done.

☞ EFFICIENT Gen Why is remarkable at achieving maximum results with minimal effort and resources in minimal time.

☞ DESENSITIZED Because they have experienced so much so early in life, Gen Why has a "been there/done that" attitude.

☞ DISENGAGED As mosaic thinkers, Gen Whys do not inherently buy in to structure and conventional processes.

☞ SKEPTICAL Gen Why has been conned, manipulated, cheated, and exploited, so they don't automatically believe what they hear or read.

☞ RESILIENT As a generation that has experienced a lot of negativity and is used to disappointment, Gen Whys have learned how to roll with the punches and land on their feet.

☞ DISRESPECTFUL Gen Whys feel that they are owed respect from others but that their respect must be earned by others.

☞ BLUNTLY EXPRESSIVE Gen Why has been urged to freely speak their minds no matter what they are thinking and feeling, and they do it bluntly, boldly, and loudly.

➣ TOLERANT Gen Why does not buy in to age-old prejudices and is readily willing to accept individual differences. They make great additions to diverse teams.
➣ COMMITTED Gen Why is fiercely loyal to causes and purposes they believe in. They can make great long-term employees.

P A R T   T W O :

Employing Generation Why

Introduction to the specific management issues of recruiting, training, managing, appearance, fun, recognition and rewards, and retention.

Chapter 4: Recruiting For Gen Whys, jobs appear plentiful. It takes creative thinking to attract the best to your company.

☞ SELL YOURSELF FIRST Why should Gen Why want to work for you? Know why and be able to convince them.

☞ CAST A WIDE NET The only effective recruiting strategies are those you actively use. Don't rely too heavily on any one method.

☞ CHANGE YOUR GLASSES Get to know your Gen Why customers, and look at them as potential employees.

☞ STREAMLINE THE PROCESS Cut out everything that might be unnecessary in your application process—forms, steps, red tape, etc.

☞ SNOOZE AND LOSE Build relationship with your applicants immediately. Reduce the time between application and interview and interview and job offer.

☞ GO WHERE THEY GO From bathroom ads to skateboard parks, from rock concerts to Internet cafes—be visible and accessible where Gen Why is.

🔑 FORM AN ALLIANCE Develop an inside track with key people from local high schools and colleges; let them know you are hiring; they can recommend potential employees.

🔑 BUILD A BRIDGE FOR YOUR FUTURE CEO Tell the stories of how your managers have grown with the company; introduce new employees to the corporate headquarters. Help them to visualize employment with your company as a career, not just another job.

🔑 WORK THE NETWORK Develop an employee referral plan, offering a reward to your Gen Whys whose friends and family are ultimately hired.

🔑 STANDING ROOM ONLY For effect, make it easy to apply, but not so easy get hired. Be rigorous in your hiring process.

🔑 THE FIRST RESPONDER Have current Gen Why employees be the first follow-up contact with your Gen Why applicants.

🔑 CYBER RECRUITING Gen Why jobseekers are on the 'Net—develop a good job description, respond quickly, make sure your corporate website is easy to access and navigate.

Chapter 5: Training There is a paradox between Gen Why's lack of basic skills and their incredible business and money savvy, which creates both challenging and exciting training situations.

🔑 MAKE IT FUN For the stimulus-junkie Gen Whys, increasing the Fun Quotient enhances learning throughout the training process.

🔑 ENGAGE THEM Actively involve Gen Whys in their own learning in whatever ways you can—it'll pay off on the job.

❧ MAKE IT FRESH Find new ways to convey the necessary material and make sure that what you teach them is indeed necessary right now.

❧ KEEP UP THE PACE Train a concept and move on. Let Gen Why apply the new skill before training another.

❧ REWARD SKILL DEVELOPMENT Publicly recognize skill development and training completion, or it loses its effectiveness.

❧ ORIENT BEFORE YOU TRAIN Insert an orientation program between hire date and training to help Gen Whys connect with their new coworkers and feel comfortable with their new surroundings.

❧ EXPLAIN THE WHY Examine the concepts and processes you want to train, and be clear about not only what and how to do something, but also about why it is important, including how it ultimately affects Gen Why.

❧ LET THEM FIGURE IT OUT Explain a situation, the boundaries of time or resources, and the desired outcome, and let Gen Why figure out how to achieve the desired result.

❧ USE EYE CANDY Make training materials interesting by adding color and varying the medium of delivery—lecture, video, interactive CD-ROMs, etc.

❧ BRIDGE THE GAP IN SERVICE Providing great customer service is almost impossible for a generation that hasn't received it—start with the basics and build on what they observe.

❧ STAY A CHAPTER AHEAD Involve each member of the training class in both learning and teaching.

Chapter 6: Managing Throw out the old rulebook and sharpen up your management skills. Prepare to be even more up front, authentic, and connected.

🔑 LAY OUT THE BIG PICTURE IN SMALL TERMS To effectively manage behavior of Generation Why, you need to clearly lay out your expectations in simple terms.

🔑 REVISIT YOUR RULES Be sure that your rules, principles, practices, and procedures are a prerequisite to profit. If not, get rid of them.

🔑 SINK YOUR POSTS DEEP Keep your rulebook light and tight: edit out unnecessary items and rigorously enforce those that are critical.

🔑 TUNE IN TO THEIR FREQUENCY Watch, listen, and read what they are watching, listening to, and reading, to stay current with their interests and trends.

🔑 GET THEIR HEADS IN YOUR GAME Share as much information and responsibility as possible, training and teaching as situations arise.

🔑 THE FLEXIBILITY FACTOR: ATTENDANCE & PUNCTUALITY Revisit your policies on work schedules and develop a win-win environment for Gen Whys that scratches their itch for flexible hours without compromising your needs.

🔑 WAGE A BATTLE AGAINST BOREDOM If you want to keep them tuned in to the job, vary the tasks, procedures, and environment to the greatest degree possible.

Chapter 7: Appearance Hair, clothing, and music are only the start of the commercialized youth culture, and Gen Whys resent being judged by their often-outrageous identity.

🔑 INSIDE OUT Examine your dress code from the inside out, determining validity and necessity. Keep abreast with the ever-changing trends and update your dress code as you are able.

🔑 COMMUNICATE THE CODE Clearly define your appearance standards. Display photographs or posters of acceptable work attire.

⚷ DEBUTING A NEW CODE Make an occasion of your new dress code; set rules but try to be flexible. Involve Gen Why in its introduction.

Chapter 8: Fun Work is not just work anymore; it's an experience. Making that experience fun will pay off in productivity and retention.

⚷ MAKE FUN THROUGH COMPETITION Pit employees against an achievable goal, not each other. Use a variety of games and activities to generate excitement and energy.

⚷ MAKE FUN THROUGH PARTICIPATION Create opportunities for Gen Why to show off their talents, skills, and ideas to an audience, whether coworkers or customers.

⚷ MAKE FUN THROUGH INTERACTION Gen Why likes to work with friends; create an atmosphere that is conducive to social interaction and let them have a hand in creating their own fun.

Chapter 9: Recognition and Rewards Get the best out of your Gen Whys by developing a system of recognition and rewards that helps them feel like a valued employee.

⚷ THE FOUR PS OF WISE R&R Make your recognition and reward system personal, proportionate, punctual, and public.

⚷ THE MAGIC OF SENDING A LETTER HOME A simple, but heartfelt letter is inexpensive but can return remarkable results. Simple things mean a lot.

⚷ THREE FREEBIES THAT STRIKE GOLD

1. Name Identity–know and use their names.
2. About Face–use employees in billboards, TV ads, catalogs, etc.
3. Golden Rule–do for them what they do for you.

THE PRIZE PATROL Assemble a contingency of coworkers to serve as the presenters of recognition and reward incentives.

CASH IS KING Use on-the-spot cash for performance and retention incentives and make the presentation memorable.

KEEP TRACK OF THE EXCELLENCE Develop a performance scorecard program and acknowledge desired work behaviors and outcomes. Involve employees and customers in the scorekeeping.

Chapter 10: Retention Always looking for a better deal or a change of pace, Gen Why is in a perpetual job-seeking mode. Retaining them is difficult but not impossible.

FILL THE RUTS Gen Whys will get itchy feet when the workplace becomes too monotonous. Look for ways to keep necessary tasks from seeming too routine.

THE MAGIC OF THE SLOW REVEAL Spread perks, benefits, and responsibilities out over time; keep Gen Why looking to the future.

READ THEIR MINDS Ask Gen Whys what they think and how they feel—they'll be direct and honest. Have an open door and develop an employee response system for new hires.

KEEP TABS ON YOUR COMPETITORS When they jump ship, find out where your Gen Whys are going, and why, and always offer more! Take steps to protect your business against employee robbery.

EXPAND THE CIRCLE OF BENEFITS Offer employee benefits to your employees' families and consider periodically providing their friends discounts on merchandise and services.

ROTATE TO MOTIVATE Sprinkle responsibility for the dirty jobs throughout the staff chart to make everyone feel like part of the team.

🗝 CHRISTMAS IN JULY Schedule frequent celebrations, both small and large, throughout the entire year. You don't need a holiday as an excuse to throw a party or an employee event.

PART THREE:

Connecting Points

Discover the principles for generating new ideas and strategies to remain Why2K Compliant.

Chapter 11: Eight Surefire Ways to Connect and Remain Connected

🦕 Keep positive.

🦕 Know and show the why before telling them what to do.

🦕 Always tell the truth.

🦕 Get to know them as people by tuning in to their frequency.

🦕 Look for opportunities to reward positive behavior.

🦕 Zag and look to break patterns that lead to monotony and boredom.

🦕 Make them the star of your workplace.

🦕 Be a living example of what you want them to be.

Chapter 12: Seven Surefire Ways to Disconnect

🦕 Be inflexible with schedules.

🦕 Be rigid with rules.

🦕 Prejudge them based on their appearance or other factors.

🦕 Take away their personal identity and try to clone them into yours.

🦕 Put company profits before your employees and your customers.

🦕 Pigeonhole them and don't give them training or advancement opportunities.

🦕 Put them on hold and delay their growth and learning.

TRUCKDOGS

Picture books by the same author

TRUCK DOGS

A NOVEL IN FOUR BITES

Graeme Base,

As told to him by his dog Molly

Amulet Books
New York

Library of Congress Cataloging-in-Publication Data has been applied for.

ISBN 0-8109-5031-6

Text and illustrations copyright © 2003 Graeme Base

Published in 2004 by Amulet Books, a division of Harry N. Abrams, Incorporated, New York.
All rights reserved. No part of the contents of this book may be reproduced
without the written permission of the publisher.

Set in 13/19 point Joanna
Printed and bound in China
10 9 8 7 6 5 4 3 2 1

Amulet Books
100 Fifth Avenue
New York, N.Y. 10011
www.abramsbooks.com

Abrams is a subsidiary of
LA MARTINIÈRE
G R O U P E

For William

CONTENTS

GLOSSARY

AUGER   *a tool used for boring holes*

BILLABONG   *a water hole*

CHOOKS   *chickens*

PETROL   *gasoline*

SPANNER   *a wrench*

TIP   *a junkyard or dump*

UTE   *a small pickup truck*

YABBY   *a freshwater crayfish*

List of

ILLUSTRATED PLATES

PAW WORD

What is it with dogs and cars? Dogs love cars, love chasing after them, love traveling in them, love peeing on the wheels, love barking as they roar by. At least our dog Molly does. So it shouldn't have come as such a shock when I found a stack of dog-eared paper at the back of her kennel that turned out to be a first draft manuscript entitled TruckDogs.

As I pawed through the pages, brushing away dog hair and the occasional flea, it all fell into place—the furtive notes I had seen her making on long road trips, the twelve-month subscription to Big Rig magazine that I know wasn't mine, and the paw prints on the kids' computer keyboard. They say everyone has a novel in them and clearly our Molly was no exception.

But when she announced she wanted her book published I had my doubts and I told her so. She was barking up the wrong tree, I said. Publishing was a dog-eat-dog world, no bones about it. But she ignawed me.

Finally, I relented and agreed to show the work to my publisher. The reaction was as I had feared. "TruckDogs?" they asked. "What are they? Where did they come from? And how do they do all those things like pump petrol and throw spanners without the benefit of opposable thumbs?"

I confronted Molly but she had no answers. Perhaps if I was to draw some pictures it would help? she suggested. I told her it was out of the question. Then she did that thing dogs do with their big doleful eyes and long floppy ears and tail half-wagging in forlorn hope. And I rolled over.

So here it is—Molly's first novel. With pictures. Every dog has its day.

—Graeme Base, 2003

BITE **ONE**

"This is such a bad idea," said Bullworth, peering out from the long, dry grass that swept down from the hill toward the dam. He flicked an ear nervously and fidgeted with his rear drive wheels. "We shouldn't be doing this."

Bullworth was big as TruckDogs go, a bulldog/dozer with a huge mouth, chunky caterpillar tracks and a thick stumpy tail. Like all TruckDogs he was half vehicle, half dog. He ran on diesel, plus some oil for his hydraulics, but unlike his Mongrel Pack friends who scarffed dog food and gnawed on old bones, Bullworth was a vegetarian and ate cabbages by the ton.

The other TruckDogs were silent, intent, crouched low in the grass. They were a motley collection of makes and breeds, young enough to still have their original tires, old enough to be sporting lots of scratches and several impressive dents.

None of them had much fat on their bones, however. Without homes of their own they had to fend for themselves, sleeping under the stars, picking up meals where they could, getting by on the smell of an oily rag.

Beyond the fence at the bottom of the hill, a flock of TruckSheep grazed quietly on the lusher grass that grew near the water. It was a peaceful scene, the morning sun glowing on the fence posts that ran from the paddock up to Farmer Howell's farmhouse on the neighboring hill.

"Relax," said Prudence, seeing Bullworth's worried expression. "We're only chasing them, not eating them."

Prudence was a slender dachshund/fuel-tanker road train. Her shiny black bodywork was set off by purple fenders and underbelly and a pair of tall chrome exhaust stacks behind her long ears. She turned to Bullworth with a smile. "Unless you *want* to eat them instead?"

"No!" he said, shocked. He looked again at the TruckSheep. "But they're huge—and they've got horns. I don't wanna get hurt."

Zoe, the other girl in the Mongrel Pack, a streetwise dalmatian/cement mixer with blue spots and purple eyeshadow, shook her head and shoved the gum she was chewing to the side of her grill. "Aw, don't be such a sook, Bullworth. You're made of solid iron and you're worried about getting a couple of dents?"

"He's right, y'know," offered Digger. "Sheep-leaping can be dangerous—but only if you get caught."

Digger was a labrador/back hoe, good-natured like all labs, sand-colored, with a brown nose and a ready smile. He winked at Bullworth, his long pink tongue lolling out. "C'mon, mate, those TruckSheep are no match for you." He scratched suddenly behind his ear with his rear excavator shovel. "Flies are driving me nuts."

"Flies?" said Prudence. "What you've got there is *fleas*. When's the last time you had a car wash?"

Digger shrugged. "I dunno. What month is it?"

"Zip it, you lot." Hercules frowned at the other TruckDogs. He was the self-appointed leader of the Pack, a massive great dane/ore truck. "Let's see if we can retain the element of surprise here, all right?"

"Sure, Herc," said Zoe, revving coyly.

"Sure, Herc," said Prudence and Digger, winking at each other.

Bullworth looked unhappy.

Hercules nodded. "Okay. Everyone together. Ready . . . Set . . . Go!"

The TruckDogs burst from cover and raced down the hill toward the grazing TruckSheep, baying like wolves, horns blaring, engines roaring. The TruckSheep looked up at the noise and scowled, baring old, yellow teeth. These were no lambs— meek and easily frightened—but big, tough TruckSheep.

"Woo hoo!" yelled Digger as he dropped himself into overdrive and slewed round an outcrop of boulders.

"Yeehaa!" cried Prudence, leaping right over the outcrop, ears flapping in the wind as she carved a graceful arc through the air.

5

The TruckSheep baaa-ed angrily, turned toward the intruders, put their heads down and charged.

"Okay, split up!" yelled Hercules.

The TruckDogs fanned out, racing across the paddock in big sweeping curves, drawing the TruckSheep in different directions until there were sheep and dogs zooming everywhere.

A TruckSheep veered away from the main flock.

"That one's got your name on it, Digger!" called Prudence.

Digger dropped back a gear, dug in his wheels and made a sharp turn to bring himself alongside the galloping TruckSheep. He dodged this way and that as the beast tried to skewer him with its horns or trample him under-wheel, then, pulling away slightly, he slowed and gathered himself for a leap. But suddenly Hercules roared past him, springing over the TruckSheep with a huge bound and crashing to the ground on the other side. He just missed Bullworth, who was rumbling by in the other direction trying to get out of the way.

The TruckSheep bleated in surprise and took off.

"Hey, watch it. You nearly hit me," said Bullworth.

"If I'd meant to hit you, you'd be on your roof," replied Hercules.

"One to our great leader," said Prudence.

"You are just so good at this, Herc," said Zoe. Hercules looked pleased with himself.

Digger shrugged and looked around for another target.

The game continued. The young TruckDogs dodged and revved, swerved and leapt, chancing their luck with the angry TruckSheep, and adding several new scratches and dents to their bodywork.

Prudence raced along in a great curve, pursued by three furious TruckSheep. Suddenly she twisted and launched herself into the air, bounding across all three of them, one after the other, zigzag, like a big move on a checkerboard.

"Three!" she yelled. "Now who's looking good?"

"Nice one," called Digger. "But I've got seven."

"Herc is up to ten," said Zoe.

Bullworth shook his head as he watched the other Mongrels racing around the paddock. "They're all nuts."

On the far side of the dam, on a low rise, lay an old tanker hulk, rusting in the sun. From the top another TruckDog was watching the Mongrel Pack, his short tail wagging at high speed. He was a little Jack Russell/ute, brown and white, very excited, with a bright red collar and a shiny name tag. His name was Sparky.

He bounced up and down on his springs, trying to get a better view. "Oh, boy! Sheep-leaping. I love this!"

He jumped down from the tanker and squeezed through the fence wire, disappearing into the long grass as he sped around the edge of the dam toward the others.

7

Sparky knew the Mongrels were what his mum called "problem kids"—always in trouble, a source of constant irritation to the good townsfolk of Hubcap—but he couldn't help liking them. It wasn't their fault they had no homes of their own. They were just regular kids. And they had the best fun doing cool things like sheep-leaping.

"Hey, guys! Hi! Can I play?" he yapped as he burst out of the tussocks and skidded to a stop, tail wagging faster than ever.

The TruckSheep had given up the chase for the time being and were standing together at the other side of the paddock, breathing heavily.

Prudence looked at Sparky and shrugged. "Sure, why not?"

"Because he's too small," said Hercules. "Because he'll probably get killed. Because he's not part of the Pack."

The wagging tail slowed.

"Come on, Herc," said Digger. "Worst that can happen is he gets totally written off. Or caught."

"Hey, Sparky" said Zoe. "Does your mum know you're here?"

Sparky winced. "She thinks I'm cleaning out my kennel."

He was an obedient son, as a rule, but today he felt justified in skipping this chore—he'd cleaned his room just the other week. Well, back in February anyway. Besides, the day was too good to spend indoors.

"You're going to get it," said Prudence. "Tell her we kidnapped you."

"She'd believe it," said Sparky. His mum was the mayor of

Hubcap—and she didn't approve of him hanging around with the Mongrel Pack, even though he was only a year or so younger than they were.

"Hey, look," said Digger, nodding toward the TruckSheep. They had gathered together by the fence in a rough line. "Y'know, I reckon I could clear the lot of them in one go the way they are now."

"Not if I get there first," said Hercules. And he sped away, shoving Digger to one side.

"They're mine, you dirty sheep thief!" called Digger. He crunched into gear and roared after him.

"C'mon, Zoe," laughed Prudence. "We can't let the boys have all the glory!"

They tore off, leaving Sparky and Bullworth behind.

"Count me out," said the big bulldozer.

The TruckDogs hurtled toward the TruckSheep. But all at once Hercules skidded to a stop.

"Hold on, I smell a ram."

The others put on the brakes. Suddenly Sparky shot past, yelling excitedly. "Come on, guys! What are you waiting for?"

He raced up to the TruckSheep, yapping like mad. The sheep looked at him balefully, then moved apart. Behind them stood a huge, snorting beast, solid muscle and steel, cruelly curved horns mounted above massive bony fenders: the TruckRam from hell.

Sparky gulped.

The huge TruckRam tore at the ground with his front

wheels. Sparky slammed his gearbox into reverse, spun around in a cloud of dust and bolted back across the paddock. The TruckRam set off after him.

"Not this way, you idiot!" cried Hercules.

"Go left!" yelled Prudence.

"Or right!" added Digger.

"Anywhere but here!" screamed Zoe.

The TruckDogs turned and fled, Bullworth with them. But Sparky quickly caught up, terrified, the huge TruckRam breathing down his exhaust pipe.

"Help!"

"Head for the dam!" yelled Digger.

They raced across the paddock, shock absorbers crashing and bouncing on the uneven ground, and launched themselves into the air. The TruckRam lunged at Sparky as he leapt, sending him tumbling.

A moment later the still waters of the dam erupted in a series of huge splashes as the TruckDogs disappeared into the muddy depths.

The TruckRam skidded to a stop at the water's edge and snorted in satisfaction as the intruders floundered in the middle of the dam. Then he turned and motored back across the paddock with his nose in the air.

The TruckDogs reached the far side of the dam and hauled themselves out, coughing and spluttering. Bullworth sat sobbing in the shallows.

"I'm . . . all . . . wet. I'm going to die of rust."

Zoe dragged herself up the bank, dripping and covered in weeds, muddy water sloshing out of her mixer.

"Look at me!" she screeched. "I'm filthy!"

She splashed angrily, sending more mud flying into her own face, and burst into tears. The others scrambled up the slope and collapsed in a sodden heap. Prudence looked around.

"Where's Sparky?"

"Who cares?" sulked Zoe, turning on her wipers but only managing to smear mud all over her windscreen.

Digger reached down with his back hoe and felt around in the water. After a moment he scooped Sparky out and dumped him on the grass.

"Here he is."

"Thanks," said Sparky, gasping.

"No worries."

But Hercules was not so easygoing. "Should have left him there. Brainless dipstick."

Sparky hung his head. The others shook themselves dry like dogs do. Zoe screeched as she got spattered with mud again.

"Hey, look on the bright side," said Digger as they sat there, dripping.

"And what bright side would that be exactly?" inquired Prudence.

"We could've been caught by Windy Howell."

Prudence laughed. "Yeah, downwind. That old pickup can backfire like no other TruckDog alive."

At that very moment a bang rang out across the paddock like a gunshot. They looked at each other with dread.

On the hill beyond the TruckSheep paddock, an old red heeler/Ford pickup emerged from his run-down farmhouse. The screen door slammed behind him. He revved his engine and let rip another deafening backfire. Flames and smoke billowed out of his exhaust pipe, as he looked across the fields toward the dam.

"It's that flea-bitten Mongrel Pack again," growled Farmer Howell. "I'll teach them to worry my sheep!"

He unleashed another flatulent masterpiece, setting fire to a stump by the outhouse and at the same time propelling himself down the hill toward the dam.

Prudence watched Farmer Howell career across the field toward them in a cloud of billowing oily smoke and shook her head.

"One of these days he's going to blow himself up."

"I'm getting out of here!" cried Bullworth.

"Too right," said Digger, and the others agreed. Angry TruckRams were one thing—Farmer Howell on the warpath was something else altogether.

They turned tail and fled.

☺

TRUCKDOGS

Reg No.
485865
K9

NAME: SPARKY

BREED/MAKE: Jack Russell/Ute
COLOR: Brown and white
IDENTIFYING MARKS: Bright red collar, waggy tail
TEMPERAMENT: Very enthusiastic

FILE INFO:
11 years old. Son of Mayor Plugg. Lives with mother (76 Boneo Rd, Hubcap). Father deceased. Good kid but overly influenced by local street gang (Mongrel Pack).

SPECIFICATIONS:
Engine: 4-cylinder, 1600cc
Fuel Requirements: Unleaded petrol, standard dog food plus the occasional bone
Maintenance: 12-month oil change and flea treatment Regular worming (monthly)

"The trouble with the youth of today is they have no respect," said Edna Fleasome as she bustled out of Hubcap general store with a roof rack loaded with groceries.

"No respect," agreed her sister, Ida.

"They don't even have homes."

"No homes."

"They don't belong here."

Ida nodded.

"And they're dirty," Edna said with conviction.

"Dirty," echoed Ida.

The two sisters motored out into the main street, a wide, dusty strip of red dirt flanked by a ragged line of weatherboard and corrugated-iron buildings. Next door to the general store was the local bone depot. Across the road stood Scratchly's Fencing Supplies. Farther up was the Country TruckDogs' Association building and a couple of houses with low verandas shielding their windows from the desert sun. The only permanent-looking building in the street was the Town Hall that stood on the corner of Memorial Park. It had an entrance porch with two white pillars and a curved ramp leading to its double doors.

The only other notable features of the town were the park itself (a statue of Lord Hubcap stood in the middle behind a rope fence), a creaking windmill, and several rusty water tanks. At the far end of the main street stood Hubcap Garage. It was the only petrol station in town (two pumps: one standard, one diesel). A fuel shed stood to one side and a large mechanic's workshop was set back to the right.

Beyond the petrol station the road stretched out to the distant horizon—the Great Outback Highway that led to Combustion City far to the south.

Edna and Ida drove past some young TruckPups playing in the road, laughing and rolling about in the dust. Edna shook her head.

"They should be in obedience school," she tut-tutted.

"Obedience school," agreed Ida.

At that moment the sound of thumping music was heard, growing louder. Edna looked up the street and scowled.

"Come, Ida. We don't need to listen to this." They turned and drove off.

The Mongrel Pack rolled into town. A sign hanging over the roadway said "Welcome to Hubcap" and beneath, in smaller letters, "Hubcap is a Tidy Town. Please dispose of your droppings thoughtfully." One by one the TruckDogs sprang up and hit the sign with a wing mirror as they passed underneath. The hinges squeaked in protest as the sign swung back and forth. Sparky, following the older TruckDogs at the end of the line, jumped up as well. He didn't quite reach it.

Zoe's radio was on full blast. The TruckDogs shimmied from side to side in time with the music, stirring up clouds of dust, as they came down the street. Thump! Thump! Thump!

Mr. Scratchly, a rather deaf bitzer/hatchback, came out of the fencing-supplies store and scowled at the noise, fiddling with his hearing aid. "Twurn that racket down!" he called.

"Eh, what's that?" shouted Hercules. "Can't hear you."

"Bah!" Mr. Scratchly turned and went back inside. The Mongrels motored on.

Edna and Ida turned and watched from the roadside, tut-tutting as the Pack went by.

"Morning, Miss Fleasome, Miss Fleasome," said Digger pleasantly, nodding at the two sisters.

Edna turned away primly. "Insolent pup, talking to an adult that way. You can tell their parents never taught them manners. And all that ruckus," she continued. "Wasting fuel—goodness knows there's barely enough to go round as it is. I don't know what this town is coming to."

Ida's echo was lost as the Mongrel Pack rolled by and continued on down the street. *Thump! Thump! Thump!*

🐾

The Pack passed the Town Hall and turned left into Memorial Park.

Sparky followed, but as he went past the Town Hall a matronly Irish setter/Land Rover Discovery called out from the top of the steps. She was wearing a blue sash with a large gold medallion of office. Mayor Plugg. Sparky's mum.

"Sparky. Here, boy."

Sparky pretended not to hear.

"Sparky, I know you can hear me. I've just had a call from Farmer Howell . . ."

Sparky cringed.

⊕

Mrs. Plugg looked across her desk at her son. He squirmed uncomfortably. A photo of him as a TruckPup stood to one side of her desk. On the other side was a photo of Mr. and Mrs. Plugg on their wedding day.

"Sparky, I've told you a hundred times about that Mongrel Pack," said Mrs. Plugg. "I know they're, well, disadvantaged . . . but they'll only get you into trouble."

"We were just having some fun," protested Sparky. "Having a bit of a run . . . and jump."

Mayor Plugg looked squarely at her son. "Farmer Howell says you were harassing his TruckSheep."

"More like them harassing us."

Mayor Plugg shook her head. "What am I going to do with you?"

"That's the problem, Mum—there's nothing to do around here."

"Well then, I'll find you something to do," she said briskly. "Go over to the petrol station and collect those drums of anti-rust I ordered. That new mechanic, Rex Whatever-his-name-is, should know about it. Then you can tidy your room—I assume you haven't done it yet? It looks like a DesertDog has been holed up in it. And clean out the food bowls from breakfast. Go on now. I've a mountain of work to get through."

Mayor Plugg busied herself at her desk. Sparky rolled his eyes.

"Don't roll your eyes at me," said Mrs. Plugg without looking up.

How do mothers do that? wondered Sparky as he headed back into the street. He dragged his wheels as he went. Mrs. Plugg glanced at the photo of her and Mr. Plugg.

"A pup needs a father," she sighed.

🐾

The sun was beating down. Sparky crossed to the shady side of the street. He paused to sniff a couple of veranda posts on the way. The posts heading in the other direction were more interesting and he began to wander back up the street.

Soon he had made his way up to the general store. A little TruckBug buzzed past his ear. Sparky snapped at it, springing up and bumping into a water trough by the veranda. The trough slipped off its footings onto the ground and tipped over, sending water sloshing across the veranda and up against the walls.

"Oops."

The storekeeper was out in a flash. He was a bad-tempered corgi/delivery van with a squint in one eye.

"Look at this!" snapped Mr. Barker, nostrils flaring indignantly. "Don't you know there's a drought?"

"Sorry," said Sparky. "It was an accident." He pushed the trough back upright with his bumper bar. The remains of the water splashed out over Mr. Barker's wheels.

"Watch it!" cried the storekeeper, jumping back. "Kids. Should be banned." He turned, shaking his rear wheels dry, and disappeared irritably back into the shop.

A middle-aged basset hound/mobile crane and his wife, a spaniel/tray truck with a handy scissor-lift attachment, chugged up the street. They looked at hapless Sparky and shook their heads good-naturedly.

"The Plugg boy," observed Mr. Dogsbody.

Mrs. Dogsbody nodded and sighed. "Poor Mayor Plugg. It can't be easy."

Sparky hurried now down to the petrol station and across to the workshop. The workshop was a big weatherboard building with wide barn doors and a high window above. A faded banner read "Smash Repairs—All Models, Makes and Breeds. Mechanic on duty." An "Open" sign hung on a nail underneath.

The big doors were open wide. Just inside, an old and weatherworn red setter/tractor was working on the engine of a border collie/combine harvester. The tractor was a scruffy sort—patches of rust showing through faded red paintwork, mismatched wheels with worn tires, a bent funnel sticking up above his graying snout. As Sparky approached he looked up and wiped his front wheels on an oily rag.

"Hiya, Rex!" said Sparky. "What are you doing? I've been hanging out with the Mongrel Pack. Boy, we had fun! We were sheep-leaping, and we got chased by this huge ram right into the dam, and Farmer Howell nearly caught us, but we got out of there really fast, I can tell you! And then Mum found out—that's the not-so-good bit—but she was pretty cool about it, and she told me to come over here and get some, er, axle grease or something that she's ordered so"—he stopped for a breath— "so I've come over to get it." He noticed the combine harvester. "So what're you doing? Fixing someone?"

Rex was already back working on the engine, delicately adjusting the fanbelt with his worn old front tires. "Yup."

"Got him working yet?"

"Nope."

Sparky looked with interest at the engine.

"Think you can?"

"Yup."

"Can I help?"

Rex turned and regarded Sparky for a moment. He crossed to the cluttered workshop wall where some cans were stacked in long rows, nudged three drums of anti-rust off the shelf with his snout and into Sparky's tray. He looked at the little ute from under his bushy eyebrows, waiting for him to go, but Sparky just smiled and wagged his tail.

Rex sighed and turned back to the harvester. "You can pass me that spanner."

Rex had only been in Hubcap a week or two. He had turned up out of nowhere, a drifter, it seemed, who moved from town to town, picking up odd jobs where he could find them. He was good with engines and could fix just about anything given a little time and a few spare parts to work with. Sparky had warmed to him the moment he arrived. The old tractor looked shabby and down-at-wheel, yet there seemed to be a deep understanding and kindness beneath his battered rusty panels.

Sparky looked around the workshop. Various bits of rusty machinery lay scattered all around, some in pieces on benches, some under old tarpaulins. A big silver spanner lay on the work-bench. Sparky looked at it and whistled. It was the most beautiful spanner he had ever seen. The shaft was long but perfectly balanced, the hand-finished grip inlaid with mother-of-pearl, the jaws bisected by a sure, sharp edge. It was a work of art, a real beauty. And it was heavy too! Sparky could hardly lift it.

"Here you go, Rex," he gasped, struggling across from the bench.

"Thanks." Rex took the spanner and deftly tightened a bolt, just so. He straightened up. "That should do it."

He closed the engine cowling, reached in and turned the key. The harvester roared into life.

"How's that feel?" he asked.

TRUCKDOGS

NAME: HERCULES

BREED/MAKE: Great Dane/Ore Truck
COLOR: Gray cab, yellow tray
IDENTIFYING MARKS: Red/white safety bars on side walls
TEMPERAMENT: Headstrong

FILE INFO:
14 years old. No fixed address. Whereabouts of parents unknown. Self-styled leader of Mongrel Pack street gang. Problem with authority. Tends to be bossy.

SPECIFICATIONS:
Engine: 12-cylinder, water-cooled turbo
Power Output: 735kw at 2100rpm
Fuel Requirements: Diesel (direct injection), high-carb dog food with regular calcium top-up
Mainten... monthly flea drench, auto-worming System (AWS) stand... no service required

"Much better," said the collie, stretching and revving a little. "Feels great! Many thanks." He rolled off up the street. Rex nodded in satisfaction.

"I wish I could do that," said Sparky.

Rex looked at him. "You could learn."

Sparky's tail wagged eagerly. He wanted to be a mechanic more than anything in the world. Maybe even more than being a member of the Mongrel Pack.

"I want to learn how to grind out cylinder heads and recondition gearboxes and—"

"Whoa there," laughed Rex. "Let's start with looking after your tools. Do you own a spanner?"

But before Sparky could answer, a horn beeped announcing the arrival of a customer at the pump. Rex holstered his own spanner and went outside. Sparky looked out and recoiled. It was Farmer Howell.

"Morning," said Rex.

"Hrmph," said Farmer Howell. "Fill it up. Regular."

He released his fuel cap with a little pop of pressure from within and looked sidelong at Rex. "So you're the new mechanic, eh? Planning on staying long?"

Rex flipped the nozzle off its hook and began to pump fuel. "No plans."

Farmer Howell grunted as he took on the tank load. Rex looked at him from under his brow and checked the pump. He added a little more, then stopped.

"Reckon that'll do."

"I said, fill it up," Farmer Howell growled. "And give me a couple of cans of two-stroke as well."

Rex continued to pump in silence for a while longer. He replaced the cap and crossed to the fuel shed near the workshop to get the cans of two-stroke, catching Sparky's eye as he did so. Sparky thought he saw the slightest raising of an eyebrow.

Farmer Howell grunted again as he adjusted himself, clearly uncomfortable with a full tank sloshing about inside. He had the unmistakable look of one about to pass wind. Sparky shrank back into the workshop and closed his air vents.

Just then, Mr. Scratchly rolled up at the pump, stopping with a jerk. He looked around impatiently, then took the nozzle and began to serve himself, first checking that the pump was working by squirting some fuel on the ground. It splashed around the pump and trickled toward Farmer Howell.

Farmer Howell was meanwhile looking more and more uncomfortable, clearly working up to a real beauty. Sparky's eyes widened in horror. Rex locked the fuel shed and glanced back toward Sparky. He saw the look in Sparky's eyes and turned around, instantly registering the spilled fuel and Farmer Howell's look of discomfort.

Rex hurled himself at Mr. Scratchly, grabbing the nozzle and knocking him clear across the garage forecourt. At the same time he spun Farmer Howell around with his rear wheels so the pickup's backside pointed out across the street. A second later a huge tongue of flame shot out of Farmer Howell's exhaust pipe, accompanied by a loud bang. A clump of grass growing by the roadside went up in flames.

Rex turned and sent his silver spanner flying toward the pump. It flashed in the sun as it spun through the air, locked onto the fuel-flow lever and flipped it around, turning it off.

Sparky looked on, openmouthed. He hadn't even had time to bark.

"What in Dog's name do you think you're doing, you cwrazy halfbwreed?" cried Mr. Scratchly.

A crowd began to gather. He turned to them, fumbling with his hearing aid. "Darn twractor went and attacked me!"

"Got rabies by the looks of him," said Edna Fleasome from amongst the onlookers. "Thought so the minute he arrived in town. He's got shifty eyes."

"Shifty eyes," said Ida.

Rex retrieved the spanner and headed back toward the workshop. "Flames and fuel don't mix," he said as he went. "Basic safety."

Farmer Howell looked guilty.

Mr. Scratchly called out after Rex. "I'll be pwressing charges, you hear? I'll . . . I'll have you put down!"

"Then we won't have a mechanic again," said Mr. Dogsbody dryly. "A town has to have a mechanic, you know. Who'll run the petrol station? Windy Howell? Now that would be asking for trouble."

The others chuckled. Farmer Howell went red.

"I could run it," said Mr. Barker the storekeeper in a low voice that no one heard.

"That was amazing!" said Sparky as Rex rolled back into the workshop. "How'd you do that?"

Rex didn't answer. He carefully wiped the spanner, checking the barrel and closing the jaws. Then he spun it with the ease of a practiced tool-slinger and holstered it snugly by his rear wheel. Sparky was deeply impressed.

Rex's off-side rear hubcap fell off with a clang and rolled into the dirt, somewhat undermining the moment.

Rex sighed. He retrieved the hubcap and hung it on a nail outside the door next to the "Open" sign.

"I'm falling apart."

He looked out the side window at the dispersing crowd and shook his head. "I don't need this kind of aggravation."

"You're not leaving, are you? You only just got here."

Rex was silent.

"I don't want you to go," said Sparky. "You're my friend. I haven't really got any others."

Rex thought for a moment, then turned back to Sparky with a half-smile.

"You and me both."

☻

The next day dawned as hot as ever. The corrugated-tin roofs sizzled and popped in the heat and the old peeling paint on the veranda posts curled, hard and brittle. The few TruckDogs who ventured out stayed in the shade of the verandas, squinting their eyes against the glare. Even the buzzing TruckBugs kept to the shady side of the street.

Prudence, Digger, Zoe and Hercules were kicking an empty oil can around in the main street, outside the general store. The can made a terrific amount of noise, clanging off the water troughs, whanging off the guttering and kerthunking off the wooden veranda posts as they whacked it with their wheels and bumper bars.

Mr. Scratchly winced at the racket as he went past.

Bullworth stood with his big mouth open wide, opposite the store. He was the goal.

Sparky watched from across the street as the others played, following every move, waiting for the can to come his way.

Digger had the can. He dribbled around Zoe and was about to pass it to Prudence when Hercules thumped into him and sent him sprawling. The big ore truck lined up Bullworth and flicked the can skillfully with his front wheel, sending it spinning into his open mouth.

"Good shot, Herc!" cried Zoe. "One, nil."

Bullworth spat the can out onto the ground and felt around his back teeth with his tongue. "Ow. Not so hard."

"How about a free kick for shoving?" said Digger.

"That wasn't shoving. It was a nudge," said Hercules. "You wanna see a shove?"

"Save it," said Digger.

Prudence flipped the can back into play with a shrug of her fender. Digger slewed sideways and smacked the can with his back hoe. Hercules was ready but the can glanced off Zoe's mixer and popped up into the air, over his roof. Quick as a flash Sparky jumped—straight up in the air like little dogs do —and caught the can in his teeth.

"Hey, way to go, Sparky," said Prudence.

"Nice leap," nodded Digger.

"Yeah, nice," said Hercules. "Just watch I don't squash you by mistake, okay?" He put a heavy wheel on Sparky's roof and pressed him right down on his springs.

"Yeah, okay," said Sparky with difficulty. "I'll watch out."

He passed the can up to Hercules. The big truck let him go and the game continued. Sparky sat down again.

Rex, who was on his way to pick up some supplies, stopped under the store veranda and watched. He smiled as he remembered playing similar games long ago when he was a pup. The can clanged down nearby and he bent to retrieve it.

But Hercules was quickly there. "Make way, old-timer. You'll burst a gasket if you're not careful."

Hercules flipped the can up into the air with his front wheel, spun around and caught it in his tray. He pointed at

Rex, then at the can—"Old dog, new trick." He winked and drove off, looking to the others for their approval.

Rex watched him go with a slight smile. Sparky looked from Rex to Hercules, then back again, amused and puzzled. He knew what Rex was capable of.

The can was back in play again.

"Keep that mouth open wide, big boy," Prudence called to Bullworth. "I'm about to level the score!"

"Caregul og ny teeg, okay?"

Prudence whacked the can with her tail, sending it rocketing into Bullworth's mouth. It hit the firewall at the back of his mouth and went straight down his gullet.

Bullworth's eyes bulged. "Euuurgch. Hclg! I'g chokngg!"

The others looked on.

"I think he's choking," said Zoe.

"Yup, looks like it," said Digger. He came up behind Bullworth and squeezed the big dozer's undercarriage with his back hoe.

"Yeeeee!" squealed Bullworth. The can shot out of his mouth, straight across the street, over Sparky's head, and smashed through the window of the general store.

"Whoops," said Prudence. "Time to go."

"Do we get extra points for that?" asked Digger.

Mr. Barker was outside in a flash. "You hoodlums!" he cried.

"Sorry," said Prudence with an apologetic shrug. "Accidents happen."

"Accidents?" yelled the storekeeper. "You brats are the accidents! You did that on purpose!"

They began to protest but to no avail.

"This town would be a better place without mongrels like you," snapped Mr. Barker.

"Come on," said Hercules to the others, turning his back and heading up the street. "You're wasting your breath."

"It was an accident," said Rex quietly as the Mongrel Pack drove off.

Mr. Barker turned on Rex. "You keep out of this! Those mutts are nothing but vandals. Vandals and delinquents!"

"No, they're just kids."

Mr. Barker looked at the old tractor with narrow, bigoted eyes. He saw a scruffy hobo, a drifter with an unknown past and no future. A troublemaker.

"You're no better than they are," he spat. As he turned back to the store, his eyes fell on Sparky.

"You again! I might have known. Well, your mother is going to hear about this!"

●

Later, Sparky found himself once again in Mrs. Plugg's office.

". . . and if I catch you messing about with that Mongrel Pack again, you won't be moving from your room for a week! Do you understand?"

Sparky winced.

TRUCKDOGS

NAME: PRUDENCE

BREED/MAKE: Dachshund/Fuel-Tanker Road Train
COLOR: Black and tan (with purple highlights)
IDENTIFYING MARKS: Small birthmark on front left wheel arch
(Oh yeah, and she's really, really long.)
TEMPERAMENT: Ironic

FILE INFO:
13 years old. Address: longdoggy@woofermail.com
Parents separated. (Mother resides Combustion City.
Father's whereabouts unknown.) Member of Mongrel Pack.

SPECIFICATIONS:
Engine: 8-cylinder, water-cooled
Power Output: 250kw at 2000rpm
Trailers: 3 12.5m general purpose tankers
Fuel Requirements: Multi-fuel capacity, regular dog food
Maintenance: 12-month grease, oil change and good scratch on belly

"It—"

"I don't care if it wasn't your fault," she said. "You were there with them and you shouldn't have been. They are a bad influence. Do I make myself clear?"

Sparky hung his head. "Yes, Mum."

Mr. Barker looked on smugly from one side of the desk. Mrs. Plugg's eyes flickered in distaste. She had never much liked the storekeeper.

"The cost of fixing the window will be reimbursed," the mayor told him coolly, "out of miscellaneous street repairs."

Mr. Barker nodded, satisfied, and departed.

Mrs. Plugg looked at Sparky and her tone softened. "Just try to keep out of trouble, all right? I know I'm a little hard on you sometimes." Her glance fell for a moment on the photo of Mr. Plugg. "Go on now."

Sparky headed off.

Mayor Plugg's face was a mixture of exasperation, concern and despair as she watched him go.

A week later the Mongrel Pack was hanging around Memorial Park. The statue of Lord Hubcap stared out at the windmill from behind its rope fence. There was some shade under the big spreading gum trees that were scattered through the park but the TruckDogs weren't concerned about keeping cool. They were doing time trials on the circular gravel path that ran around the statue.

Sparky looked on from across the road, his mother's words still ringing in his ears. He made a sad sight, sitting there, tail wagging occasionally as one of the Pack did a particularly good lap. He was dying to join in. He was trying to be good.

"Whoa, steady there, oh great leader," called Prudence as Hercules roared around the track. "You're going to cause a dust storm."

"One lap to go," called Zoe, checking his time on her trip computer.

Hercules put on a burst of speed, sending gravel and stones flying. Bullworth flinched. "Ow, you're chipping my paintwork!"

Hercules completed the lap and skidded to a stop. Zoe checked the time. "Thirteen point seven seconds. You're just the best, Herc!"

Hercules did a lap of honor. Zoe grabbed on to his rear bumper with her grill. "C'mon, everyone. Conga line!"

Digger fell in behind Zoe with a happy "Woo hoo," dragging Bullworth after him with his back hoe. They slewed from side to side alarmingly.

"This is going to end in tears," said Prudence. But she shrugged and joined in anyway.

The conga line got faster and faster, spinning round and round the statue. Sparky watched, his tail thumping the ground in excitement. Unable to contain himself any longer, he bolted across the road, leapt the corner of the rope fence and began racing around behind them, unnoticed.

But in his excitement he didn't see that the rope had snagged on his rear axle. The rope tore away from the old posts, one after the other, but the last one held fast. The rope went tight for a second, then the post broke off. It flew inward, glancing off Bullworth's head, and smashed into the statue. One of Lord Hubcap's concrete ears went flying, never to be seen again. The rest of the head spun through the air and hit the ground with a thud, ten yards away.

Sparky was flung high into the air. He landed in the fork of an overhanging tree and hung there, wheels dangling, looking very surprised.

The Mongrels came to a stop, bumping into each other like shunting trucks as they became tangled up in the rope.

"Ow!"

"Ugh!"

"Ooof!"

"What happened?"

"Yeowwwwww!" cried Bullworth. A large welt had appeared on his head, surrounded by bare metal where the orange paint had come off. Tears welled in his eyes.

"Get this off me," said Hercules, revving angrily against the rope that had wrapped itself around his wheels. There was a loud crack from above. The TruckDogs looked up to see the statue teetering on its base. Bullworth stopped in mid-sob, mouth open.

They watched, transfixed, as the statue teetered back and forth, working its way to the edge where it balanced for an impossibly long moment. Then, like a felled tree, it toppled earthward.

"Watch out!" yelled Prudence.

Zoe scrambled out of the way with a yelp as it crashed down. A cloud of cement dust billowed out over the park, coating everything in a layer of white.

Slowly the cloud cleared. The Mongrel Pack emerged coughing and spluttering. They looked like ghosts, completely white with dust. Prudence turned on her windscreen wipers and looked around.

"Er, guys," she said. "We have company . . ."

The others washed their windscreens, blinked and looked up. They did indeed have company. The entire population of the town in fact.

Mayor Plugg came forward and surveyed the broken statue in silence. Eventually she spoke.

"Is my son here?"

Up in the tree, Sparky bit his lip.

"No, just us," shrugged Prudence.

The Mayor sighed. That was something at least. She looked at the statue, then squarely at the Pack.

"This is not an isolated incident," she said sternly. "You are fast becoming a public nuisance. And that's something this town can do without."

"They broke my window," put in Mr. Barker. "They're vandals."

"They've been worrying my sheep," said Farmer Howell.

"They're rude and noisy," said Mr. Scratchly.

"Impudent!" exclaimed Edna Fleasome. "Impudent and far too young." She looked at her sister. "Isn't that right, Ida?"

Ida hesitated. She vaguely remembered being young herself once, but she nodded. If Edna said so, then it must be right.

"Too young."

"Quite a list," remarked Digger.

"They left out 'bored to death' and 'totally lacking in opportunity,'" remarked Prudence. "But otherwise that just about covers it."

"All right, yes, thank you," said Mayor Plugg to the towns-folk. "Please let me deal with this."

"No, no, they've done a great job," said Hercules. "You don't want us here. And we don't want to be here. So fine. We're leaving."

Prudence raised her eyebrows. "And where would we be going exactly?"

"Anywhere but here."

"Wait," said Mayor Plugg. This wasn't what she had meant to happen. As mayor of Hubcap she had a duty to maintain law and order, but she was also a mother. The Mongrel Pack some-times seemed practically adults themselves—with no proper homes they had grown up quickly—but in reality they were still just bored kids. She thought about Sparky, how he seemed to have nothing to do—nothing better than hang around with the Mongrel Pack. She frowned. They *were* a bad influence.

"Let 'em go," snapped Mr. Barker. "We don't need 'em."

Hercules turned and drove away across the park and out onto the street. He was followed by the others.

The townsfolk mumbled amongst themselves. Some, like Mr. and Mrs. Dogsbody, shook their heads worriedly. Others murmured their approval. A town had to have its standards.

"They need to be taught a lesson," said Edna.

"At least my sheep will be safe," said Farmer Howell.

"Maybe now we can all get a bit of peace and quiet," said Mr. Scratchly.

Farmer Howell backfired as he headed off.

"Not with him around," remarked Mrs. Dogsbody.

Mayor Plugg looked after the departing Mongrel Pack and didn't know what to think.

☉

Rex was tinkering with an old gearbox, adjusting the tension with a screwdriver clenched between his old yellow teeth, when Sparky rushed into the workshop.

"They've gone!" gasped Sparky. "The Mongrel Pack. I don't believe it."

Rex put down his spanner. He followed Sparky to the door and looked out across the desert, squinting into the sun. He scanned the horizon, but all he could see was the faintest shimmer of a dust cloud out toward the west.

Sparky told him what had happened.

"Those young hotheads are going to get themselves killed," the old tractor muttered. "There are DesertDogs out where they're heading."

He looked for a while longer, then shook his head and turned back to the town. He spoke softly, as if reciting:

"A town that turns away its youth,

Will surely turn to dust.

And all that's left is fleas'n'weeds,

Some memories—and rust.

"I'm an old dog, Sparky. I've seen a lot of towns slowly fade away, eaten up from within, until there's nothing left but rust and resentment. I don't want to see any more."

He flipped a saddle pack off its hook with a shrug of his wheel arch, and swung it up across his cab. He cast an eye around the workshop. "Never did finish that gearbox," he murmured regretfully.

"If you're leaving, I'm coming with you," said Sparky.

Rex looked at the youngster and saw the lower lip jutting out, stubborn but trembling ever so slightly.

"You're young," he said kindly. "Believe it or not, I was once a pup myself. It was a long, long time ago. But I still remember. So I understand how you feel."

He took down a couple of water bags, and his tool kit and the big silver spanner. "But a TruckDog should stay put as

35

long as he has a job to do, a kennel to lie in and a bone to gnaw on."

"And unless I'm mistaken, there're a few more bones here for you to dig up yet, young fella—maybe more than you know. As for me . . ." He spun the spanner and slipped it into his tool kit and trundled off down the hill.

"Are you coming back?" called Sparky.

Rex paused. He didn't look back. "You take care."

He left the road and headed off across the desert, westward.

Sparky turned despondently to the workshop. He pushed the big doors closed. There, hanging on a nail next to the "Open" sign, was Rex's old hubcap. Sparky looked at it for a moment, then hung his head.

Then with a sad shrug he turned the sign around to "Closed."

TRUCK**DOGS**

Reg No.
436861
k2

NAME: BULLWORTH

BREED/MAKE: Bulldog/Bulldozer
COLOR: Safety Orange
IDENTIFYING MARKS: Blue eyes, blue collar, big mouth
TEMPERAMENT: Surprisingly timid considering size

FILE INFO:
13 years old. No fixed address. Parents deceased. Member of Hubcap street gang the Mongrel Pack.

SPECIFICATIONS:
Engine: 4-stroke cycle, water-cooled, direct injection
Power Output: 300kw at 1800rpm (flywheel horsepower)
Operating Weight: 15,200kg and growing
Fuel Requirements: Diesel, oil and cabbages (note: vegetarian, no bones please)
Maintenance: 6 month oil and worm. 12 month flea powder

ex chugged slowly and steadily through a harsh landscape dotted with low, rounded boulders. Brittle bushes and clumps of dry grass grew close to the rocks where there was some shelter from the relentless sun. He scanned the ground as he went, looking for tire tracks, but there were few signs to be read in the hard, stony ground.

Late in the afternoon he came to a billabong. A solitary gum tree stood with its gnarled branches hanging out over the pool. The water level was low. A few thirsty TruckRoos hopped away as he approached. Rex looked at the tree and noticed a small branch hanging down—freshly broken. Tire prints were visible by the water's edge. He looked out to the west. The Mongrels were nowhere in sight. But he knew he was on the right track.

Rex filled his water bags and topped up his radiator, rolling right into the billabong to find deeper water. Just then he heard the sound of engines approaching. Lots of engines. He reversed out of the water and waited quietly under the shade of the tree.

Soon the thunder of engines was so loud it made the surface

of the billabong shimmer. Over a low rise, coming out of the north, appeared twenty or so huge, aggressive-looking TruckDogs. They were a mangy lot, flecked with rust and spattered with mud. Some were standard models—utes mostly, a few twin cabs and tray trucks. Others were weird hybrids, sporting modifications of various kinds. Oily black smoke spewed from unsilenced exhaust pipes and boiling water dribbled from slavering grills and overheated radiators.

They were the RottWheelers—a bunch of highway bandits and car thieves, led by the meanest TruckDog that ever hit the highway—the notorious Mr. Big.

Each vehicle was loaded with supplies—spare parts, maintenance equipment, tires. Some towed tarpaulin-covered trailers. They looked hot and tired but there was no sign they were going to stop at the billabong. They were driving hard.

Rex stood quietly under the gum tree as they passed, his dull, rusty panels blending in with the rocks and red earth. Most of the band had thundered by when one spied him and shouted an order. The other RottWheelers came about, tires squealing, gearboxes crunching, and circled round the billabong to where Rex stood.

The sharp-eyed one was a greyhound/drag car with off-road wheels and suspension, powered by a rear-mounted aircraft-style ramjet engine. She was flame red with a wide yellow stripe down the roof and hood. Her grill was styled in a permanent sneer. Her name was Throttle. She was Mr. Big's lieutenant.

"Hey, Brake, come and look at this."

An enormous mastiff/monster truck came up beside her. Patches of bright electric blue showed through the mud that was spattered over his huge frame. He had a lot of amateur paint detailing on his door panels and multiple piercings on his wing mirrors and wheel arches. A heavy black leather collar with silver studs was fastened tightly around his girth and he sported gigantic tires meant for a vehicle several times his size. But for all his bulk, Brake had a teeny weeny cab. Definitely not the brightest car in the auto pool.

Throttle nodded toward Rex, who remained motionless, eyes averted. "Is this pile of junk dead or alive?"

"You want I bite it and find out?" said Brake in a guttural growl.

"Sure, go ahead. 'Course, it might be poisonous. Or rotten. Certainly looks flyblown."

Brake thought for a minute, then grunted. "I bite it anyway."

But as he rolled forward another voice broke in, altogether smoother, infinitely more unpleasant. "Thank you, Brake. That won't be necessary."

The crowd of slavering TruckDogs parted and a little chihuahua/Isetta rolled forward. Apart from being one of the smallest TruckDogs ever conceived, he was also clearly one of the nastiest. He had a nasty face, all pinched and sneering— nasty thin lips, nasty buggy eyes and nasty little pointy teeth. And he was painted a particularly nasty shade of blue, too.

This was Mr. Big.

He regarded Rex with distaste, then extended his antenna and, from a safe distance, poked the tractor sharply in the side. Rex remained motionless. Mr. Big leaned forward and sniffed at him. It was a nasty sniff.

"Well, it certainly smells dead. But you can never tell with these old strays." He turned to Throttle. "Maybe he just needs a wash?"

Throttle grinned. "You got it, Boss."

She kicked out suddenly with her rear wheels, sending Rex sprawling into the billabong.

"Clean him up, boys."

The RottWheelers drove into the billabong, hooting and hollering. They circled Rex, churning up the water, covering him in mud, then emptied his water bags over his cab.

"That will do," said Mr. Big. The RottWheelers stopped obediently.

Rex groaned slightly as he lifted himself upright, flexing a dented wheel arch.

"Well, well—he's alive after all," said Mr. Big. "What a shame we can't stay and play longer. Relieve him of his tools, Throttle my dear, and we shall be off. We still have a ways to go." He turned to Brake. "What's the name of the next lucky town?"

Brake produced a map, unfolding it clumsily (his thick tire tread pattern wasn't designed for such work), and read slowly. "Uh, PacbuH."

"And if we turn the map up the other way?"

"Er, Hubcap."

Throttle rummaged through Rex's tool kit with her snout, discarding most of the tools—nothing but worthless old junk —but she eyed the spanner with interest.

"Now, that's a nice tool."

Rex's eyes flickered.

"Your spanner?" she asked.

Rex nodded.

"Not anymore." She stowed it in her tool compartment.

At that moment Mr. Big rallied the RottWheelers, whipping the closest rump with his antenna. "Let's ride!"

They revved their engines, a huge confusion of sound and smoke, and thundered off. Throttle circled Rex.

"Have a nice day, now." She gave him a wink and followed the others.

Rex hauled himself out of the water and watched as they disappeared towards the east. After a long moment he looked west, in the direction the Mongrel Pack was headed, as if judging the distance. He paused, weighing things up. Then he collected his other tools from where they lay scattered on the ground, wiped them clean, refilled his water bags and set off after the Mongrel Pack.

The spanner would have to wait for later.

Sparky sat by himself in Hubcap Memorial Park, glumly contemplating the statue of Lord Hubcap lying in the dirt. The head lay some way off, looking rather surprised. A little TruckPuppy out with his mother strained at the leash to sniff at it. He lifted a wheel. His mother hastily dragged him away, scolding. Sparky laughed hollowly.

"Go for it, kid."

Just then, the roar of engines filled the air. Sparky lifted his head, filled with a sudden hope. Was it the Mongrel Pack coming back? And Rex?

The cause of the commotion came into view, and his hope turned to sudden interest and then, just as quickly, alarm, as twenty huge TruckDogs came rumbling into town.

The townsfolk hurried inside, drawing blinds and bolting doors, as the cavalcade rolled up the main street.

Mr. Big pulled in at the petrol station and looked around. Under the "Closed" sign on the workshop wall hung another, reading, "Mechanic Wanted."

Mr. Big sounded his horn. There was no response. The other RottWheelers joined in, circling the garage forecourt, honking and beeping. Eventually a very nervous-looking Mr. Barker emerged from the general store, hurried down the street and across to the petrol station.

"Er, can I help you?"

Brake stuck his big grill right in the storekeeper's face. "You delivery boy, huh?"

TRUCKDOGS

NAME: ZOE

BREED/MAKE: Dalmatian/Cement Mixer
COLOR: Peacock blue with mauve highlights
IDENTIFYING MARKS: Lots of beauty spots
TEMPERAMENT: Sassy

FILE INFO:
12 years old going on 18. No address, no parents. Mongrel Pack member. Often seen parking with Hercules (file 00228302).

SPECIFICATIONS:
Engine: 6-cylinder, d/i
Power Output: 112kw at 2300rpm
Fuel Requirements: Something nice, preferably unleaded
Maintenance: Monthly wax, polish and furcleanse; weekly tire trim and windscreen debug (no harm in dreaming!)

Mr. Barker blinked nervously. "No, actually I own the general store. I'm looking after the garage until—"

Throttle grabbed him by the collar and spun him around to face her. "Can you pump petrol?"

Mr. Barker nodded meekly.

"So pump."

He looked around at the assembled RottWheelers. "Which one?"

Mr. Big rolled up and tapped him on the cab with his antenna. "All of us, Mr. Delivery Boy. All of us. You can start with Brake here. He takes his unfiltered with plenty of lead."

Brake loomed over Mr. Barker, grinning. Mr. Barker reached for the fuel nozzle but hesitated. Mr. Big looked at him with narrowed eyes and smiled to himself—he'd seen this type before. He retracted his antenna, came alongside and spoke confidingly.

"You're a smart one, I can see that. You and I are not as different as you think. We all need fuel. And we all need friends—preferably big, powerful ones."

Mr. Barker's eyes flicked across to the RottWheelers and back. Mr. Big raised an eyebrow. "We understand one another, yes?"

The storekeeper swallowed. Just at that moment Mayor Plugg arrived.

"Ah, the official welcoming committee," said Mr. Big. ". . . numbering exactly one. Tell me, where is everyone else? Come out, come out, wherever you are!"

Mr. and Mrs. Dogsbody and a handful of the more stalwart townsfolk appeared and gathered behind Mrs. Plugg. A few others emerged timidly, staying near their doors, keeping their distance.

"That's better," said Mr. Big. "Come in closer now. We're not going to bite, you know."

"Heh, heh, heh," chuckled Brake.

The townsfolk shuffled their wheels, and kept their distance.

Mayor Plugg came forward and cleared her throat. She smiled in what she hoped was a friendly but firm way.

"Good afternoon to you all. And welcome to Hubcap. Is everything all right? If it's fuel you need, you only have to say. I am sure we can spare enough to see you on your way."

Mr. Big feigned surprise. "Really? Why, that would be wonderful, wouldn't it, boys? The kind people here will let us have some of their precious fuel—'enough to see us on our way.'"

Throttle smirked.

Mayor Plugg pressed on. "You will understand, of course, that we're only a small town with limited supplies . . ."

"Well, that's going to be a problem, isn't it?" interrupted Mr. Big. "You see, lady, we're not here for 'enough to see us on our way.' We're here for 'all that we can take'!"

Mayor Plugg bristled. "Now listen here, just because there are a lot of you . . ." She looked around. "Quite a lot of you— it doesn't mean you can just roll into town and take over."

"Actually," smiled Mr. Big, "it does."

He clicked his door handles and several RottWheelers instantly lunged forward and sideswiped Mrs. Plugg, wrapping a rope around her hood and tying it off on the roof racks. Others attached heavy wheel clamps to her wheels. Throttle tightened them with the big silver spanner.

Brake bit the lock off the workshop doors and Mayor Plugg was shunted roughly inside.

"Now just a minute—" started Mr. Dogsbody, the mobile crane moving forward, but he too was instantly grabbed, bound and hurled into the workshop.

"You leave him alone!" cried his wife, the scissor-lift. Then "Ow! You leave *me* alone!" And she soon joined her husband.

Mr. Big looked around at the stunned townsfolk. "Anyone else?"

From the back of the group came a voice. "Yeah. Me."

It was Farmer Howell.

A pair of RottWheelers made to tackle him but he was ready for them. Before they knew what was happening he reared up on his back wheels, grabbed them in his front wheels and banged their cabs together. They staggered away, reeling. Farmer Howell turned to face Mr. Big. The little Isetta held his antenna out in front of him and put himself into reverse.

"Keep him away from me!"

The other RottWheelers, led by Throttle and Brake, piled onto Farmer Howell. The crusty old pickup put up a good fight, giving several of the thugs dents they would long remember, but there were too many for him. Soon he was trussed and clamped and thrown in the workshop with the others.

Mr. Big looked again at the townsfolk. "Anyone? Anyone at all?"

The townsfolk hung their heads.

Satisfied, Mr. Big turned to Mr. Barker. The storekeeper lifted the fuel nozzle off its hook and held it up in readiness. But Throttle snatched it from him.

"Forget it, Delivery Boy. We prefer self-service."

She smashed the pump's glass window with Rex's spanner and, pointing the nozzle skyward, shot a fountain of fuel high up into the air.

"It's party time! Yeeeha!"

The RottWheelers honked and revved, pushing and shoving to get at the free petrol. Suddenly a flash of white and brown flew through the air, snatching the nozzle from the unsuspecting Throttle.

Sparky landed squarely on his wheels, bristling and growling, his jaws clamped around the nozzle.

"This is our fuel," he said through clenched teeth. "And this is our town. And that . . ." he nodded toward the workshop doors, "is my mum! Now you let her go or . . . or . . ."

He looked around at the huge and very unfriendly thugs who had encircled him. The rush of fuel to his carburetor subsided. Mr. Big rolled forward and relieved him of the nozzle.

"Or what? You'll nip me on the axle?" He tapped Sparky with his antenna. "You are a naughty puppy. And naughty puppies need to be disciplined."

He motioned to Throttle. She pulled the tarpaulin cover off one of the trailers. Underneath was a big iron cage. And inside the cage was a monster.

From the sloping hood that began almost at the roof-line, it appeared to be a bull terrier/heavy-haulage hybrid but it was hard to tell for sure. The rear-drive wheels were enormous. A huge engine protruded from behind the cab, the exhaust stack sticking up vertically from the block. Wild albino eyes stared out from a heavy leather-and-steel muzzle.

Throttle pulled the bolt on the cage door. The monster sprang out with a roar and hurled itself at Sparky, who stood rooted to the spot. But suddenly the beast gave a choked yelp, pulled back in midair by a heavy chain attached to the cage. It landed with a solid thud but immediately scrabbled to its wheels again and began barking insanely at Sparky, pulling at the end of its chain.

Mr. Big tapped the monster on the nose with his antenna. "Clutch. Sit."

Clutch looked at Mr. Big, uncomprehending. Mr. Big held up a Doggy Bite on the end of his antenna.

"Sit . . ." Clutch sat down.

"Good boy." He flicked the Doggy Bite toward the monster. It vanished down its gullet in an instant.

Clutch looked up expectantly.

"Still hungry? Dear me, I seem to be out of Doggy Bites." Mr. Big half-turned and spoke confidingly to Sparky. "You should run away now—it makes it so much more fun for him."

Sparky looked with horror at the monstrous TruckDog. Long strings of oily saliva drooled from the leather-encased grill. Mr. Big undid the strap at the back of Clutch's harness and let it fall to the ground. The steel muzzle remained, fixed in place by a pin. A thin string hung from the pin. Mr. Big held it in the tread of his front wheel.

"Steady . . ."

Clutch remained sitting, eyes fixed on Sparky, shaking in anticipation.

Sparky backed away, fumbling to find reverse gear, then turned and fled. Mr. Big waited until he had made it as far as the general store. Then he pulled the pin. The steel muzzle fell to the ground.

"Fetch."

Clutch sprang away, howling.

Sparky knew his life was on the line. He could never out-run the massive beast. His only chance was his size. Quick as a flash, he scurried down the narrow space between the general store and the bone depot next door, his wing mirrors folded back so they didn't hit the walls. He reached the far end and glanced back.

Clutch flung himself headlong into the narrow space and

accelerated forward. There was a rending, screeching sound as he became wedged between the walls. He spun his wheels furiously, tearing up the dirt, but he was stuck fast.

Sparky poked out his tongue. Clutch roared in fury and surged forward, bringing half the store wall with him in an avalanche of splintered weatherboards and corrugated iron.

Sparky fled up the lane, back into the main street and across into Memorial Park. An instant later Clutch roared round the corner in pursuit.

Sparky was breathing hard. He couldn't keep running much longer. He saw Lord Hubcap lying headless in the dirt. He glanced up at the sheared-off base of the statue. Then Clutch was upon him. He scurried to the other side of the statue base. Clutch leapt after him. Soon they were racing round and round the path, throwing up a great cloud of white dust.

Sparky could hear Clutch roaring and snarling right behind him, but the dust cloud was so thick he couldn't see him. All at once he sprang up onto the statue base. Below him, Clutch continued to go in circles. After a few more laps the monster veered away, staggering dizzily, and thudded into a tree which shuddered at the impact. He shook his head violently to clear it and looked around.

Up on the concrete base Sparky froze, statue-like, under a thick coating of white dust. Clutch prowled about below him, growling, sniffing the ground.

Sparky's nose began to tickle. He started to sweat.

At last Clutch moved away, following Sparky's trail back across the park. Suddenly the sound of a muffled sneeze came from behind him. He spun back with a snarl. He looked up at the statue. A faint cloud of dust floated above it. Clutch cocked his head quizzically to one side. Sparky remained absolutely motionless.

Then, with a grunt, Clutch looked around the park again. His prey was nowhere in sight. With a bark of frustration he roared away.

Sparky waited until he was sure the monster had gone. Then he blinked, jumped down and scurried off.

Far out in the baking desert, the Mongrel Pack was a long way from home. A merciless sun beat down upon their unprotected roofs. Their tongues were hanging out. Digger had excavated several holes as they went along, looking for water, but without success.

Bullworth was panting. "My tracks are burning. I've got blisters on my drive wheels."

"Try hopping on one track," Prudence suggested.
Bullworth tried but he couldn't keep his balance.

"Actually, I was only joking."

"Can't we stop soon, Herc?" pleaded Zoe.

"Yeah. I'm starving," said Digger. "I haven't eaten for hours."

TRUCKDOGS

NAME: DIGGER

BREED/MAKE: Labrador/Back Hoe
COLOR: Sort of dusty yellow
IDENTIFYING MARKS: Well, there is that big orange light on top of his head.
TEMPERAMENT: Easy-going

FILE INFO:

Age: 12 years old. Address: nope. Parents: Got a couple—just doesn't know where they are right now. Member of Mongrel Pack gang.

SPECIFICATIONS:

Engine: 4-cylinder, 3990cc
Power Output: 84kw at 2600rpm
Loader: Standard bucket (2270mm)
Lifting Capacity: 4400kg
Fuel Requirements: Anything that's going
Maintenance: Nah

"You could try eating leaves and berries," suggested Bullworth.

"If there were any," added Zoe.

Hercules looked ahead and spied a rocky outcrop shimmering in the distance. "We'll stop at those rocks. At least there'll be some shade."

"You can't eat shade," said Digger.

"Depends what's making the shadow," remarked Prudence.

The outcrop was closer than it at first appeared. They were soon making their way between the rocks, clambering over them where necessary. Suddenly Hercules stopped and listened.

"Wait here," he said to the others. "Digger, come with me."

Hercules and Digger crept quietly forward. The sound of growling and scuffling could be heard coming from somewhere not far ahead. They peeped out from behind a boulder to see an open, sandy area. A pool of water lay to one side, flanked by some trees. By its edge lay the dried-up remains of a wild TruckSheep. Digger licked his lips.

But around the carcass, gnawing on the bones, was a pack of dingo/4x4s. They were mainly old Land Cruisers and Patrols, single cabs with large bullbars and ragged, patched-canvas covers that hung from scrawny roll bars on their pickup backs. They snarled and growled at each other as they fought over the carcass. There were seven or eight of them.

"DesertDogs," whispered Hercules. "Could be tricky."

"Food," said Digger, looking at the TruckSheep carcass and licking his lips again. "Who cares?"

Hercules gazed at the carcass too and his gearbox rumbled. He thought for a moment.

"Okay, we're going to need a diversion."

An old TruckSheep skull—just the hood, roof and front window frames—lay nearby.

"Grab that," said Hercules. "And let's get back to the others."

🐾

"You've gotta be kidding!" said Bullworth as Digger and Hercules outlined the plan. "We're talking DesertDogs here. They eat things like us for breakfast."

"For once I'm with Bullworth," said Prudence. Zoe nodded.

"Listen," said Hercules, "without food we are going to die. It's a dog-eat-dog world out here."

"Not an expression I would have used under the circumstances," remarked Prudence dryly. "But I guess you're right—we gotta eat. Lead on, O great one."

🐾

A little later the DesertDogs were gnawing away on the carcass, growling and snapping at each other, when something vaguely resembling a TruckSheep popped up from behind a rock on the far side of the clearing. It bleated, not very convincingly.

The DesertDogs looked up curiously. The TruckSheep bleated again and moved up and down a bit.

Behind the rock, Digger held up the TruckSheep skull with his back hoe, bobbing it up and down. The skull had been dressed up with some dried grasses and leaves which the Pack hoped looked a little like wool from a distance.

Zoe was doing the bleating.

"I can't keep this up much longer," gasped Digger. The skull was heavy and sweat was trickling into Digger's eyes.

"Baaa! Lift it up a bit more," hissed Zoe. "Not that much, your bucket's showing. Baaaaa!"

Behind a boulder further round the clearing Hercules, Prudence and Bullworth were watching. The DesertDogs left the carcass and went to investigate the decoy TruckSheep.

"Looks like they've swallowed it," said Hercules.

"They'll swallow us if we're not careful," remarked Prudence. But Hercules wasn't listening.

"Okay, you two . . . Go."

Prudence and Bullworth edged away from the boulder and made their way around the back of the outcrop, coming up on the carcass from the far side. It was half buried in the sand. With a quick glance to be sure the DesertDogs were fully occupied with the fake TruckSheep, Prudence took one of the carcass's horns between her teeth and tugged. It didn't budge. Bullworth took the other horn. They pulled together. Nothing.

"A little harder," said Prudence.

They pulled a little harder and the head came right off.

"Oh, great," said Bullworth. "Now we'll never get it out."

At that moment they heard a low growl. They looked up to find a DesertDog standing on a rock above them. Prudence and Bullworth grinned stupidly.

"Sorry, our mistake," said Prudence. She replaced the head, arranging it neatly, and backed away. The DesertDog snarled, revealing a gleaming set of dagger-like incisors.

Bullworth and Prudence squealed and fled.

A short time later, Prudence and Bullworth stood huddled together within the ring of rocks, guarded by three ferocious-looking DesertDogs. They were soon joined by Digger and Zoe and Hercules. The TruckDogs were no match for the lithe and powerful desert dwellers.

The leader, a big brute with one yellow eye and a scar that ran down his fender from windscreen to wheel well, came forward and regarded the captives greedily. His gaze fell on Bullworth and he licked his lips.

Bullworth's eyes grew wide. "No no no," he protested. "I'm tough—all gristle and cogs. I'll taste terrible. I'm a *vegetarian*, for pity's sake!"

The leader advanced on the hapless dozer but suddenly a rock crashed down on his roof, leaving a large dent. He yelped in pain and surprise. Everyone looked up. Atop the rocky outcrop, sharply drawn against the westering sky, stood the dramatic silhouette of a TruckDog—a tractor with a wonky funnel.

"Sorry to have to do that," called Rex, "but I needed to get your attention. Now, I'd like you DesertDogs to leave these young pups alone and go back to your lawful business. They've no right to be here, I know, but they're no threat to you and they're no good to eat, seeing as they're not dead yet."

The one-eyed leader snarled savagely and barked an order. The DesertDogs howled furiously and leapt up the rocks. Rex sighed and waited, immobile on the ridge. The leader lunged at him. Rex caught him by the scruff of the neck with his teeth and with one fluid motion threw the 4x4 behind him over the rocky ledge. The DesertDog disappeared with a yelp and a distant thud.

A second 4x4 came at Rex from the side. Rex raised a thin, sinewy front wheel. The DesertDog crunched into it as if it were made of iron. Rex took hold of the beast's nose between his front wheels and twisted sharply. The DesertDog flipped over with a surprised yelp and disappeared over the ledge.

Two more DesertDogs attacked. Rex spun around and struck out with front and back wheels together, catching one of them under the sump and sending it, wheels flailing, into a prickly mass of sagebrush. The other Dog soared off in the opposite direction into a rock face and crumpled to the desert floor, senseless.

The one-eyed leader reappeared behind Rex.

"Watch out!" cried Bullworth. Rex turned and faced the DesertDog, alert, ready.

The leader paused, and for a moment their eyes met. Then the DesertDog lowered his gaze and slunk away, limping, descending to the desert floor. He looked back at Rex with his one baleful eye. Then he barked an order and the DesertDogs dragged themselves upright and retreated, licking their wounds, into the desert.

The Mongrels watched them go, then looked back at Rex, gob-smacked.

Prudence broke the silence. "Well, that was impressive."

"Strewth!" enthused Digger. "That was awesome! Who says you can't teach an old dog new tricks, eh, Herc?"

Hercules looked uncomfortable.

Rex clambered down to the desert floor. He rotated his left front wheel painfully.

"Old tricks. Even older dog." He looked at Hercules and the others from under his eyebrows. "You might need a few extra tricks yourselves if you're planning to stay out here for long."

"Planning has not been high on the agenda so far," said Prudence.

Zoe looked at Hercules. "Can't we go home now, Herc?"

"We're not going back to Hubcap. They don't want us— and we don't need them. And we don't need your tricks either, Mr. Mechanic. We can look after ourselves."

"So I see," said Rex. He looked up at the sky. "Well, I'll be going, then. I for one don't plan to be out here when it gets dark. Those DesertDogs will be back, and in greater numbers. This is their territory, not ours."

The TruckDogs glanced around, noticing the lengthening shadows. A distant, chilling howl came floating across the desert. Bullworth's eyes bulged. Prudence's hair stood on end all the way along the back of her trailers.

"Yeeesh! Now that's a sound you could learn to hate."

She sidestepped across to where Rex stood. "I'm with the tractor. No offense, Herc, but there's only so much abject terror a girl can take in one day."

Bullworth, Zoe and Digger gulped nervously and gathered close together with Prudence.

"C'mon, Herc . . ." pleaded Zoe.

Another howl punctuated the night, closer this time and off to the left. Hercules struggled with himself, trying to be brave, wanting to act like a leader. But in reality he was scared too.

"Okay, so we find somewhere safe for the night."

The others breathed a sigh of relief.

"But tomorrow we keep moving."

The streets of Hubcap were deserted. The townsfolk had been ordered to stay indoors and RottWheelers patrolled the streets, growling ferociously at anyone who showed so much as a headlight.

The rest of the gang had made themselves at home in the workshop. Empty cans of engine oil and brake fluid lay scattered across the floor and more were being emptied at an alarming rate.

Mayor Plugg, Farmer Howell and Mr. and Mrs. Dogsbody sat bound and clamped at the back of the workshop, looking on helplessly as the gang gorged themselves on the precious fuel.

"Hey, Delivery Boy, more brake fluid," called one RottWheeler.

A harried Mr. Barker hurried across to the shelf.

"It's all gone."

"Then go to the shed and get some more," growled the RottWheeler.

"And a can of diesel," added another.

"Two-stroke. Step on it!" ordered a third.

Mr. Big looked on with a mixture of amusement and distaste as Mr. Barker hurried off.

"It's a dog's life."

☻

Meanwhile, Sparky was sneaking along the back lanes of Hubcap, headlights off, engine just ticking over, toward the sound of the RottWheelers' celebration. There was a full moon (he suppressed the desire to howl), which cast an eerie blue light over the landscape. He came to a corner, peeped around and ducked back quickly as a RottWheeler patrol motored by.

TRUCKDOGS

NAME: REX

BREED/MAKE: Red Setter/Tractor
COLOR: Used to be red.
IDENTIFYING MARKS: Bald tires, loose funnel, missing hubcaps, leaky exhaust, out of rego, not roadworthy—stuff that just happens when you've done that many miles.
TEMPERAMENT: Quiet type

Reg No.
83845
VJ

FILE INFO:
Age: Can't remember exactly. Pretty old.
Address: c/o Hubcap Garage.

SPECIFICATIONS:
Engine type: 4-cylinder
Power Output: About 50hp last time he checked
Requirements: No preference
nce: Self-service

When it had passed he crept on to the workshop, slipping down the side of the building and round the back. The shadows were deep there, almost black. He wondered if he dared turn on his lights.

Suddenly he heard a noise. It sounded like a large bag of air being deflated. He stopped dead. It came again, then silence. Sparky remained motionless, straining to see. After a long while he decided to risk a little light. He flicked on his low beam—and nearly yelped in fright.

There, barely a few feet from his nose, was the huge and unmistakable shape of Clutch. The monster was asleep, snoring, chained to a stake in the ground. An empty packet of Doggy Bites lay next to him. Slowly Sparky began to back away, eyes fixed on the sleeping beast. Clutch rolled over, drooling a long string of saliva, growled something unintelligible and belched right in Sparky's face.

Sparky gasped and staggered back into a sheet of corrugated iron that was leaning up against the wall. It fell with a clatter. Sparky froze. Clutch grunted and half opened a bleary eye, then slurped in the saliva, rolled over and fell back into another demented dream.

Inside the workshop, Throttle looked up. She had heard something. She nudged Brake, who was drinking noisily from a bucket.

"You hear something?"

"Huh? No. Nothing. Just this." He slurped noisily again

from the bucket. Throttle whacked him on the back of the cab, dunking his snout in the fuel dregs. Brake spluttered angrily.

"Now, now, settle down," said Mr. Big. "It was probably just Clutch pining. He's been a bad dog, letting that little mutt get away. But you know, I just can't see him suffer. Throttle, you can untie him now"

"Okay, Boss."

Mr. Big turned to Brake, whose face was back in the bucket, and sighed.

"Try to use some manners, will you?"

Brake looked up quizzically, covered in slop. He had no idea what the boss was talking about.

Outside, Sparky gave Clutch a wide berth and snuck up to the back of the workshop. He sniffed along the wooden plinth until he found what he was looking for.

"Psst! Mum," he whispered. "Can you hear me?"

"Sparky, is that you?" whispered Mayor Plugg from the other side of the weatherboards.

"Move closer to the wall. I'm going to try to unlock your wheels."

Mayor Plugg and the others shuffled carefully to the workshop wall, glancing nervously at the RottWheelers. But the RottWheelers were too busy with their refueling to notice.

Sparky found a loose weatherboard. He flipped a tire lever

out of his tray and, holding the lever between his teeth, inserted it under the board.

Inside, one of the RottWheelers had flooded his carburetor and began misfiring noisily, much to the amusement of the others.

Sparky pressed down on the tire lever, prying off the loose board. It squeaked and snapped but the sound was lost in the general noise of hooting and laughing inside.

He stooped down on his suspension and peered inside. He could see the captives' wheel clamps.

"Hold still . . ."

He poked his nose in as far as he could, a screwdriver clamped between his teeth, and by feel began to pick the locks on the wheel clamps, starting with Mr. Dogsbody. Soon the left-hand pair were loose.

"Turn around."

Mr. Dogsbody wriggled around to face the other way. After a moment he was free. Next Mrs. Dogsbody was released, then Farmer Howell. Sparky started work on Mayor Plugg.

"Sparky, where did you learn to do this?" she whispered.

"Hanging around with bad influences."

He had three of Mayor Plugg's wheel clamps off and was working on the last when Throttle came round the corner, headlights on. Sparky was caught in the beam.

"Hey, you!" yelled Throttle.

Sparky released the last bolt, dropped the screwdriver and

fled. He skidded around the corner and ran straight into Clutch, whose sleeping form now straddled the whole lane. The monster woke with a start, jumped up and looked groggily this way and that. He didn't have his muzzle on. Sparky stood right in front of him, horror-struck. Clutch snarled and lunged forward, pulling the stake right out of the ground.

"ROOOOAAAAAR!"

At the same moment Sparky leapt past him with a yell that was an equal mix of terror and determination.

"YAAAAAH!"

Inside the workshop Mayor Plugg heard the commotion and instinctively cried out.

"Sparky!"

The RottWheeler gang looked around.

The unbolted wheel clamps lay on the ground for all to see.

"Run!" cried Mayor Plugg to the others. She quickly scooped up the screwdriver. The others made a dash for the door but it was blocked by a wall of snarling RottWheelers.

Mr. Big rolled up to the captives. "I am disappointed in you. I go out of my way to be reasonable—I don't kill anyone or burn the place to the ground—but then you try to escape. I'm afraid I shall now have to deal severely with you."

"Lock them in the fuel shed," he told Brake, then turned to Mr. Barker. "Keys please, Delivery Boy."

Mr. Barker glanced at Mayor Plugg, then held out a big bunch of keys. Brake snatched them in his grill. Mayor Plugg held Mr. Barker's eye as she and the others were led off.

He looked away.

☻

"YAAAAAAAH!" cried Sparky.

"ROOOOAAAAARRR!" bellowed Clutch.

Sparky ran flat out, driving blind. He scurried around a corner into the main street. Clutch, free of his muzzle but with the chain flailing wildly behind him, was right on his tailpipe. Sparky could feel his hot breath. He nearly gagged at the smell.

But a full bag of Doggy Bites was having its effect on Clutch. He swung out wide on the corner, right through a veranda post. The heavy chain whipped around as he sped off, taking out the rest of the posts one after the other.

A moment later, Throttle came racing around the corner, just in time for the veranda to collapse on top of her in a mass of rubble.

Sparky raced past the old windmill. Digging in his wheels he made a tight curve around the water tank and sped off again in the opposite direction. Clutch followed, wheels scrabbling, carving up a huge arc of dirt as he slewed out wide. The swinging chain smashed through a row of old sheds, reducing them to flying splinters and taking the top clean off a low-roofed TruckChook roost. Startled TruckChooks flew everywhere, squawking and flapping their wings.

Sparky tore up the road toward the "Welcome To Hubcap" sign. But Clutch was gaining on him. The big beast was not good on corners, but he was a lot faster than Sparky on the straightaway. His head was clearing and he had his prey in his sights now. Sparky was tiring, out of tricks, desperate. The monster bore down on him as they approached the sign.

Sparky could feel Clutch at his back. The terrible jaws opened, ready for the kill. At the last minute Sparky veered off the road onto the shoulder and ducked down on his springs under one of the big iron beams that flanked the sign. Clutch swerved to follow—and slammed headlong right into the beam with a sickening crunch. The heavy posts splintered and the iron beam rang like a bell as the vibrations ran up and down its length.

Clutch staggered back onto the road, eyes rolling up into his head. He fell sideways into a ditch by the roadside, a stupid smile across his face, and lay with his wheels in the air.

Sparky reversed back and sniffed at him gingerly. He was out cold. Sparky fixed the chain securely to the beam and scuffed up the grass—satisfied at a job well done—then headed off back into town. As he passed by, he jumped up at the swinging sign.

And he hit it.

🎱

Mr. Big watched as Brake and four burly RottWheelers

reclamped Farmer Howell and the Dogsbodys and pushed them roughly into the small fuel shed next to the workshop. A sign on the door read "Danger—Highly Flammable—No Naked Flames." Mrs. Dogsbody looked at the sign with alarm.

"Mr. Howell, you are going to have to control yourself."

Farmer Howell nodded and gulped.

Mayor Plugg was being wheel-clamped when Sparky arrived, stealing up behind a bush, close enough to see and hear what was going on. He watched helplessly as Mrs. Plugg was forced toward the shed.

"As lawfully elected mayor of Hubcap I demand you release me and my companions immediately," she said.

Brake looked at Mr. Big questioningly.

Mr. Big rolled his eyes. "We're in charge here, you idiot. Don't listen to her."

"Okay, Boss. Don't listen to her," he told the others. They kept pushing Mrs. Plugg toward the door. At that moment Throttle arrived.

"It was that little mutt again, Boss—the mayor's son. But Clutch is after him." She grinned nastily. "He won't get away this time."

"Sparky! No!" cried Mayor Plugg as she was pushed inside and the door slammed.

"Excellent," said Mr. Big. "Now let's get rid of Mummy Dear."

Mr. Big produced a lighter and flicked it on. He held it out gingerly toward the shed with one wheel. Sparky's eyes grew wide. He was about to spring out when Throttle spoke.

"Hang on, Boss. This shed is loaded—it'll blow sky high."

"That's the whole idea."

"But it's gonna take the petrol station with it. It's too close. There's lots of fuel in those tanks yet."

Mr. Big considered this for a moment, then flicked the lighter off.

"You're right." He turned to the RottWheelers. "You four, guard this shed. We"ll save the fireworks as a parting gift *after* we've relieved Mayor Plugg and her friends of all the fuel. And I mean *all* of it—every last drop.

"Go and find something big to pump it into," he told Throttle. "Something really big. We're gonna squeeze this town dry."

The four RottWheelers took up positions on each side of the shed as Mr. Big motored off. Throttle turned to Brake.

"Okay, you heard him—something really big. Come on."

They departed, leaving the other RottWheelers standing guard. From his hiding place Sparky looked on in despair. He cast around desperately—and saw the battered hubcap hanging on the workshop door.

"Rex . . ."

⚙

The sun had dipped below the horizon and the vast desert sky had begun to glow a deep indigo when Rex and the Mongrel

TRUCK**DOGS**

NAME: MAYOR PLUGG

BREED/MAKE: Irish Setter/Land Rover Discovery

COLOR: Green with white stripe

IDENTIFYING MARKS: Mayoral Badge of Office

TEMPERAMENT: Stern but fair (she hopes)

Reg No. 913881 02

FILE INFO:

Age: Confidential

Address: Mayoral Office, Hubcap Town Hall, Hubcap, 0860

Tries to be fair and reasonable but is over-protective of son Sparky (file 00228301).

SPECIFICATIONS:

Engine: 8-cylinder, 5.2 liter

Fuel Requirements: Unleaded petrol

Maintenance: As per service booklet

Pack came to a sudden dip in the ground before them.

"Looks promising," said Rex.

At first it seemed little more than a depression in the desert floor, but as they traveled along it became a rocky gully. The shadows grew deeper as they made their way downward, the last light of the day fading from the sky. Suddenly the gully opened out into a broad hidden valley set below the level of the surrounding desert. The Mongrel Pack stopped and gaped. Before them lay a huge junkyard. Rusted-out vehicle hulks rested amongst ancient farm machinery, pumping equipment, traction engines and other old and broken contraptions. As night came on and the shadows grew into black pits, it looked very spooky indeed.

"So this is your idea of a nice safe place to spend the night, hey, Rex?" said Prudence. "Very cozy. Love the graveyard theme."

"I'd say it was the old tip from years back when Hubcap was still a thriving town. Hasn't been used in decades, by the looks of it. DesertDogs wouldn't come here. They'd think it was haunted."

Prudence looked around at the twisted metal wreckage that loomed out of the twilight all around. "You don't say."

Hercules grunted and went on ahead of the others. He was being brave and silent, still smarting from the confrontation earlier that afternoon.

Bullworth and Zoe peered around at the junk and gulped. They crept forward nervously, winding their way between towering piles of contorted steel frames, warped and torn panels and rusting body parts.

The leering grill of an ancient Buick loomed out of the darkness, rubber pipes spilling out from the engine block like entrails, the windscreen gaping like an empty eye socket. A TruckRat scuttled out from behind the dashboard and disappeared into the darkness. Zoe screamed. Bullworth backed away, bumping into something behind him. He turned as the skull-like bucket of a huge, old steam shovel tipped out toward him. Muddy water sloshed out of the shovel over his terrified face.

"Aaargh! Get it away from me!" he squealed.

Digger went up to the shovel and smiled. "Don"t worry, Bullworth. It's just my old Grandpa Fergus. He always was a bit of a dribbler."

Prudence looked at the old steam shovel with a mixture of horror and curiosity.

"Your grandpa? You've got to be joking!"

Digger smiled wickedly and moved on. Prudence realized she'd been had. "You *were* joking, you beast! I'm the one who says things like that, not you!"

But the mood had been lightened. They pressed on deeper into the valley, laughing as they came across old bits and pieces that reminded them of folk back in Hubcap.

"This one looks like Farmer Howell," said Zoe, pointing at a large pickup truck with a smashed-up rear end.

"Just as long as it doesn't smell like him," said Prudence.

"Here's Mr. Barker," called Digger, coming across a particularly unappealing van. He worked the hood up and down from behind like a ventriloquist. "You did that on purpose, you vandals! Yap yap yap, blah blah blah."

"Put a lid on it will you?" growled Hercules, coming back. "This stuff is nothing but trash—old junk, dead and gone."

Rex raised his eyebrows and regarded him thoughtfully. "Old, yes. Dead, maybe—but not gone." A rusty pump engine stood nearby. "That old heart has life in it yet." He turned the flywheel and they could hear the pistons move inside the engine block.

He pointed at the heavy boiler plate of a huge traction engine. "This steel is still strong."

He ran his wheel over the blade of an old plow. "The edge of these plowshares still have work to do."

"So what are you now, some kind of cosmic oriental mystico?" said Hercules. "It's all just junk."

Rex was silent. The others stood by uncomfortably.

Hercules snorted, breaking the silence. "I've had enough of this. Come on, guys."

He rumbled off toward the cleft leading up to the desert floor and looked back.

"I said, 'Come on!' Am I the leader of the Pack or what? Are you going to stay and listen to Mr. Deep-and-Meaningful here? You want to be the Cosmic Tractor Gang now, huh?"

The other TruckDogs looked at him unhappily. Rex spoke

quietly.

"No, Hercules, they want to follow you. But you have to learn how to lead them."

"What's that supposed to mean?" asked Hercules. "Ah, just forget it." And he stormed off. Zoe made to go after him but Rex gently restrained her.

"He needs a little time to work this out for himself. We can stop here for the night."

Hercules had not gone far. He stood fuming by a tangled pile of steel reinforcing rods. Rocks that had fallen from the surrounding cliffs lay scattered amongst the steel rods. He stomped angrily on the edge of a rock, flipping it up into the air and catching it in his tray.

"It's a good trick," said Rex, rolling up behind him. Hercules glanced at him, then looked away. Rex continued.

"You're a strong TruckDog, Hercules, and you're clever. But there are still things you can learn. A leader can always learn."

"Yeah? Like what?"

"Like not forcing your friends to choose between their heads and their hearts," said Rex sharply.

Hercules thought a bit and grunted. Rex went on more softly.

"Like not trying so hard to *act* like a leader—just *be* one. Make room for the others, Hercules. Everyone has their own role to play, their own talent. The smallest is as worthy of respect as the biggest." He picked up a piece of junk, an old camshaft. "And the old just as useful as the new."

"And I thought you meant learn something practical," said Hercules sullenly.

"Yes, practical is good, too."

He pointed to a huge boulder with the camshaft. "Flip that one up into your tray."

Hercules looked at the rock, judging its weight. "It's too heavy."

"Throw it then," said Rex casually. "As far as you can. Over the junk pile."

"Don't be ridiculous."

Rex rammed the camshaft under the edge of the boulder, jumped into the air and came down hard on the end of the shaft, catapulting the rock high over the junk pile into the darkness beyond.

Hercules was impressed. But he tried not to show it.

"With your strength and ability you could learn to throw it twice as far," said Rex. "With a little help from this 'junk' that you think so little of . . ."

Hercules looked around at the junk pile, then back at Rex. "Okay," he said. "I'm listening."

Meanwhile, back in Hubcap, Mr. Big was standing outside

the workshop, whistling and calling. He rustled a packet of Doggy Bites.

"Clutch! Here boy. Where is that blasted dog?"

He heard a clinking sound and out of the darkness came Clutch, looking extremely groggy. He was dragging his chain which was still attached to the big iron beam. He dropped down at Mr. Big's wheels, exhausted.

"Where's the puppy, Clutch? Did you eat him all up like a good boy? Did you?" Mr. Big paused, looked at the chain and beam, then said in a very different voice, "You didn't let him get away again, did you?"

Mr. Big extended his antenna. Clutch cringed and crawled away on his belly, whimpering. But all of a sudden he stopped and began to sniff the ground. He got up and sniffed some more, circling round and round until he reached the bushes where Sparky had been hiding. Growling, he followed the trail to the edge of the garage forecourt, looked out into the desert and started barking like crazy.

"What is it?" said Mr. Big. "He's gone? Where? Out into the desert to get help? How can you possibly know that? What are you, Lassie or something?"

Clutch whined desperately. Mr. Big undid the chain.

"All right. If that's where he is, go get him!"

Clutch bolted off in a cloud of dust. Mr. Big shouted after him as he went.

"And don't come back until you find him!"

74

First light was dawning as Sparky came to the billabong where Rex had met the RottWheelers. He sniffed around, puzzled by all the criss-crossing paths, but eventually picked up Rex's scent.

"Rex! Where are you?"

His voice echoed amongst the rocks but there was no answer.

He went down to the water's edge. A couple of TruckRoos hopped lazily around to the far side of the pool. As Sparky drank, the TruckRoo reflections shimmered amongst the spreading ripples, then vanished. A moment later they were replaced by another, larger reflection. Sparky looked up. Clutch stared back at him across the water.

Sparky leapt backward with a yell. He spun around in midair and hit the ground running. Clutch launched himself into the waterhole and surged forward, sending a huge wave across the pond. He hauled himself out and set off howling after his prey.

Sparky was out of luck. There was nowhere to hide.

No, wait in the distance was a rocky outcrop. He couldn't tell how far. He fled toward it . . .

In the inner circle of the rocky outcrop a big meeting of

DesertDogs was under way. The whole tribe was there, thirty or more. The one-eyed leader snarled and growled in the snarly growly language of the DesertDogs.

Suddenly the sound of a high-revving engine, accompanied by a long, terrified yell, broke into his speech, and Sparky hurtled into the clearing. He skidded to a halt right in the middle of the DesertDogs and looked around in utter confusion. They stared back, equally surprised. A second later, Clutch burst into the clearing and slammed into the one-eyed leader, bowling him over. In an instant the DesertDogs were all over him—a biting, scratching, howling ball of teeth, claws and metal. Dog hair and car parts began flying everywhere.

Sparky watched for a moment, then realized no one was paying any attention to him at all. He edged away, backward, until he was outside the ring of rocks.

Then he turned and bolted.

Up at Farmer Howell's place, Throttle and Brake were sniffing around, looking for something big to carry the fuel in, as Mr. Big had instructed. The stump by the outhouse was still smoking. Throttle wrinkled her nose.

"This place stinks."

Brake sniffed and shrugged. It smelled all right to him. Suddenly, Throttle stopped and looked out across the paddock.

TRUCKDOGS

NAME: Norman J. Snitt (Alias: MR. BIG)
BREED/MAKE: Chihuahua/BMW Isetta
COLOR: Light blue/gray
IDENTIFYING MARKS: Permanent snarl, wonky eyes
TEMPERAMENT: Horrid

WARNING
DANGEROUS DOG
DO NOT APPROACH
CALL AUTHORITIES ON SIGHTING
1800BADDOG

FILE INFO:
Leader of RottWheeler Gang. Numerous convictions for theft. Wanted for questioning in regard to recent fuel scams in Combustion City and neighboring towns. Seriously unpleasant character. No redeeming feature whatsoever. Probable small-dog inferiority syndrome.

SPECIFICATIONS:
Engine: 1-cylinder, 298cc
Power Output: 13hp
Fuel Requirements: Yours
Maintenance: On demand

She tapped Brake with the spanner.

"Bingo."

In the middle distance lay the rusty old tanker hulk that Sparky had stood on to watch the Mongrels sheep-leaping. The flock of TruckSheep was grazing nearby. Throttle noticed one with a set of large curved horns. She frowned.

"Hmmm. We'll have to deal with that big one first. Shouldn't be a problem . . ."

●

Three minutes later, Throttle and Brake were flying through the air. They came down in the dam with two huge splashes. The TruckRam snorted in satisfaction as they dragged themselves out on the far side.

Throttle shook herself dry, her suspension squeaking as she wriggled her hindquarters.

"Okay," she said through clenched teeth. "Plan B."

Brake shook his head to get the water out of his wing mirrors and squirted a stream of muddy water from his grill. A TruckYabby popped out and clamped onto Throttle's snout.

"Yaaaah!"

●

Not long after, the TruckRam was back grazing with the TruckSheep when Brake's head appeared from behind a hedge in the next paddock. He went cross-eyed and poked out his tongue. The TruckRam snorted and charged toward him, head down. Suddenly a gate swung shut in front of it. The TruckRam slammed into the gate, entangling its horns in the steel bars of the gate. It struggled furiously to free itself but was caught fast.

Throttle emerged from her hiding place and looked at the TruckRam.

"That should do it. Stupid sheep. Let's get to work."

They soon had the tanker fastened to Brake's tow bar and were heading back. The big truck sweated and puffed as he hauled the heavy load out onto the road.

"Doing a great job there, Brake," said Throttle.

Brake just grunted.

The TruckRam was still struggling to disentangle itself from the gate. After they had gone it had one more go at freeing itself, and suddenly the whole gate came off its hinges. The TruckRam tugged again, twisting from side to side, and the lock sheared off, leaving the beast free but with the gate still firmly attached to its head. It looked around in surprise, as if wondering what to do next, then trotted out onto the road and headed off.

❽

Inside the fuel shed, Mayor Plugg and the Dogsbodys were in a huddle, talking urgently.

"So we're all agreed then," Mrs. Plugg was saying. "We can't just sit here and wait any longer." She looked around. "How're you doing, Mr. Howell?"

Farmer Howell was in the corner, looking as if he was about to explode. He gave a little shake of his head.

"Just hold on as long as you can," said the mayor.

"What are we going to do?" asked a worried Mrs. Dogsbody.

Mayor Plugg held up the screwdriver that she had scooped up in the workshop.

"I'm going to try a little trick my son showed me."

🐾

A little later, as the RottWheeler guards snored, one on each side of the fuel shed, there was a slight bump, a pause, and the shed slowly began to rise up into the air. As it lifted up off its foundations, Mayor Plugg's nose stuck out.

"They're asleep," she whispered. "All right, Mrs. Dogsbody, lift . . ."

The fuel shed rose up into the air, teetering a little as Mrs. Dogsbody's scissor-lift reached its full height. Mayor Plugg, Farmer Howell and Mr. Dogsbody crept out from under it. Farmer Howell hurried off.

"At least a hundred yards if you can, please, Mr. Howell," Mayor Plugg called after him in a whisper.

Mr. Dogsbody turned back to the shed and reached out with his mobile-crane hook, holding it while Mrs. Dogsbody lowered her scissor-lift and joined them outside. Then, carefully, he placed the shed back on its foundations just as a muffled explosion came from the direction of Farmer Howell. It had been a close thing. The four escapees hurriedly crept away.

The RottWheelers stirred, woke and looked around at the shed. They saw that the door was still bolted. All was well.

Mr. Big rolled up.

"What was that bang?"

The RottWheelers shrugged. Mr. Big looked at the fuel shed suspiciously. Had it moved a bit to the left?

"Check the shed."

But just then Throttle arrived. "We found it, Boss—the perfect thing! One fuel tanker as requested."

Behind her came Brake, laboring under the weight of the tanker hulk. He was exhausted.

Mr. Big practically skipped with delight. "Excellent! Let us begin!"

He headed off toward the petrol station, Throttle and Brake following.

"It's good to see the boss so happy," remarked Throttle.

Brake just grunted.

After they had gone, the silhouette of a TruckRam with a gate stuck on top of its head trotted past in the distance, framed against the early morning sky.

☻

Bullworth, Zoe, Prudence and Digger were sitting around a very smoky campfire surrounded by piles of junk. Up above in the desert it was already fully light and beginning to grow hot but the valley was in shadow and still wreathed in the chill of the night.

Digger threw another tire onto the fire. Prudence coughed as the smoke billowed out.

"Well, that's the last of Cousin Edward," said Digger. "He always was a heavy smoker."

"Ha, ha," said Prudence.

Zoe looked around the junk piles. "Where do you reckon Rex and Herc have got to? They've been gone ages."

Just then, they heard a scrabbling sound above them. A stealthy figure was silhouetted against the light on the ridge above them. It began to make its way down the steep cliff.

"It's a DesertDog!" said Zoe in a frightened whisper. Prudence's hair stood up all the way along her back. Bullworth backed away, eyes bulging. The figure was halfway down the slope when it stumbled and fell, sprawling in a heap at the foot of the stunned TruckDogs.

"Oof!" said Sparky.

"Sparky! What are you doing here?" said Digger.

"And why were you trying to scare us?" added Zoe indignantly.

"I wasn't. Sorry. Ow!" He got up painfully. "That hurt."

"I'm not surprised. That was quite an entrance," said

Prudence. "So, what brings you all the way out here, may I ask?"

"It's Mum—they've got her prisoner—and they're stealing all the fuel—and I got away—and I was looking for Rex—and—"

"Whoa there, slow down. Who's got your Mum prisoner?"

"Mr. Big."

"Mr. Who?"

"No, Mr. Big. He's a thief. And he's stealing the town's fuel, and Mum has been locked up, and Farmer Howell, too. And—"

Suddenly a large rock came whistling out of the darkness. It thudded into the side of the cliff. A moment later a second rock slammed into Bullworth, breaking into several pieces and knocking the big dozer right over onto his roof.

"Yeeeow!" cried Bullworth.

The others looked around in alarm.

"Sorry, Bullworth!" came Hercules's voice. "But I told you before that if I meant to hit you, you'd be on your roof!"

The others gawked as Hercules rolled into sight. Two long iron beams ran along either side of his body, attached to his tray by large pivots. A pair of big metal baskets had been bolted onto the ends. The beams were linked to two hydraulic pistons which were in turn hooked up to a large compressor.

"Dual air-powered catapults," he explained in answer to their baffled expressions.

He jiggled his rear suspension, flipping a couple of rocks out of his tray, one into each basket, then took aim at a tall crane that was sticking up out of the junk piles and fired. The first rock hit the crane, spinning it around and sending the dangling hook swinging on its cable. The second rock hit the hook which wrapped itself tightly around the crane. Then the whole thing collapsed.

The onlookers whistled appreciatively.

"Hey, could someone help me up?" called Bullworth. He wiggled his caterpillar tracks helplessly, like a turtle on its back, but the others were too engrossed in Hercules's new toy.

Prudence examined the contraption. "Where'd you find this thing anyway?"

"Rex made it."

"Rex built this?" said Prudence.

"Awesome!" exclaimed Digger. "Why?"

Rex chugged up behind Hercules. He looked at Sparky. "It seems the answer to that has just arrived."

"Rex!" cried Sparky joyously.

"Things beginning to heat up back in town, eh?"

Sparky nodded.

Behind them, Bullworth was still struggling. "Hey, guys— help me up!"

"What's going on?" asked Hercules, noticing Sparky for the first time. "What are you doing here?"

Sparky told his story again, more slowly this time. When he finished they sat for a moment in silence.

Then Rex spoke. "All right, listen to me, all of you. Here

comes the speech. In every machine there are many parts, each with its own purpose. Even the smallest cog in the biggest machine has a vital job to do. It is part of the whole. Without it the machine does not work as it should. You youngsters have energy to burn. It's what got you in trouble back in Hubcap. It's also your greatest strength. Well, now the time has come to put all that young energy to good use. Your home is in peril. And you have a job to do."

Digger looked puzzled. "Maybe I'm missing something but didn't those old fleabags just run us out of town?"

"We're a public nuisance," said Bullworth.

"Rude, impudent vandals, as I recall," said Prudence.

Sparky looked at Rex in despair. But Rex's eyes were unreadable. He remained silent.

"They ran us out of town all right," said Hercules. "They're narrow-minded, selfish, intolerant, gutless—and old." He paused. "Which is why they need us. Hubcap is our town too. They may be living in the past—but we are the future!"

"Yay!" cried Zoe.

"Woo hoo!" hooted Digger.

Rex smiled.

"Yeah, great," said Bullworth. "And I'm still upside down. Come on, guys!"

Hercules turned to Sparky. "How much time do we have?"

"Not much. They're going to take all the fuel—every drop, they said—then blow up the fuel shed. We've got to save

TRUCKDOGS

Reg No.
0863

NAME: THROTTLE

BREED/MAKE: Greyhound/Drag Car

COLOR: Red with broad yellow stripe

IDENTIFYING MARKS: Large mole on right hand front panel, fake ruby-studded collar

TEMPERAMENT: Arrogant, vicious and immoral (but otherwise she's really delightful).

FILE INFO:

Member of RottWheeler Gang. Second in command to Mr. Big (file 00228309). Wanted for questioning in regard to recent fuel scams in Combustion City and neighboring towns. Numerous convictions for speeding.

SPECIFICATIONS:

Engine: Single rear-mount Aerospace ramjet

Power Output: Enormous

Fuel Requirements: Designed for high-grade aviation fuel but modified to run on premium unleaded instead

Maintenance: General overhaul every Wednesday afternoon

Mum!"

"All the fuel?" said Rex. "They'll have to find something to carry it in . . . and pumping it out will take time . . ." He thought for a moment. "We've got maybe twenty-four hours. Come on, we have to prepare ourselves."

"Does that mean I get a catapult, too?" asked Digger hopefully.

"No. The catapult is for Hercules. It is an extension of his natural strengths. I made it for him alone."

"So what do we get?" asked Prudence.

"Well," said Rex, "let's see what you're good at."

They headed off, leaving Bullworth still upside down.

The Pack gathered around Rex in an open space between the junk piles.

"We'll start with rocks," said Rex. Digger whooped enthusiastically and bounded off to find some big ones.

Zoe found a small boulder nearby but try as she might she couldn't flip it up at all. The rough edges of the rock were giving her blisters on her tire walls. Prudence had no more success, though she eventually managed to roll a small round one down a slope with her snout, hitting a still-upside-down Bullworth on the nose.

"Sorry, Bullworth. What are you doing lying down on the job?"

"Yeah, c'mon, Bullyboy. We've got work to do," added Hercules.

"Very funny."

Sparky was about to have a go at the rock when they heard Digger's voice. "Watch this!" he called, struggling up to them with a huge boulder loaded into his back hoe. "Hold still, Bullworth."

"Don't you dare!"

But before Digger could fire, he over-balanced backward and found himself staring skyward with his front wheels in the air.

With a huge effort Bullworth at last managed to roll himself right-way up.

"Right, it's payback time!" He scooped up Prudence's rock in his mouth, crunched it into gravel and sprayed it out like a scatter gun.

"Yeow!" cried Digger, scrambling back to his wheels. The others squealed and ran for cover. Bullworth charged off after them.

After the others had gone, Sparky tried to move Digger's boulder with his snout.

Not a chance.

Digger was determined to get the rock-throwing right. After all, he figured, he already had a built-in catapult in his back hoe. Zoe watched with amusement as he shunted another huge boulder into his hoe and struggled to lift it.

"C'mon, Digger, put some effort into it."

Digger gritted his teeth and strained mightily. Suddenly the whole back-hoe arm came off, sending him tumbling forward.

"Ouch—that must have hurt," winced Zoe. "Hey, Herc, can you come here a moment? Digger seems to have been rendered armless."

In response to the pathetic joke, Digger shoved her into the side of a nearby water tank. Dirty water sloshed out all over her just as Hercules came up.

"Yeeeee! I *hate* that!" she cried. "I just *hate* it!"

Hercules laughed. Zoe glared at him. Then she looked up at the tank with a cunning smile.

Rex was busy, meanwhile, showing Bullworth how to move large objects by a combination of leverage, body placement and sheer force of will. Thin and weedy though he was, the old tractor put his wheel to a huge old pumping engine and shifted it backward a good two yards.

"Remember, you have to *want* to move it. Decide you are going to do it—then do it."

Bullworth nodded, took a couple of deep breaths and put his head down. He strained until he was blue in the face and his teeth hurt. The pumping engine didn't budge an inch.

"Ow. My eef urt," said Bullworth, feeling around his mouth.

"Hmmm" said Rex. "Looks like some dental work is in order. I'll get back to you."

Zoe trundled by with a length of garden hose and some baling wire between her teeth. She carried it to the water tank and added it to her stash, which already included a compressor and a big brass nozzle from an old fire engine. Her plan was coming together.

Later in the day, Hercules was practicing with his catapult when suddenly a stream of freezing water hit him in the face.

"Bleargh! Hey, what the . . ." He spun round to find Zoe looking innocently at the sky, whistling. Mounted on her roof was the water tank and compressor. A length of garden hose ran from her mixer, which was full of cold water, to the compressor. Another length was looped around a garden rake at the end of which was tied the brass fire-engine nozzle.

He frowned at her sternly. "Now, listen here . . ."

But she just pointed the nozzle at him and fired another burst of water, then fled, laughing, with the big ore truck in hot pursuit.

On the other side of the junkyard Rex stood back and admired his handiwork. He had fitted Bullworth with a reinforced dozer front bucket made from the old plow and a huge truck gearbox. He adjusted it, checking that the circular plow blades spun freely, and pronounced it finished. It looked very fearsome indeed.

"All right, now you have no excuse. You can do it—so do it!"

Bullworth lowered his head, lined himself up with the huge pumping engine and pushed. He shunted it right across the junkyard, and crunched into the cliffs on the far side. An avalanche of rocks rained down, burying him up to his roof. His exhaust stack, which was poking up out of the rocks, belched smoke as he revved his engine. He engaged his gearbox, spun the plowshares like a massive blender, and the rock pile was rapidly ground down into gravel. Bullworth emerged, one happy and proud dozer.

"I'm unstoppable!" he cried.

"Yes," laughed Rex. "I believe you are."

Darkness fell and still the TruckDogs worked. Rex moved between them offering advice and encouragement.

Prudence was searching through the junk looking for inspiration when she came across a firebox belonging to an old traction engine. She filled it with coals from the camp fire and blew through it from behind. A cloud of black smoke erupted from it, making Digger cough and choke just as he was trying yet again to get a rock into the air.

The rock came down on his cab, squashing it flat.

Digger held his breath and blew through his gaskets, popping his cab back into shape. He found Rex watching and shaking his head. "I think we're barking up the wrong tree here, Digger. A rock-thrower you most definitely are not. Can you dig?"

"Can I dig? Hey, I'm a labrador!"

Rex nodded toward an enormous auger lying amidst the junk—a giant drill bit used to dig post holes. "You, my friend, are going to dig like no other labrador in history!"

Dawn was not far off as Rex finished attaching the auger to Digger's back hoe, tightening the bolts with his teeth.

"You could do with a spanner," remarked Digger.

"I've got a spanner," replied Rex. He paused. "I just don't have it with me right now."

The auger was linked to Digger's main drive shaft with a series of belts and pulleys. Digger held it poised over his head like a scorpion's tail.

"This is great!" he said excitedly. "I've gotta dig something!"

He lifted the auger high above his head and quickly gouged a deep hole in the cliff face. Rex nodded, satisfied. Digger pointed the drill downward and within moments had dug a six-foot-deep hole in the rocky ground.

"Awesome!" He put the drill into reverse and revved, but the bit jammed, spinning him around in circles instead. Rex shook his head—there was more work to do yet.

Sparky had been watching. Digging holes was surely something all TruckDogs could do. He waited until they had gone off to make some improvements to the auger, then set to work. But when Rex and Digger passed by a little later, the hole he had made was only a tenth of Digger's effort and he was exhausted.

Digger looked rather smugly at Sparky's hole in the dirt but before he could comment, there was a deafening roar from behind him. Digger leapt in fright and spun around to find himself enveloped in a huge cloud of acrid smoke. He coughed and gasped. A vast armor-plated dragon with horns and a visor like a knight's helmet appeared out of the cloud, snorting and smoking. The long body was lined with steel plates, like scales topped with jagged points all the way down the spine. The firebox, slung in front of the grill, was filled with coals and smoldering tires.

The dragon raised its visor. "So, what do you think?"

Digger circled Prudence's outfit and nodded appreciatively. "Smokin'!"

The two went off together to plan tactics, leaving a rather forlorn-looking Sparky behind.

"Why so glum?" asked Rex. "Seems you've lost all your bounce."

"It's nothing." Sparky scuffed his wheels in the dust. "It's just that I'm not really good at anything."

Rex considered this for a moment, then seemed to come to a decision. "Yep, that's definitely the problem. You've lost your bounce. Come with me."

He led Sparky to another part of the junkyard, beyond the steel girders and wrecked vehicles.

"I bet we can find your bounce somewhere here."

Sparky gazed up at a mountain of coiled springs, shock absorbers and suspension struts of every size and shape. His tail began to wag.

The sun was rising over the rim of the world, casting a golden glow over the desert, when at last the Mongrel Pack were all gathered together in their armor—proud Hercules with his catapults, Bullworth with his plow blades, Zoe with her water cannon, Digger with his auger and Prudence in her dragon suit.

"Where's Sparky?" asked Digger.

"Here!" cried Sparky, bounding in. He was wearing a safety helmet with a flashing light and a new power-spring suspension system featuring four massive hydraulic shock absorbers.

"Watch this!" He crouched down, then leapt straight up—eighteen feet clear off the ground.

"Whoa!" he cried as he struggled to maintain control, bouncing several times before landing dangerously close to Bullworth's new rotor blades.

"Impressive ground clearance," said Digger.

"Matched by enviable ride and handling," said Prudence.

"And ready for anything!" cried Sparky.

Suddenly a terrible howling broke out. They looked around in alarm as twenty or more DesertDogs swarmed down the slopes above them and over the piles of junk. The one-eyed leader snarled in puzzlement at the TruckDogs' strange outfits. But then he barked an order and the DesertDogs attacked.

The Mongrel Pack's new accessories gave them a definite advantage over their attackers. The DesertDogs yelped and howled as they fended off hurtling boulders, jets of water,

TRUCK DOGS

File No: 00228311

NAME: BRAKE

BREED/MAKE: Mastiff/Monster Truck

COLOR: Blue

IDENTIFYING MARKS: Numerous self-inflicted tattoos and piercings

TEMPERAMENT: Thick as a ten-ton-truck tire

FILE INFO:
Senior member of RottWheeler Gang (chief navigator).
Wanted in connection with 376 outstanding parking tickets.

SPECIFICATIONS:
Engine: Twin V12 turbos
Power Output: 500kw at 5000rpm
Fuel Requirements: 2 1/2 gallons per 300 feet
Maintenance: Duh?

spinning plowshares, razor-sharp augers and clouds of blinding smoke. But they were ferocious fighters and greater in number. They swarmed over the junk toward their foes.

Rex was especially targeted. Sparky saw him surrounded by ten or more DesertDogs. He set his new suspension to maximum clearance and sprang to his aid, but couldn't control the new springs and went bouncing wildly all over the place. On a couple of bounces he connected with a DesertDog, but just as often landed on one of his fellow TruckDogs (with a cry of "Sorry!"). At one point he scored a direct hit on the one-eyed leader, coming down hard on his tailpipe. The DesertDog spun around yelping in pain and fury but couldn't work out where the attack had come from as Sparky had already bounced off again over the junk piles.

The battle raged back and forth, but at last the DesertDogs were beaten. They retreated, howling, scrabbling back up the cliffs into the night. The Mongrel Pack cheered in victory.

Hercules flexed his catapults. "Hey, Rex, these things are not bad—not bad at all!" He looked around. "Rex?"

The old tractor was nowhere in sight.

"Rex! Where are you?" called Sparky. A familiar hubcap lay in the dirt. A little farther on was Rex's funnel. Sparky was filled with a sudden dread.

They searched urgently, calling out Rex's name, until at last they found him lying amongst the junk. His old body blended in with the battered old machinery so well he was almost invisible. Around him lay the wrecks of several DesertDogs. He was badly damaged, a deep rent in one wheel arch, a gaping hole at his funnel outlet. The left rear wheel had been ripped off at the axle and was nowhere in sight. Engine oil seeped from a puncture in his sump.

The Mongrels gathered around him anxiously.

"Rex! Say something," cried Sparky. "Anything!"

"Woof," said Rex weakly.

"Okay, that'll do," said Prudence. "At least he's alive."

Hercules frowned. "We need to get him to a mechanic. Come on, guys. Help me lift him."

But Rex shook his head. "There's no time. You have to get back to Hubcap. Besides," he managed a smile, lifting himself with some effort up on one axle, "I'm a mechanic. It'll just take me . . . a little time . . . to fix myself up."

"We can't just leave you here," protested Sparky. "What if the DesertDogs come back?"

"I doubt they will. But if they do I'll be ready for them." He looked at the junk lying around him. "I've plenty of good material to work with."

Sparky hesitated, unwilling to leave his friend, but Hercules nodded. "Rex is right. We have to go. Hubcap needs us." He turned to Sparky. "And we need you with us, partner."

Sparky looked at Hercules, then the other TruckDogs. "You mean . . . I'm a member of the Mongrel Pack?"

"Sure," smiled Prudence. "Unless you'd rather join the Cosmic Tractors?"

Sparky beamed. "Oh, boy! I always wanted to be one of you guys!" He looked back at Rex in concern.

"I'm all right," said the old tractor reassuringly. "Your town needs you. Go."

The Mongrels looked at each other, a team, bonded by their past, their present and their future. Then they revved their engines, crunched themselves into gear and roared off into the sunrise.

BITE THREE

eanwhile, back in Hubcap, things were looking grim. Up at the garage the fuel-pumping operation was well underway. One of the Rott-Wheelers monitored the flow at a valve connected to the underground fuel-storage tank. Another held the hose steady, pouring the fuel into the rusty old tanker. Brake was still attached to the tanker. He was sweating heavily.

Throttle was overseeing operations, practicing spinning the big silver spanner with one wheel. She fumbled and it fell to the ground.

"Stupid spanner—out of balance," she muttered.

The townsfolk were all staying safely indoors, but on the far side of the workshop, Mayor Plugg, Farmer Howell and the Dogsbodys were watching, their hoods poking out from between a row of low shrubs. An engine approaching from farther up the street made them pull back quickly.

It was Mr. Big.

The little chihuahua rolled up and surveyed the scene,

nodding in satisfaction. At that moment there was a gurgling sound and the RottWheeler monitoring the valve called out that the tank was empty. The other RottWheeler held the hose up, dripping.

Throttle turned to Mr. Big. "That's it, Boss."

Watching from their hiding place, Mayor Plugg whispered hopefully to the others. "They don't know about tank two!"

Out on the forecourt, Mr. Big turned to Mr. Barker, who was hovering nearby. "Open up tank two."

Mr. Barker gulped. "Er, we only have one tank," he said, unconvincingly.

"Listen, Delivery Boy, I do a lot of this kind of thing. I know you have a second tank. Now open it up or we'll drain you dry as well."

Mr. Barker pushed aside an engine-oil display rack, revealing the access hatch to the town's emergency fuel-storage tank.

"I'll kill him," hissed Mrs. Dogsbody.

"Not if I get to him first," said Farmer Howell.

"Without fuel this town is as good as dead," said Mayor Plugg. "We have to make a stand. Let's go and spread the word." She and the others headed off.

"That's better," said Mr. Big as the two RottWheelers slid the access hatch off. He turned and snarled at Mr. Barker. "Now get out of my sight."

Mr. Barker skulked off. The RottWheelers connected the

TRUCKDOGS

NAME: CLUTCH

BREED/MAKE: Bull Terrier/Heavy Haulage Hybrid
COLOR: Albino
IDENTIFYING MARKS: Leather restraining muzzle, wild red eyes
TEMPERAMENT: Totally insane

WARNING
DO NOT APPROACH
CALL AUTHORITIES ON SIGHTING
1800BADDOG

FILE INFO:
Mr. Big's "pet." Used for tracking work and hunter/killer missions. Very dangerous.

SPECIFICATIONS:
Engine: Marine diesel/steam-engine composite
Power Output: 30 knots into the breeze
Fuel Requirements: Diesel and coal in equal parts
Maintenance: None to date

hose to the second tank and started pumping again. The tanker creaked under the weight.

"Heavy. Getting . . . heavy," groaned Brake.

"Don't be such a wuss," said Throttle, then to the RottWheelers, "Check the level."

The tanker was three-quarters full. Throttle looked questioningly at Mr. Big.

"I want all of it," he growled. "Every last drop. Keep filling."

"You got it, Boss." Throttle went to spin the spanner again but thought better of it.

Mayor Plugg, Farmer Howell and the Dogsbodys moved quietly and quickly from house to house, keeping out of sight, taking the backstreets, spreading the word amongst the townsfolk.

Farmer Howell found Mr. Scratchly outside his shop.

"We're going to stand and fight," he said conspiratorially. "Meet at the statue in one hour."

"Eh? What's that?"

Farmer Howell spoke a little louder. "We're going to make a stand. The statue. One hour."

Mr. Barker wandered by on the other side of the street. He stopped and watched.

"Spweak up, will you?" Mr. Scratchly fiddled with his hearing aid. "Stop mumbwing!"

"I said meet at the statue, you deaf coot!" shouted Farmer

Howell. "They're stealing all our fuel! We've got to stop them!"

"All wight, there's no need to showt," said Mr. Scratchly crossly and went back into his shop. Farmer Howell rolled his eyes and motored off. Across the street, Mr. Barker thought a moment, then, with a shifty look, turned and headed back towards the petrol station.

A moment later the TruckRam trotted by, the gate still firmly entangled in its horns.

The townsfolk gathered at the remains of the statue in the Hubcap Memorial Park. Mayor Plugg stood by the big tree flanked by Farmer Howell and Mr. and Mrs. Dogsbody and addressed the crowd.

"All right, everyone. If I can have your attention please. It's come down to this: either we make a stand or we lose our fuel—and if we lose our fuel, our town cannot survive. We have no option. We have to fight."

A murmur ran through the crowd.

Edna Fleasome tut-tutted. "Fight? For ourselves? We should have police or an army or something to fight for us. Really, this town is going to the dogs."

"Going to the dogs," echoed Ida.

"It's going to its grave if we don't do something," said Mrs. Dogsbody sharply. "Stop whining."

"Well!" said Edna in her most affronted voice.

"Well!" said Ida.

"And stop repeating everything she says! Why don't you think for yourself?"

Edna and Ida were most indignant. But they shut up.

"Listen, everyone, please," said Mayor Plugg. "We must work together. United we stand—"

"And divided you fall," came Mr. Big's voice.

Everyone spun around. To their horror they found the park surrounded by a snarling ring of RottWheelers. Mr. Big rolled forward.

"Was that what you were going to say, Mayor Plugg? Because divided you most certainly are."

Mayor Plugg looked past Mr. Big and saw Mr. Barker standing behind him.

"Thank you, Mr. Barker, for your most useful information," said Mr. Big. "Paid for in full with one tank of premium unleaded, as agreed, and a year's supply of brake fluid. I trust you are satisfied?"

Mr. Barker did not reply.

Mayor Plugg looked at him and shook her head. "Why, Mr. Barker?"

Mr. Barker's eye twitched. He answered angrily, defensively. "We all need fuel, you know. This town is finished without it." He jerked his head toward the desert. "It's a long way to the next pump."

Mrs. Plugg nodded slowly. "It is indeed, Mr. Barker. It is indeed." Her voice became hard. "Drive safely, won't you?"

The townsfolk glared at Mr. Barker in silence. He looked around, then averted his eyes and drove off. Mr. Big returned his attention to Mayor Plugg.

"Now, where were we? Oh, yes . . ." He paused. "This is a little embarrassing, actually. I would normally ask Clutch to tear you to pieces at this point, but he has been unavoidably delayed—doing exactly that to your son, Sparky, I believe."

He paused for a reaction from Mrs. Plugg but her face remained fixed, her expression unreadable. Mr. Big continued with a shrug. "So anyway, I have asked the rest of the gang to fill in for Clutch. So now we're going to tear the whole town apart!"

The RottWheelers bared their teeth and began to move in on their prey. Mayor Plugg, Farmer Howell and the Dogsbodys prepared themselves.

"Stay calm," called Mayor Plugg to the frightened townsfolk. "Don't run or they will chase you."

Suddenly the noise of other engines was heard over the sound of the RottWheelers, a huge roaring that seemed to be everywhere, echoing off the buildings, filling the air. Mr. Big looked around in puzzlement, unable to work out where it was coming from.

Then suddenly it stopped.

Into the silence came a voice, speaking through a megaphone.

"Attention, Mr. Big and accomplices. You are surrounded. Switch your engines off, put your gearboxes in neutral and turn your wheels to the curb."

Mr. Big whirled around but could not find the source of the voice.

It spoke again, this time without the megaphone. "Up here, shorty."

Mr. Big looked up to find Sparky standing atop the Town Hall.

"You!"

"Sparky! You're alive!" cried Mayor Plugg.

"Hi, Mum." He motioned toward Mr. Big. "That little yap dog down there causing a problem?"

Mayor Plugg looked at Mr. Big and his thugs. "Well, kind of . . ."

"Don't worry. We've got everything under control." He raised the megaphone again and addressed the RottWheelers. "You have made a big mistake taking on this town. Drive away now and no one gets hurt."

Throttle sneered. "Hah! Says you and what army?"

"This one," came a voice. There was a mighty revving of an engine. Hercules drove into view and everyone looked with amazement at his spectacular refit.

Throttle scoffed. "That's no army. It's just a kid with a catapult."

Hercules's twin compressors burst into life, catapulting a pair of enormous boulders into the air. They came crashing down, one just in front of Throttle's nose, one just behind her tailpipe. She was clearly rattled but managed another sneer.

"Missed."

"If I'd meant to hit . . . " began Hercules.

". . . you'd be on your roof," finished Bullworth, rumbling into view from the opposite direction. The crowd gasped at the sight of his spectacular plowshare dozer blade.

"What is this?" demanded Mr. Big. "A freak show? Where's the next clown going to pop out from?"

As if in answer, a deep rumbling was heard. The ground shook like an earthquake and a huge drill burst up directly under one of the RottWheelers, sending dirt flying everywhere. The unfortunate vehicle squealed in surprise. When the townsfolk looked again, a dirt-encrusted monster was clambering out of a gaping hole in the ground. Even Mr. Big's eyes bulged. The creature shook itself off, revealing itself to be Digger. He nodded to the watching crowd.

· "G'day, folks. How's it going?"

"This is ridiculous," snapped Mr. Big. "Who are you? Where did you come from?"

Sparky replied from the rooftop. "Around here actually. We're just little cogs in a big machine. But today we plan to make a difference."

Prudence appeared in her armor. Mr. Big rolled his eyes. "Oh, great. And what are you supposed to be?"

"Guess."

Prudence roared through her firebox, singeing Mr. Big's whiskers to stubble and covering him in a thick coat of smoke and ash. He blinked stupidly and coughed out a puff of ash.

"A dragon?" he said weakly. He sneezed violently. An instant later a huge burst of water hit him in the face.

"Ergch!"

Zoe rolled up with her water cannon dripping. "Getting a little hot under the collar? There you go, little fella. Bath time."

Mr. Big shook himself, looking very much like a drowned TruckRat. The RottWheelers stood looking at him, grills gaping.

"Don't just stand there gawking, you idiots," Mr. Big screeched. "Get them!"

"Attack!" yelled Throttle, who was still pinned by the two boulders. As if released from a trance, the RottWheelers surged forward and the battle was joined.

The Mongrel Pack was ready and waiting. Zoe turned as a RottWheeler charged at her, snarling. He got her water cannon full in the face and backed off, choking and gagging. Another RottWheeler launched himself at Digger's flank. Digger spun his back hoe around and drilled into the RottWheeler's windscreen, scratching across it with an ear-splitting skritchchchch. The RottWheeler bolted, squealing.

Bullworth scooped up a rock in his huge jaws, chomped it into gravel and, with his plowshare blades spinning, pumped it out. The stones hit the spinning plowshares as he adjusted the blade angle, sending stinging shrapnel ricocheting this way and that. The RottWheelers yelped and ducked.

Sparky leapt from the Town Hall roof, howling like a DesertDog. "Howoowooowooooo!"

He landed full on a RottWheeler, crushing the cab flat, and bounced off again, high into the air, out of control. "Whoaaaa!"

Throttle, meanwhile, was struggling to extricate herself from between the boulders, but she was stuck fast. She smashed at them with Rex's spanner, with no result except to mark the otherwise pristine tool.

Mayor Plugg rallied the townsfolk, who had been watching openmouthed. "Come on, everyone! This is our town. Let's fight for it!"

The townsfolk erupted in a battle cry, howling and revving, and surged forward to join the Mongrel Pack. Even Edna and Ida joined in.

"Let's bag ourselves some RottWheeler," cried Ida. Edna looked at her sister in shock.

At that moment a huge, slavering RottWheeler bore down on them. It snapped at Edna viciously. She swung the handbag that hung on her wing mirror and whacked the TruckDog sharply on the nose.

"How dare you, you disgusting creature," she scolded. "What would your mother say? You are a disgrace! Now, get out of my sight!"

TRUCK**DOGS**

NAME: FARMER HOWELL
BREED/MAKE: Red Heeler/Ford 50 Pickup
COLOR: Burgundy—or is it claret?
IDENTIFYING MARKS: More of a smell really
TEMPERAMENT: Well-ventilated

FILE INFO:
Age: No one's willing to ask.
Address: Up at the farm, but he
don't want no visitors, you hear?

SPECIFICATIONS:
Engine: 8-cylinder, 5.0 liter
Fuel Requirements: Continuous
Maintenance: Whenever. Whatever.

COMMENTS
Crusty old fart but decent enough deep, deep down

(Note also: Poultry/Seed Planter TruckChook)

The RottWheeler backed off, utterly intimidated, as another gang member passed by.

"She's horrible!" he said, glancing at Edna, tears welling. "She says the most awful things!"

Edna turned to Ida triumphantly. "There. That'll teach him."

"You said it, sis! Woo hoo!"

Edna stared at her. Ida shrugged.

Across the park, Mr. Scratchly had been pinned against a tree by another RottWheeler. Mr. Dogsbody came up behind the thug, lifted him bodily off the ground with his crane and hooked him to a branch by his collar.

"Stay," he said sternly.

Mrs. Dogsbody, meanwhile, found herself confronted by a particularly large and ugly brute. She backed away until she was hard up against the side of the Town Hall. The RottWheeler grinned nastily. She continued to back up the wall until she was vertical, facing the ground, then suddenly shot out her scissor lift like an extendable boxing glove. *Boof!* The RottWheeler was sent reeling.

Mr. Big looked around at the confusion. Throttle was still struggling between the boulders.

"Hey, Boss!" she called. "Help me."

But the fighting was getting too hot for Mr. Big. Ignoring her, he called to some nearby RottWheelers.

"You two, come with me back to the petrol station. Everyone else, help hold them off. We'll, er . . . wait for you down the road."

He took off in a hurry. Throttle saw him go. With a furious effort she struggled up and clambered over the front boulder. She had almost made it when there was a cry of "Whoaaaa!" from above and Sparky landed right in front of her, bouncing off again with another cry. Throttle fell backward onto her roof and found herself stuck upside down between the boulders. She wriggled her wheels in fury.

Bullworth rolled up to her. "Hey, I know what it's like," he commiserated. "You've just got to relax. Think like a turtle."

"What? Shut up, you overgrown Tonka toy!"

Bullworth shrugged, put his dozer blade to the boulders and pushed them even more tightly together.

"Eeech! You're squashing me!"

"It's what I'm good at."

○

Mr. Big and the two RottWheelers returned to the petrol station. Brake was there, waiting, still attached to the tanker. "What's happening, Boss?"

"Where were you when we needed you, you big oaf?" panted Mr. Big.

Brake struggled under the weight. "Too heavy. Can't . . . move."

"Is all the fuel on board?"

Brake managed to nod.

Mr. Big turned to the RottWheelers. "Okay, get him moving—give him a push."

The RottWheelers drove up to the back of the tanker and pushed, but he wouldn't budge. Just then, Throttle arrived, having at last managed to free herself. She looked a mess, her paintwork scratched and dented, her rear wheels wobbling on their axle. Mr. Big glanced at her, then back at the struggling RottWheelers.

"Come on! Push!"

"No really, I'm fine," said Throttle sarcastically. "Thanks for asking."

"Yeah, whatever. I'm getting out of here."

"What happened to Clutch?"

"Who knows? Damn dog has disappeared, useless mutt. Never liked him anyway."

"No," said Throttle with emphasis, looking behind Mr. Big's shoulder. "I mean, *what happened to Clutch?*"

Mr. Big turned to find Clutch standing there, bruised and battered, his collar hanging half off, torn and tattered. The huge beast looked at Mr. Big, puzzled, hurt. And for the first time he spoke.

"Master—no—like—Clutch?"

"Oh, there you are," said Mr. Big. Then he looked around and frowned. "No puppy again? I told you not to come back without him."

He tapped his antenna but, rather than cringing, Clutch started to move forward, his red albino eyes fixed on Mr. Big.

"Master no like Clutch. Cruel master. Bad master!"

"Now, now. That's not what I meant. I meant . . . er . . . Throttle, what did I mean?"

Throttle shrugged. "Don't ask me."

Mr. Big fumbled for a packet of Doggy Bites but his glove box was empty. He backed away, holding his antenna out in front of him. He stumbled on a tree root, regained his balance and began to slash wildly as Clutch bore down on him.

"Get away from me, you monster!"

Clutch caught the antenna in his mouth, bit off the end and chomped it up. Mr. Big wet his wheels, turned and fled. Clutch sprang after him with a roar.

"Yipe! Yipe! Yipe! Yipe!" squealed Mr. Big.

One of the RottWheelers standing by the tanker looked at Mr. Big, then at Throttle. "Should we, like, save him or something?"

Throttle looked at Brake, "What do you reckon, Brake?"

Brake grunted. It sounded like no.

The battle between the townsfolk and the rest of the RottWheelers was getting closer. A flying RottWheeler landed at Throttle's wheels with a thud.

Throttle looked at the senseless vehicle in alarm. "Okay. I say we save the fuel and get out of here. Brake, *get moving!*"

Brake strained mightily. "Aaaaaargh!"

There was a grinding noise and a loud clunk and he collapsed onto his springs, smoke billowing out of his engine.

"Brake broke," he groaned.

"Oh, this is just great," muttered Throttle. She glanced up at the approaching townsfolk. The time had definitely come to be somewhere else.

Mr. Big fled into the workshop and slammed the door. He looked around in desperation and scurried under a tarpaulin by the back wall. A moment later Clutch smashed through the door, splintering it into a million pieces. He stopped, looked around and saw the tarpaulin trembling . . .

"Master no like Clutch. Clutch no like Master!"

But as Clutch stood looking down at the quivering lump, Mr. Big leapt up and threw the tarpaulin over him. Clutch fell back with a roar, struggling to free himself. He knocked a half-full can of diesel over, soaking the sheet.

Mr. Big got out his lighter. He flicked it alight, held it over Clutch and dropped it.

"Oops."

The tarpaulin erupted into flames. Clutch began to thrash about wildly.

Mr. Big hurried to the doorway, poked his nose out to check the coast was clear, and hurried off.

Mr. Scratchly scurried down a narrow lane pursued by a huge RottWheeler. He turned a corner and skidded quickly into a hiding spot between two water tanks. A moment later the RottWheeler roared past.

"Now!" he yelled.

A huge jet of flame shot out from the other side of the lane, accompanied by a juicy bang, roasting the passing RottWheeler. It disappeared into the desert, yelping. Farmer Howell emerged, smoking. The two TruckDogs did a high five.

"You're really firing today, Farmer Howell!" said Mr. Scratchly.

Farmer Howell winked. "It's what I'm good at."

Most of the fighting was still centered around the Memorial Park and farther up the main street, but Sparky had bounced across to the petrol station. He was busy flattening out one of the RottWheelers when suddenly he smelled something. He looked up and saw a wisp of smoke rising from behind the garage.

"The workshop's on fire!" he cried.

He bounced once more on the RottWheeler, knocking him out cold. Prudence looked up from over the road as he raced off.

At the workshop door, or what remained of it, Sparky was greeted by billowing smoke and tongues of fire. He tried to see into the building but the smoke was too thick. Was that whimpering he could hear?

"Hello!" he called. "Is anyone in there?"

He cocked his head and listened. The sound of whimpering was clearer this time. Gathering himself, he sprang over the flames to the far side.

Clutch was cowering at the back of the workshop. Sparky skidded to a halt.

"Aaagh! YOU!"

He scrabbled round and made to leap back to the doorway. Clutch stared at him, shaking in terror, a pitiable sight.

Sparky paused, confused.

"C'mon," he said, keeping his distance. "Just smash your way out! You can do that." But the monster was immobile, petrified.

By now the fire was making its way along the back wall. Sparky looked through the rising flames toward the doorway— it was now or never.

Clutch whimpered again.

Sparky could not leave him to die. Clutch might be a psychotic monster with a murderous bent, but he was still a living creature. Sparky knew what he had to do.

A ramp along the side wall led up to a mezzanine floor where old timbers and junk were stored. The fire had not reached it yet.

"Listen . . . Clutch. Look at me. We're going up that ramp, okay? Come on."

He held Clutch's eyes and began backing up the ramp, speaking softly. "Come on."

Clutch moved forward slowly. He began to climb up the ramp. An overhead beam collapsed in a shower of sparks. The ramp sagged alarmingly. Clutch froze, terrified.

"It's okay," Sparky said soothingly. "We can do this. Come on now."

Clutch continued to creep forward . . .

Outside, Prudence came up to the warehouse just as a huge cloud of sparks billowed up into the air. She jumped back in alarm.

"Zoe! Fire-engine duty! Zoe, where are you?"

Near the windmill, Zoe was bailed up by a pair of Rott-Wheelers, one in front of her, snarling, the other behind, snapping at her axle.

"Get away from me, you ugly beasts!" she cried, and kicked out at them with her rear wheels. She fired her cannon but they were too close, ducking under the water jet.

Down the hill Hercules saw her peril. He scooped up a boulder, took aim and fired.

"Zoe, duck!" he yelled.

Zoe ducked. So did the first RottWheeler. The second one didn't. The boulder slammed into him, shunting him backward

TRUCK DOGS

File No: 00228314

NAME: TRUCKRAM

BREED/MAKE: Merino/VW Kombi
COLOR: Aqua and cream two-tone
IDENTIFYING MARKS: You mean apart from the enormous horns?
TEMPERAMENT: Very baaaad-tempered

FILE INFO:
Age: Unknown—looks Jurassic. Property of Farmer Howell.

SPECIFICATIONS:
Engine: 4-cylinder, air-cooled
Fuel Requirements: Grass, and lots of it
Maintenance: Yearly dip and dedag if you're brave enough

(Note also: Merino/VW Beetle TruckSheep)

into the windmill, which shuddered on its foundations. The first RottWheeler looked up at the windmill, then back at Hercules just in time for a second boulder to slam into him. Zoe sidestepped nimbly as he was shunted into the other RottWheeler. The windmill buckled and toppled, crashing down on the two RottWheelers in a tangled mess of iron.

Hercules rolled up to Zoe.

"You okay?" he asked in his best screen-hero voice.

"Oh, Herc, you saved me!" Zoe swooned.

He bent over for the kiss he so clearly deserved—and instead got a face full of water as Zoe squirted him and wriggled away.

"No way, you big Alfa Romeo!"

"Bleargh! Come back here!"

She spun away, laughing, and he raced after her.

⚙️

Sparky and Clutch reached the mezzanine. Bright tongues of flame licked around the timbers. Suddenly a huge section of floor fell away, leaving just a pair of beams intact—twin tightropes across empty space. At the far end was the loading-bay window, directly above the front doors. It was the only way out. Sparky swallowed hard.

"Okay. We can do this," he said to himself. "I think . . ."

He edged out into space, high above the flames, his tires feeling along the edge of the two beams.

"Don't look down, don't look down, don't look down."

He looked down. A swirling firestorm boiled below, fiery tendrils reaching up at him. He squeezed his eyes shut.

After a moment he continued on, eyes still shut, judging the width of the two beams with the outer rims of his tires. At last he reached the far end and gasped with relief.

"Okay, Clutch, now all we have to do is jump out this window . . ." He looked back over his shoulder. "Clutch?"

Clutch was still back at the other end of the beams.

"Come on!" he called desperately, but Clutch shook his head. Sparky looked out the window to safety. He hesitated, then called back over his shoulder.

"Okay, hang on. I'm coming back."

Gritting his teeth, he gingerly turned on the two beams, one wheel at a time—a delicate high-wire balancing trick. The flames were starting to lick around his fenders. One wheel slipped and for a terrible moment he teetered above the inferno. Then he regained his balance, steadied himself and headed back to Clutch.

"Listen to me, Clutch," he said urgently. "It's about to get really hot in here. Do you understand? You've got to believe in me. We can do this, together. Now, come on . . ."

He headed out again, backward this time, keeping his eyes fixed on Clutch's face. Clutch edged out after him. The beams creaked and groaned. The flames roared higher and higher all around.

It didn't look like they were going to make it . . .

☺

Prudence was in a terrible state when she saw Zoe and Hercules coming her way.

"Zoe! Quickly. The workshop is on fire!"

They hurried up to the burning building. Zoe tried dousing the flames with her water cannon, but the searing heat drove her back. The workshop was beyond saving.

A moment later, Digger and Bullworth raced up. Prudence turned to them with dull eyes.

"Sparky's in there . . ."

They looked on helplessly as the flames roared higher.

The sound of breaking glass came from overhead. The watching TruckDogs looked up. Amidst a shower of shattered glass, Sparky burst through the window high above them, surrounded by a halo of flames. Clutch followed, bringing the window frame and most of the wall with him.

Sparky sailed through the air and, for a moment, the scene seemed to go in slow motion. The Mongrel Pack watched openmouthed as he floated silently earthward, wheels spinning, ears flapping.

Then sound and motion returned. Sparky thudded to the ground with a sickening crunch. His new suspension shattered, retaining bolts and air-hoses shooting off the ends of the hydraulic pistons with a hiss and whoosh. But apart from being bruised, winded and somewhat overheated, he was otherwise unharmed and very much alive.

He staggered a little, then regained his balance amidst the cheering of his friends. A moment later Clutch slammed down in a shower of falling debris and sat there dazed, amongst the rubble.

Prudence eyed the monster uncertainly.

"And this would be . . . ?"

"His name's Clutch," said Sparky, patting the monster on the cab.

Clutch gave him a big wet lick across the face. Sparky screwed up his nose and laughed.

"And I think he's my friend!"

Suddenly Zoe called out. "Sparky, look. Your mum's in trouble."

Up the road at the Town Hall, Mayor Plugg stood on the porch as a particularly unpleasant-looking RottWheeler slowly advanced up the ramp toward her, snarling.

"I am warning you, in my official capacity as mayor, to stay where you are," she was saying, "or you will feel the full weight of the law." She held up her big mayoral medallion on its blue sash. The RottWheeler glanced at the medallion, grinned and kept coming.

"Right, then." Mrs. Plugg whipped off the medallion with her teeth, swung it round and caught him a terrific blow on the side of the cab. The RottWheeler stopped in surprise, smiled stupidly and rolled over, senseless.

"Heavy, isn't it?" said Mayor Plugg.

"Way to go, Mum!" Sparky called, then turned to his friends. "My mum can look after herself. She's cool."

They nodded in agreement.

But the other townsfolk were still in the thick of things. The RottWheelers had regrouped and were mounting a fresh attack from the hill behind the remains of the windmill.

The Mongrels headed off to help and Sparky made to follow. Suddenly Clutch growled. Sparky looked at him in alarm but then saw what the huge brute was looking at— Mr. Big slipping away down the narrow lane at the side of the general store. His eyes narrowed.

"Okay, I see him. Stay close."

Mr. Big peeped round the far end of the general store, checking that the coast was clear. The open desert lay beyond.

"Leaving without your fuel? But we told you we had enough to see you on your way."

Mr. Big spun around to find Sparky and Clutch standing behind him. Clutch growled and bared his teeth. Quick as a flash, Mr. Big dived through the gaping hole in the side of the store. Clutch sprang after him with a roar.

"No, boy! Heel!" yelled Sparky. Clutch stopped and looked back with a bewildered whine.

"We don't eat baddies round here. We catch them and chuck 'em in jail. Understand?"

Clutch nodded.

"Okay, then. Let's get him!"

Sparky squinted as he adjusted his eyes to the dim light inside the store. All around were dusty aisles loaded with produce. There was no sign of Mr. Big. He motioned down one of the aisles.

"You take engine oils," he whispered to Clutch. "I'll take worming tablets and flea powder. Keep your engine low."

Sparky crept down his aisle toward the back of the store.

Mr. Big meanwhile had made his way down an aisle lined with canned dog food and packets of Doggy Bites. At the back of the shop there was a storeroom door. An exit sign glowed above it. Suddenly he heard the sound of an engine in the next aisle—and snuffling. It was Clutch. Mr. Big froze, sweat trickling down his windscreen. His eyes fell on a bag of Doggy Bites.

Clutch was sniffing along the bottom of the shelving when a Doggy Bite rolled out in front of him and across the floor. He followed it, sniffed, and gobbled it up.

Another followed, and another.

In the next aisle Mr. Big listened to Clutch chomping away. He poured the rest of the bag of Doggy Bites under the shelves, then crept across to the back door, his own engine noise covered by Clutch's gobbling.

Meanwhile Sparky reached the checkout counter at the front of the store. He looked back just as Mr. Big disappeared into the back room.

He hurried down the aisle to find Clutch gorging himself. Clutch looked up, mouth full, then remembered what he should be doing and swallowed with an apologetic smile.

"He went that way." Sparky motioned toward the door. "You go around the side to the back lane and cut him off."

Clutch glanced longingly at the remaining Doggy Bites strewn over the floor, then headed off. Sparky tried the door to the back room—but it had been barred from the inside.

The storeroom was dark, the only light coming from narrow cracks in the weatherboard wall. A rear door opened out into the laneway beyond. Mr. Big made for it. But a strange sound made him stop. He peered into the gloom and could just make out a large iron gate. Strangely, there seemed to be a set of horns entangled in it. The gate rose into the air, revealing a most unexpected sight—a very large TruckRam with a thick layer of mush around its muzzle. It had been happily scarfing on a bag of feed when Mr. Big burst in. Now it snorted loudly, covering Mr. Big's surprised face in a thick layer of soggy oats.

Inside the general store, Sparky was still wondering how to get into the back room when the door suddenly exploded into a million pieces. He leapt back as Mr. Big shot out, squealing in terror, followed closely by the TruckRam.

"YAAAAH!" yelled Sparky.

"AAAAAAAAAH!" screamed Mr. Big.

"BAAAAAAAAAAAA!" roared the TruckRam.

Mr. Big landed on the Doggy Bites and spun out of control down the aisle, straight through the checkout and out the front door. He tumbled down the steps and sprawled into the street. An instant later the TruckRam burst through the front of the store, leaving a gaping hole where the door had been.

Before Mr. Big could collect himself, the TruckRam bent its head, picked him up with the gate and sent him flying clear across the road. He crashed through the roof of Scratchly's Fencing Supplies. Bales of barbed wire flew up into the air. A mighty yelp of pain came from within.

The TruckRam snorted, looked around and galloped off as Sparky skidded out of the ruined store. Clutch joined him, panting. Sparky looked around urgently but Mr. Big was nowhere in sight.

There was a crash and a curse from across the way and Mr. Big backed painfully out into the road in a tangle of barbed wire.

"Need any help?" called Sparky.

Mr. Big looked up. Clutch snarled and leapt forward. Mr. Big squealed and bolted, hoops of wire trailing from his bumpers whipped about, lashing at his rear end. Sparky and Clutch raced after him.

"Yeow! Yipe! Ow!"

Sparky and Clutch leapt after him.

After they had gone, there was a groan of splintered timbers and the whole general store teetered and collapsed in a cloud of flea powder, worming tablets and Doggy Bites.

While the Battle of Hubcap raged, Throttle had been hiding, watching. As it became clear that the RottWheelers were being thrashed, she snuck away from behind the fuel shed, slipping across the rubble and coarse grass behind the outbuildings and onto the road out of town.

She looked back. A plume of smoke rose into the air.

"Stinking town. Fuel was low-grade rubbish anyway."

She turned back to the road and gasped in shock. There in front of her, blocking the road, was Rex. His head was bowed. She stopped dead in her tracks.

"What are you doing here?"

Rex's missing wheel had been replaced with a traction-engine flywheel, and his funnel with a set of old V8 extractor pipes—pretty hot-looking, in fact. He looked up slowly and fixed her with a steady gaze.

"I've come to get my spanner back."

Up in town, the last RottWheeler sagged, defeated, to the ground. The Mongrels and the townsfolk looked around, only now able to stop and take in the smoldering workshop and the pile of rubble that had been the general store.

Hercules whistled through his grill. "Made a bit of a mess, eh?"

"Yep," nodded Digger. "It's what we're good at."

"It certainly is," came a voice.

They turned to find Mayor Plugg standing by them. They gulped, but she winked. "Don't worry about it, fellas. Never liked that general store anyway." She smiled at their stunned expressions. "By the way, it's good to see you back."

Just then Prudence called out from up by the garage. She was looking down the road. "It's Rex!"

Mayor Plugg, Hercules, Digger, Prudence, Zoe and the townsfolk all gathered at the edge of the forecourt to watch. Down on the Great Outback Highway, Rex and Throttle eyed each other— the powerful young dragster and the worn-out old tractor.

"So what are you now?" Throttle scoffed. "Some kind of road warrior?"

Rex said nothing.

Throttle laughed. "And you think you can just take your spanner back, is that it?"

Rex nodded. "Yup."

Throttle's eyes narrowed. She sized him up—the bald tires, the weedy frame, the rusty bolts. He was no match for her.

"You old fool." She held the spanner up in front of him. "So come and get it."

Rex rolled forward. Throttle leapt at him, intending to take him out in one swift move. Rex moved deftly aside and she crunched to the ground, surprised and winded.

"One—nil," said Hercules, up at the petrol station.

Throttle picked herself up and lashed out with her rear wheels. Rex grabbed her by the axle and flipped her upside down. She crashed down on her cab.

"Two—nil," said Zoe.

Throttle was up again in an instant. She and Rex circled each other, alert, watching.

"You belong in a junkyard," she spat. "You're just a clapped-out tractor, old and weak and foolish."

"While you are young and strong and arrogant," said Rex. "An interesting contest, no?"

Digger leaned across to Prudence and whispered, "He's going all oriental again."

Prudence whispered back, "I think he has a Japanese drive-train."

Down on the highway, Throttle taunted Rex. "So come on, old tractor. Bring it on. Show me what you've got."

"Patience is a TruckDog's greatest ally."

"Patience? I'm a girl who likes a bit of action!"

On the word "action" she lunged again, but Rex sent her sprawling behind him in the dirt. He didn't even look around.

Bullworth nodded appreciatively. "Double points. Four—nil."

Throttle turned with a snarl and leaped at Rex's unguarded

back. The onlookers on the forecourt cringed at the coming impact, but at the last moment Rex half turned and raised his front wheel. Throttle slammed into it like a TruckBug hitting a windscreen on the freeway. She reeled away, stunned, tottered for a moment, then slumped to the ground.

Rex rolled up to her and picked up his spanner. His eyes flickered as he noted the damage.

"You're lucky I didn't know about this before. I might have got mad."

Throttle opened a bleary eye and groaned.

"Five, six, seven, eight, nine and ten," said Hercules. "No contest. Game to Rex."

"Yay, Rex!" shouted Zoe. "Way to go!"

"Woo hoo!" hooted Digger.

Suddenly Mr. Dogsbody called out in warning. Embers from the smoldering workshop had lodged in the grass by the fuel shed. Brake, still trapped under the overloaded tanker, saw the flames begin to take hold and yelled out.

"Help . . . help me!"

Hercules, Digger and Prudence were closest. They rushed over and tried to push the stranded tanker out of danger. Mayor Plugg joined them but Brake was stuck fast under the weight of the tanker.

"Zoe! Quick!" yelled Hercules but Zoe gestured helplessly.

"I'm out of water!"

Then Bullworth rolled up to the tanker. Harnessing an

inner strength, he lowered his mighty head and began to push. The tanker slid slowly but surely away from the shed. Two yards, five yards, ten yards. Everyone watched, spellbound. Fifteen yards, twenty yards . . .

Finally Prudence called out, "Okay, Bullworth, okay! That's enough. Any more and he'll die of friction burns."

The flames licked around the fuel-shed door. The TruckDogs backed away, bracing themselves for the blast. At that moment, the TruckRam trotted around the back of the garage—a bizarre sight, its gate held high above its head. It looked at the flames in alarm and jumped clear of them—onto the roof of the shed . . .

KAAAΛΛAAA-BOOOM!

The shed rocketed straight up in the air, taking the TruckRam with it, and vanished out of sight in the clouds of smoke.

Prudence turned to Digger, not quite able to accept what she had seen. "Did you . . . was that . . . ?"

Digger was equally stunned. "Yeah. I think so."

At the other end of town, Sparky and Clutch raced after Mr. Big, hot on his tail. The barbed wire hanging off Mr. Big's bumper came loose and wrapped itself around Clutch. He stopped to disentangle himself. Sparky sped on.

Mr. Big scurried around the remains of the workshop and into the petrol-station forecourt—and found the entire town waiting for him. He screeched to a stop. A moment later, Sparky came hurtling round the corner and skidded to a halt by the tanker. Mr. Big looked around desperately. A wall of grim-faced TruckDogs looked back at him. He turned and saw Sparky by himself, without Clutch.

With the desperation of a cornered animal he flung himself at Sparky, pointy little teeth bared in a look of pure hatred. Sparky recoiled, caught unaware by the speed and savageness of the attack. Rex, who had chugged up to the forecourt, yelled out to him and sent the silver spanner spinning through the air. Sunlight flashed off it as it flew toward the tanker.

In an instant Sparky saw where it was heading. He jumped—fifteen feet clear, no hydraulic assistance—and caught the spanner between his teeth. Twisting in midair, he locked the spanner onto the pressure-release valve on the back of the tanker and turned it. Fuel blasted out of the valve, a sudden powerful jet. It hit Mr. Big right in the face, shooting straight up his nose.

Mr. Big was flung backward along the ground. He gasped, inhaling several liters of fuel, flooding his engine. There was a high-pitched screeching sound followed by a muffled pthoonk! as his motor seized and exploded. Smoke billowed from under his hood. A second, larger explosion detonated his fuel tank. His doors flew off and the gearbox dropped out onto the ground, spilling cogs and sump oil all over the road.

He lay there, a broken wreck, at Sparky's wheels, and groaned. A small black dot appeared in the center of his roof, growing rapidly larger. Sparky looked up and backed away. A moment later, the TruckRam—minus gate and looking extremely surprised—landed full on the little tyrant, squashing him flat.

"Baaaaaaaa!"

A second later the gate clanged down in front of Mr. Big's face, the vertical iron bars looking for all the world like the bars of a prison cell.

Sparky closed the fuel valve and regarded Mr. Big sternly.

"Bad dog."

Mayor Plugg came up to her son, shaking her head in wonder. "Where did you learn to do that? More bad influences, I assume?"

Sparky grinned.

Rex rolled up to join them. Mayor Plugg looked at him. The tractor shrugged. "Young fella has a natural talent."

"Thanks, Rex," said Sparky, giving back the spanner. "I owe you, big-time."

Mrs. Plugg regarded Rex with new appreciation. "You know, a pup needs a . . . well . . . a role model. Thank you, Rex."

He acknowledged her with a polite nod.

Just then Clutch arrived, chomping on the remains of the barbed wire. A murmur ran through the crowd and they backed away nervously.

"It's okay," said Sparky. "He's with me."

Clutch gave him another big lick across the face. The townsfolk looked on, gob-smacked. Then everyone began to talk at once. Clutch saw his former master behind bars and howled in approval.

"Hooray for Sparky!" called out Prudence.

The crowd barked and beeped.

"Three cheers for the Mongrel Pack!" shouted Mrs. Plugg. The crowd honked and howled.

"Let's hear it for Hubcap!" yelled Hercules.

And the crowd went totally wild.

TRUCK**DOGS**

8316

NAME: DESERTDOG (LEADER)

BREED/MAKE: Dingo/4x4
COLOR: Yellow
IDENTIFYING MARKS: Missing one eye
TEMPERAMENT: Savage

FILE INFO:
Leader of the DesertDogs that inhabit outback areas north and northeast of Combustion City. Potentially very dangerous. Doesn't like loud noises.

SPECIFICATIONS:
Engine: Generally V6 (3.2–4.3 l)
Fuel Requirements: Whatever the tribe catches
Maintenance: Not likely!

(Note also: Marsupial/Bicycle TruckRoo)

BITE FOUR

 few days later, the iron bars of the gate had been replaced by the real thing. Mr. Big, worse for wear and nastier than ever, took up residence in the Hubcap Jailhouse at the back of the Town Hall. Throttle had the cell next door. Sparky could see them looking out of their barred windows as he crossed the street, past the garage where the new workshop was already under construction, on his way to Memorial Park.

The two inmates couldn't see each other, but that didn't stop them having a lively conversation.

"Take all the fuel," sneered Throttle. "Every last drop. Nice call, Boss."

"Ah shut up, you whining mutt," snapped Mr. Big.

"Don't you tell me to shut up, you overgrown TruckRat. I could've told you all that fuel was too heavy."

"Oh, so now you're the big genius? Left your run a bit late, haven't you, you flea-bitten tramp?"

"I've *always* been smarter than you. Everyone knew that,

except you. They respected me!"

"By everyone I assume you mean that mangy bunch of ungrateful mutts who have run off and left us both to rot? Respect, hah!"

Sparky shook his head and continued on into the park where a big celebration was getting under way. A huge marquee had been set up amongst the trees, giving the park a great party atmosphere. In the middle of the tent stood the statue of Lord Hubcap, back on its pedestal, still missing an ear but otherwise intact.

Mr. Dogsbody was hanging fairy lights high up in the branches with his crane. Farmer Howell was directing operations. He called out to Mr. Scratchly, "Okay, switch them on."

"What's that?"

"We've finished. You can switch them on now."

"Eh?"

"I said . . ." began Farmer Howell, but Mr. Scratchly laughed and flipped the switch.

"I hear ya, Windy. I hear ya."

The lights blinked to life, twinkling amongst the gum leaves.

"Ooooh. Aren't they pretty?" cried Ida.

Edna looked at the lights, tut-tutting in disapproval. "Waste of energy. What is this town coming to?"

"Well, they look pretty to me," said Ida.

Edna looked at her sharply. "Ida! You're not thinking for yourself, are you?"

"Oh no, Edna," she said. "I would *never* do that."

Edna looked away, satisfied. Ida glanced at her, then looked back at the lights, smiling.

Back up on the main street, Brake rolled by, a broom and shovel in his mouth. He was hauling a wagon with a sign reading "Hubcap Pooper Patrol." Mrs. Dogsbody followed close behind.

"There's another one," she said, pointing at the ground.

Brake scooped up the offending article, plopped it in the wagon and rolled on.

"We'll make a good citizen of you yet," she said. "Look, there's another one."

Brake just grunted.

After they passed by, Clutch came cavorting across the street with a rusty old wrench in his mouth. He raced up to Sparky, dropped the wrench and sat expectantly, stumpy tail thumping the ground. Sparky threw it across the park, high into the air. Clutch bounded after it.

"This time with a double pike and turn!" Sparky called after him. Clutch leapt, somersaulted and landed with the wrench in his mouth.

"Good boy, Clutch! Off you go."

Clutch gambolled off happily. Rex rolled up next to Sparky and watched him go. "He's almost as good as you. Might make a fine member of the Mongrel Pack one day."

Sparky smiled up at Rex. Then he noticed that the old

tractor had his tool kit with him.

"You're leaving."

Rex nodded. "Yup."

"But there's so much work to do. A town needs a mechanic. You know that."

"It surely does. That's why I want you to have this." He gave Sparky his big silver spanner. "It's got a couple of dents, I'm afraid, but otherwise it's in good working order."

Sparky took the spanner wonderingly. He looked back at Rex with shining eyes. Just then, Mayor Plugg rolled up.

"So, Rex," she said. "I can't persuade you to stay?"

Rex shook his head. "No, ma'am."

"Well, I thank you for all you've done for us. This town is the richer for your being here."

Rex thanked Mayor Plugg and turned to Sparky.

"You take care, young fella."

Sparky nodded and bit his lip.

"Where are you going?" he asked suddenly.

Rex thought about it for a moment, then smiled. "Somewhere I haven't been before, I reckon. Guess I'll know when I get there."

He chugged off.

Mother and son watched him go. Mayor Plugg sighed quietly.

"A pup needs a father."

Sparky grinned at her. "Not with a mum like you around."

She looked down at him and smiled. "Come on, you—there's official business to take care of."

Sparky spun the spanner and flipped it into his tray.

Mayor Plugg was taken aback. "Where did you . . . ?" She stopped and laughed. "Never mind."

They returned to the celebrations together. Sparky went to stand with the other Mongrels to one side of the official dais. The gang was without their armor now and looking unusually clean—polished paintwork, clean tires—no dirt under the mudflaps today. Mayor Plugg addressed the townsfolk.

"Citizens of Hubcap, your attention, please. It is with great pleasure that I hereby award these six most excellent young TruckDogs the Hubcap Medal of Honor, and present them with the official Car Keys to the City."

Six cute little TruckPups trotted up, each with a medal, a key and a bunch of flowers in its mouth. Sparky's TruckPup was the one who had tried to pee on the head of Lord Hubcap. Sparky winked at him. The TruckPup wagged his tail at high speed—he was a tiny version of Sparky.

The Mongrel Pack—Hercules, Bullworth, Prudence, Digger, Zoe and Sparky turned to face the crowd. The entire town erupted in a fanfare of cheering and beeping. Sparky and his friends beamed with pleasure. Every TruckDog has its day.

"Please accept these as tokens of our thanks for your gallantry in saving our town," continued Mayor Plugg. "You are truly cherished members of this community. Welcome home!"

"Home," said Zoe. Her eyes were shining.

"It's got a nice ring to it," nodded Digger.

"I think I'm going to cry," sniffed Bullworth.

Prudence passed him an oil rag. "Take it easy, big boy." He blew his nose noisily.

And she blinked back a tear herself.

Hercules moved forward and cleared his throat. The townsfolk fell silent.

"Well," he said, "speaking for the Pack, it's no secret that we've never had a lot of time for you folks. And you've had no time for us. You're old—but that's not your fault, any more than it's our fault for being young." He paused. "So I guess if you can learn to cope with us, then we can learn to cope with you." He shrugged. "What say we start from there and see how we go?"

"Sounds good to me," smiled Mayor Plugg, and the crowd cheered in approval. "Furthermore, I hereby declare that from this day forth all TruckDogs shall have the right to rev their engines as they please . . ."

". . . play street football . . ." said Mr. Dogsbody.

". . . listen to raucous music . . ." added Mr. Scratchly.

". . . go drag racing . . ." called out Ida.

"Drag racing?" said a shocked Edna.

". . . leap the occasional sheep . . ." said Farmer Howell.

". . . and generally act like kids—loud, fast and covered in mud!" concluded Mayor Plugg. "And that includes us vintage

TruckDogs as well."

The crowd erupted again, tossing their hubcaps into the air in celebration.

🐾

Out on the highway Rex paused and smiled as the cheering and beeping wafted across the desert on the cool evening air. He sighed, looking back at the twinkling lights, and thought for a moment. Then he turned and chugged off up the road.

Back up on the hill, Sparky emerged from the marquee and looked out across the desert. He saw a figure in the distance, a lone TruckDog on an endless highway. But as he watched, the figure softly vanished, leaving the road empty. Sparky blinked. The road shifted and shimmered in his eyes. He wiped away a tear.

Then, with a deep breath, he turned and drove back toward the lights.

A moment later, the soft dusky-pink blanket of twilight closed in gently on the desert and the Great Outback Highway too faded away into the night.

THE END

LAST NIP

Far out in the desert, a lone TruckDog flees squealing from a pack of howling DesertDogs. He looks familiar—a corgi/ delivery van with a squint.

He swerves desperately this way and that, DesertDogs snapping at his heels, until the leader of the pack, a big one-eyed brute, brings him down with a crunch. The rest of the pack gather round and sniff curiously.

Suddenly he pops up again, catching the DesertDogs by surprise, and races away, zigzagging madly toward the horizon. The DesertDogs howl and set off after him, disappearing in a cloud of dust.

At least he has a full tank of fuel.

"Howowowowoooo!"

A note regarding

TRUCKBUGS

The world of TruckDogs is home to a number of other species which have evolved along similar lines to the dominant canine/vehicular life forms. They include TruckSheep, TruckRodents and TruckChooks. The most diverse group, however, is the TruckBugs. Below are some of the more common TruckBugs that can be found in the sixteen illustrated plates.

1 LADYBIRD/ROADSTER   *Coccinellidae automotum*

2 STAG BEETLE/FORKLIFT   *Lucanidae lifterupus*

3 WEEVIL/ROAD SWEEPER   *Chrysolopus cleaneria*

4 ANT/CEMENT MIXER   *Myrmecia minimixia*

5 BUTTERFLY/HANG GLIDER (PLUS ANT)   *Nymphalidae wheeee!*

6 DRAGONFLY/HELICOPTER/EXCAVATOR   *Aeshna whirli diggeri*

7 SNAIL/HOT ROD   *Helix turbochargeum*

8 DUNG BEETLE/BULLDOZER   *Scarabaeidae gruntae*

9 MOSQUITO/AUGER   *Culicidae drillium*

10 SCORPION/SCISSOR-LIFT   *Centruroides scissiori*

11 MAGGOT/BUS   *Musca commuterae*

12 WASP/JET FIGHTER   *Hemithynnus veryfastilis*

13 MANTID/ROAD GRADER   *Archimantis flattenouttera*

14 RED-BACK SPIDER/HOVERCRAFT   *Latrodectus amphibiosae*

15 GRASSHOPPER/MOTORBIKE   *Monistria brrmbrrm*

16 MOTH/AIRPLANE   *Oxycanus extrabitattheendus*